COLLECTIVE BARGAINING SYSTEMS

COLLECTIVE BARGAINING SYSTEMS

A Study of Union-Employer Responsibilities and Problems

FRANK COOK PIERSON

American Council on Public Affairs
WASHINGTON, D. C.

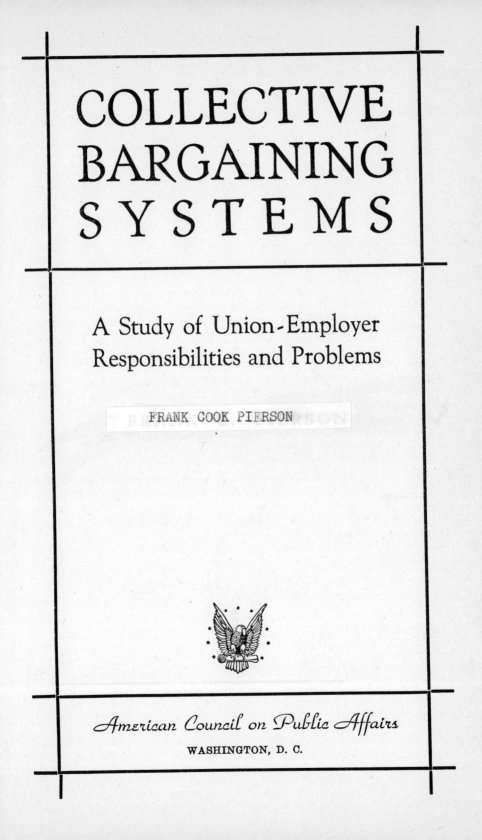

American Council on Public Affairs

Dedicated to the belief that the extensive diffusion of information is a profound responsibility of American democracy, the American Council on Public Affairs is designed to promote the spread of authoritative facts and significant opinions concerning contemporary social and economic problems.

It endeavors to contribute to public knowledge through the publication of studies and pamphlets, encouragement of adult education, initiation of research projects, organization of lectures and forums, arrangement of radio broadcasts, compilation of opinions on vital issues, and cooperation with other organizations.

The Council believes that the facts presented and opinions expressed under its sponsorship deserve careful attention and consideration. It is not, however, committed to these facts and opinions in any other way. Those associated with the Council necessarily represent different viewpoints on public questions.

The offices of the Council are at 2153 Florida Ave., Washington, D. C.

PRINTED IN THE UNITED STATES

TO MY FATHER

INTRODUCTION

The development of the collective bargaining system in the United States has been all too deeply conditioned by the extensive battle which has been fought over whether or not collective bargaining should be the accepted process for determining wages, hours, and working conditions. In that battle, the charge of "irresponsibility" as well as the actual use of "irresponsible" procedures have often been conceived by both parties as a phase of the tactics of conflict. This has been typical not only of the basic struggle over recognition of labor unions but also of operations under many first agreements, particularly those which seemed to represent a temporary armistice rather than a genuine acceptance of the collective bargaining principle.

There are strong reasons for believing that collective bargaining in the United States has today attained the stature of a recognized institution. It is significant, in this regard, that, in a public statement summarizing the activities of the National Labor Relations Board during 1941, Chairman H. A. Millis said, "It is possible, I think, to draw from these facts the conclusion that American labor, having escaped the sterile repressions of Hitler Germany, has learned to use its protected right of self-organization, and that American employers have advanced far toward making collective bargaining the accepted practice of an industrial democracy."

Prof. Pierson's competent study of collective bargaining systems is particularly timely. It becomes available just as the scene is shifting to the problem of "making collective bargaining work." That process must go on without stoppage of war production. The situation calls for the decisive use of proven procedures. This means that certain trial and error methods must largely be abandoned as non-essential luxuries.

The study made by Prof. Pierson is chiefly concerned with the question of how the fulfillment of union and employer responsibilities is related to the degree of acceptance of the collective bargaining principle and to the type of agreement which has been consummated. Although the first phase may soon possess principally historical interest, the latter is likely to have significance for many years to come to those who write collective agreements. This lasting usefulness arises from the fact that "responsibility" is not merely an intangible idea or solely a matter of good faith but a result that is at least partially dependent upon the soundness of the terms of a collective agreement. The study shows, for example, that a union commitment to forego strikes may become valueless, no matter how good the intention, unless coupled in the contract with a well-conceived grievance procedure section. Viewed in such a light, the responsibility question becomes not an emotional argument but a practical problem to be negotiated. In a similar manner, an employer's responsibility to provide steady employment cannot be divorced from the cost considerations that are jointly determined in the collective agreement.

Prof. Pierson makes it abundantly evident that the meeting of the responsibilities of each party to a collective agreement is a matter for mutual attention. Such a point of view strikes a ringing keynote as American industry and American labor join efforts to defend their heritage. For they no longer are responsible solely to each other. Pearl Harbor has made them responsible to posterity.

GEORGE W. TAYLOR

Vice-Chairman
National War Labor Board
Washington, D. C.

PREFACE

A study of labor relations, even when limited in scope, is a hazardous undertaking. Appearances in this field are often deceiving. Both union and employer spokesmen are prone to approach controversies in an emotional and vindictive spirit with the result that the issues in dispute are frequently distorted and the first-hand accounts quite likely to be misleading. Published documents bearing on labor controversies are few and none too reliable. Thus the obstacles in the path of scholarly work on the subject are serious. The impartial investigator's only recourse is to check his findings in as many ways as possible. Accordingly, the author first canvassed written materials bearing on the problem of responsibility under union agreements. He then interviewed individuals who, by training and experience, were qualified to discuss the various issues, including union and employer spokesmen as well as dispassionate observers. A subsequent step was to submit rough drafts of the chapters to persons equipped to evaluate them properly.

The documentary material for Chapters II and III, dealing with procedures for interpretation and enforcement of union agreements, was drawn chiefly from copies of union agreements on file at the Bureau of Labor Statistics of the U. S. Department of Labor. The bureau has approximately seven thousand current agreements in its records, including samples from every industry and trade in which bargaining relations have been established. Six of these fields receive special attention in the two chapters. In order to gain a broad picture of labor disputes under agreements in these industries, an examination was made of all the strike and lock-out reports sent to the bureau during the years 1937, 1938, and 1939. Upon these reports are based the bureau's estimates of the frequency of strikes and lock-outs, the number of workers involved, and the number of man-days lost; the bureau excludes all strikes and lock-outs lasting less than a day and all strikes and lock-outs involving less than six workers. Aside from this exclusion the coverage of these reports seemed adequate for the purposes of the present study. It should be explained that in order to secure comprehensive information, the bureau scrutinizes the papers and periodicals published in all cities with a population of more than 50,000, together with some from smaller centers. In addition, every known labor and trade organ is checked. Thus over seven hundred publications are carefully examined for information on industrial disputes. When a case is discovered, detailed questionnaires are sent to both parties. Though the answers are voluntary, response is, on the whole, satisfactory.[1]

In the case of each of the six industries studied in Chapters II and III, the author interviewed prominent spokesmen for both employers and unions. Several weeks were spent in and around Pittsburgh, during the summer of 1939, consulting some twenty persons in the steel and bituminous coal industries. Later that same summer, and again in 1940, he devoted a month to Detroit where he saw representatives of employers and unions in the automobile industry. During 1940 he conferred with spokesmen in the railroad, maritime, and women's clothing industries in New York City and Philadelphia.

Chapter IV deals with the law of union agreements. In part, this material was drawn from law journal articles. Many important cases were uncovered through the Labor Law Service of the Commerce Clearing House, the Labor Law Service of Prentice-Hall, Inc., and the Labor Relations Reporter of the Bureau of National Affairs. All important court decisions were studied that had been issued since 1930 bearing on this subject.

In Chapter V a number of National Labor Relations Board cases are discussed. Because of the controversial nature of the issues contained in these cases, special pains were taken to avoid inaccuracies. Accordingly, wherever the board's decision or the trial examiner's report to the board lacked sufficient detail, reference was made to the original transcript of hearings before the trial examiner. Wherever appeal was made from a board decision, the findings of the court were consulted. In one case, *The Matter of Union Pacific Stages, Inc.*, 2 N. L. R. B. 471 (1936), the court's decision threw doubt on the impartiality of the board's proceedings; the case was therefore eliminated from the group selected for analysis. In each of the seven cases finally chosen, interviews were sought with spokesmen for both sides of the controversy.

Chapters VI and VII are a survey of developments in the automobile and coat and suit industries. Here chief reliance was placed on consultations with persons identified with the two industries. Spokesmen for the United Automobile Workers of America, C. I. O., offered access to data not generally available. Copies of the minutes

---

[1] See *Strikes in the United States, 1880-1936* (U. S. Department of Labor, Bureau of Labor Statistics, Bulletin No. 651, 1938), Appendix II, III, pp. 163-172. According to this bulletin, "few, if any, strikes escape the Bureau's attention." *Ibid.*, p. 170.

of grievance committee meetings proved to be particularly helpful. With regard to the coat and suit industry, it was possible to make fuller use of documentary material. Much of this material was secured from government sources, but a portion of it came from the union and employers.

Chapter VIII deals with post-war developments in the bituminous coal industry. Of course, many phases of the period covered have been reviewed in other studies. It was enough for present purposes to confine most of the chapter to an interpretation of existing material. However, some phases of the story which have been inadequately considered by previous studies—for example, the changing competitive positions of union and non-union operators during the post-war period—are treated here.

* * * *

In the preparation of this study, help and guidance came from many individuals. Spokesmen for union organizations and employers, government officials, and research experts provided much of the material appearing in these pages. The following persons read various parts and offered numerous criticisms and suggestions: Fred H. Joiner, Bureau of Labor Statistics, U. S. Department of Labor (Chapters II and III); Professor Robert L. Hale, Columbia University Law School, and David Jaffee, member of the legal staff of the United Textile Workers of America (Chapter IV); Dr. Lyle W. Cooper, former Industrial Economist, National Labor Relations Board (Chapter V); Robert W. Conder, Director of Labor Relations, Chrysler Corporation, and George F. Addes, Secretary-Treasurer, United Automobile Workers of America, C. I. O. (Chapter VI); Harry Haskel, member of the research staff of the National Coat and Suit Industry Recovery Board, Dr. Lazare Teper, Director of Research, International Ladies' Garment Workers' Union, and Samuel F. Klein, Executive Director, Industrial Council of Cloak, Suit and Skirt Manufacturers (Chapter VII); John W. McBride, Economic Analyst, Bituminous Coal Division, U. S. Department of Interior, and Professor Waldo E. Fisher, University of Pennsylvania (Chapter VIII).

Miss Florence Peterson, Chief of the Industrial Relations Division, Bureau of Labor Statistics, and other members of the Division's staff gave valuable aid at many points in the inquiry. Dr. David J. Saposs, former Chief Economist, National Labor Relations Board, and other members of the board's staff were also most cooperative. Particular thanks are due John Dickinson, Chief Counsel, Pennsylvania Railroad Company, and Stephen M. Du Brul, Economist, General Motors Corporation, for material which they generously made available. Robert W. Bruère, Chairman of the Maritime Labor Board, and other members of his staff gave willingly of their time and energy. Harold J. Ruttenberg, Director of Research, Steel Workers' Organizing Committee, and James T. Wishard, Director of Research, United Automobile Workers of America, C. I. O., offered ready assistance. Byron H. Cannon, Secretary-Treasurer, Western Pennsylvania Coal Operators' Association, and Patrick J. Fagan, President, District 5, United Mine Workers of America, gave help at difficult points in the investigation. It is regrettable that the many other persons who took the time to answer questions and provide material cannot be listed here.

The author owes much to the advice and guidance of Dr. George W. Taylor, University of Pennsylvania. Dr. Paul F. Brissenden and Dr. Leo Wolman, Columbia University, gave invaluable aid at every stage of the inquiry. Both helped to plan the study and to improve the finished manuscript. Nevertheless, the conclusions are solely the responsibility of the writer. He also acknowledges gratitude to his wife, Marguerite T. Pierson, who participated in the early stages of the inquiry and corrected the final manuscript, both as to form and content. Without her help and encouragement the project might never have reached completion. In addition, thanks are extended to Janet M. Arnold and Marius Maken for editorial assistance. Finally, proper appreciation must be expressed to Columbia University for granting the author a University Fellowship in order to undertake this study.

FRANK C. PIERSON

Assistant Professor of Economics,
Swarthmore College, Pennsylvania.

CONTENTS

PREFACE 1

I

THE PROBLEM OF RESPONSIBILITY 7

II

ADJUSTMENT MACHINERY: NEW AGREEMENTS 12

General Characteristics 13

Recently Established Systems 16

III

ADJUSTMENT MACHINERY: OLD AGREEMENTS 26

The National Railroad Adjustment Board 36

The Bituminous Coal Industry 39

Conclusions 46

IV

THE LAW OF UNION AGREEMENTS 48

The Closed Shop 49

The National Labor Relations Act 54

Remedies Against Employers 57

The Norris-La Guardia Act 60

Remedies Against Unions 63

Individual Members 70

Conclusions 75

V

DISINTEGRATION WITHIN 78

Employer Attacks 87

Union-Employer Stalemate 94

Worker Disaffection 99
Conclusions 105

VI

RESPONSIBILITY IN THE AUTOMOBILE INDUSTRY 109
Background Circumstances 117
Disputed Issues 124
Conclusions 131

VII

ENFORCEMENT IN THE COAT AND SUIT INDUSTRY 133
Enforcement Difficulties 135
The 1924-1926 Period 144
The 1935-1940 Period 155
Conclusions 167

VIII

BREAKDOWN IN THE COAL INDUSTRY 170
Characteristics of the Industry 175
Basic Changes 178
Immediate Circumstances 182
Wage Differentials 186
The Union's Policy Appraised 188
Conclusions 197

IX

CONCLUSIONS AND RECOMMENDATIONS 199

Appendix 208
Bibliography 212
Index 221

CHAPTER I

THE PROBLEM OF RESPONSIBILITY

In current discussions of labor problems the charge is frequently made that unions are irresponsible. The usual counter-charge is that employers are the guilty parties. The term "responsibility" is an epithet dear to the heart of a partisan. Being vague, it is suitable to most occasions. It can be easily used to introduce considerations obscuring the real issues of a dispute. It invariably carries the implication that one side is utterly unreasonable and ruthless, the other wholly sensible and righteous. Manifestly, the problem of union-employer responsibility must be carefully considered in objective terms.

Organized labor now plays an important part in our economic life. Between 1933 and 1940 membership in American trade unions increased more than threefold. During this period, both veteran unions like the United Mine Workers of America and newcomers like the Steel Workers' Organizing Committee were able to organize many firms that had always been non-union. By 1940, according to convention reports of unions affiliated with the American Federation of Labor and the Congress of Industrial Organizations, as well as the independent railroad brotherhoods, paid-up membership was considerably over eight million.[1] In 1941 membership increased further, particularly in the aviation, shipbuilding, machine tool, and electrical manufacturing industries.[2] Paralleling this growth of membership there was a gain in the number of union agreements. Consequently there are at the present time more workers in American industry covered by agreements than ever before.[3]

Prior to these developments the major question seemed to be whether unions should be allowed to organize at all. Persons concerned about labor problems were prone to argue either that unions were the country's salvation or its nemesis. Today the focus has shifted to the manner in which unions are using their new-found

---

1 "Annual Conventions of the A. F. of L. and C. I. O.," *Monthly Labor Review* (U. S. Department of Labor, Bureau of Labor Statistics), vol. 51, no. 6 (December 1940), pp. 1456-1461.

2 *New York Times,* June 22, 1941, sec. 4, p. 8.

3 "Industrial Relations in 1938," *Monthly Labor Review* (U. S. Department of Labor, Bureau of Labor Statistics), vol. 48, no. 3 (March 1939), pp. 493-508. This article was written by Florence Peterson.

power and to the way in which employers are adjusting themselves to the changed industrial environment. More interest is being shown in the administration of collective bargaining systems—whether, for example, a particular wage demand is justified or whether a given seniority system should be altered. Doubtless such questions will command even greater interest as relations between unions and employers become more firmly established. Under these circumstances the problem of union-employer responsibility will surely receive closer attention.

The term "responsibility" may be used in any one of several connections. Unions and employers have certain obligations not only to each other but to the groups whom they represent. In the case of unions, it is to their members; in the case of employers, to their stockholders. Thus it is not only possible that unions and employers may disregard obligations to each other; they may also violate obligations to the groups for whom they are spokesmen. At the same time, both parties have more than these immediate commitments. They must answer to the courts of the land if any laws are broken. They must expect censure if they ignore the interests of other groups in industry—other workers or other employers. They are responsible for the economic health of industry. Nor can they overlook the interests of the public as consumers, however vague or intangible their obligations in this direction might seem. Responsibilities to these various groups are all aspects of the problem; none may be arbitrarily ruled out as unimportant or irrelevant.

The cry of irresponsibility—whether from one side or the other—is usually raised in connection with a labor dispute. Controversies between unions and employers are of two sorts: first, differences over the formulation of the terms of agreements; second, difficulties over the interpretation or enforcement of agreements. Disputes of the former type occur over demands for recognition, bargaining privileges, higher wages, seniority rights, and the like. Disputes of the latter type arise during the life of agreements, after these broader issues have been decided. For example, there may be difficulty as to the application of the wage provisions of an agreement or the administration of a seniority system. In disputes of this sort the charge is almost always made that one party or the other has disregarded his obligations under the agreement. An employer who signs an agreement with a union promises to maintain certain conditions of employment. If he is represented by officials of an employers' association in dealings with the union, he is still bound by the agreement. The union, on its part, promises to submit disputes in accordance with the grievance procedure outlined in the agreement and not to strike while the agreement is in effect. Individual workers who are represented by the union in dealings with the employer are bound by this commitment as well.[4] These are the principal obligations assumed by the parties to a union agreement. An employer, union, or individual worker who disregards them thereby disregards immediate and important responsibilities.

In order to reduce the problem to manageable limits the present study chiefly concerns this aspect of the question of responsibility. But even though thus narrowed, the study has a distinct bearing on some of the broader aspects of the problem noted above. Any adequate analysis of disputes over violations of agreements tends to show how unions and employers discharge their obligations to the groups they represent as well as to one another. It is inevitable that the material herein prescribed illuminate the relation between unions and employers and the courts. The manner in which different systems of collective bargaining are administered is, of course, discussed in considerable detail. Conflicts concerning the application of agreements bring out many of the stresses and strains to which bargaining systems are subject. Such disputes reflect important shifts in the bargaining strength of the contracting parties and they provide a valuable index to the economic soundness of a union agreement. Indeed, controversies over violations of an agreement are sometimes as weighty as disputes over its original terms. Usually, agreements set forth certain broad principles which assume meaning only on subsequent application. Moreover, the specific ways in which an agreement is applied frequently influence the attitudes of both sides toward it and shape their demands when negotiations for the next agreement are begun.

However, even after the present investigation has been restricted to this phase of collective bargaining problems, many difficulties, unfortunately, remain. Violations of union agreements are not easy to identify. What might seem to one party to be a deliberate violation of an agreement might seem to another to be a legitimate interpretation of its terms. This makes it impossible to generalize safely about the extent of the problem. Nor is it always easy to assign guilt; indeed, in many cases blame falls on no particular person or group. A step towards clarification is taken if violations of union agreements are classified. One such classification is to distinguish between substantive and procedural violations. The former relates to the standards of employment embodied in an agreement, specifying certain wage and hour rates, vacation privileges, seniority rules, and other conditions of employment; a substantive violation occurs if

[4] The relation which exists between a union and individual workers is not always clear. Sometimes it is difficult to determine whether a union is the representative of a certain group of workers. The same is true of employer associations in reference to individual employers. These issues are discussed in Chapter IV, *infra*.

any one of these clauses is disregarded. The second type of violation concerns the procedure for handling disputes that may arise during the life of an agreement. This procedure provides for a series of conferences between various spokesmen of the two parties; most agreements provide for arbitration by an outside third party if all other attempts to reach a settlement fail. Until the steps outlined in agreements are carried out no strikes or lock-outs are permitted. Any act which disregards these rules is a procedural violation.

Violations of the first type (real or alleged) occur very frequently. Agreements are necessarily framed in general terms. They must cover a variety of problems and circumstances; the process of interpretation and application begins after agreements have been signed. Employers are confronted by countless managerial decisions which often involve issues covered by the agreements. An employer might discharge a man, alleging incompetency. But this worker may have been an active union member, and the union may insist he was fired for that reason. Or an employer might hire new employees for work requiring special training, while the union contends that old employees are fully qualified. Such are some of the controversies arising over substantive violations. It is important to note that these are almost always due to some step taken by an employer, not by a union. This is so because the day-to-day decisions of management are the responsibility not of the union, but of the employer.

On the other hand, procedural violations are less frequent but generally far more serious. It is one thing for an employer to violate the substantive provisions of an agreement; it is quite another to refuse to discuss the merits of a case with union spokesmen. No less serious are actions by unions which violate procedures for handling disputes. Sometimes unions strike before all steps in the conference procedure have been completed. It is this fact which, more than any other, has given rise to the charge of union irresponsibility. Procedural violations committed by either side may have the effect of undermining or even destroying bargaining relations. But neither party chooses such a course—and this is the important point—unless it feels that there is good and sufficient reason for doing so. A union may conclude that the employer is trying to win away its members, deprive it of the benefits it has won, and break up its organization altogether. In such a case the union may therefore decide that a strike represents the only means of preserving its gains and holding its ranks intact. On the other hand, the first move in defiance of an agreement may come from an employer convinced that it renders efficient management or profitable operations impossible.

The foregoing classification of violations suggests another—one that might distinguish between those that are significant and those that are superficial. There are some disputes that have no bearing on issues beyond those immediately involved. The matter of the transfer of a single worker to a lower wage classification may be of this type, or a protest against changing the speed of production in a particular department of a plant. At the same time, the disposition of certain controversies may establish important precedents; they may affect an unusually large group of workers; or they may concern questions of a basic nature. Indeed, they sometimes raise the doubt whether collective relations between an employer and union will continue at all; for an agreement may be completely disrupted by struggles over a general reduction in wages or over a change in the method of computing piece-rates or over an effort by the union to circumvent the procedure for handling disputes.

It is clear, from this preliminary explanation, that the significance of disputes occurring during the life of an agreement depends upon the surrounding circumstances. One of our purposes here is to review the methods provided under agreements for handling controversies of this sort and to discuss the legal aspects of the problem. But the chief objective is to discover why violations are committed and why disputes occur while agreements are in force. This is done by examining specific situations where the problem has assumed an acute form. Thus, particular attention is paid to situations where the gap between standard and practice became so wide that collective dealings were broken off entirely. Such an examination should reveal in clear-cut fashion what problems confront unions and employers in their relations with one another. In analyzing these various situations a sharp distinction is made between long-established systems of collective bargaining and those that are comparatively recent. The most important conclusions of the study grow out of this distinction. For it shows that while the problem of responsibility is of equal moment in both the new and the old bargaining systems, the character of the problem changes. Proposals for remedial action must take that difference into account.

It should be pointed out that this inquiry is not primarily concerned with problems raised by the present national defense program. Emphasis is placed on background circumstances and long-term factors rather than on immediate questions resulting from the emergency. However, much of the material pertains to the existing situation. Today the Federal government is proceeding on the assumption that the best way to maintain industrial peace is for employers and unions to sign agreements covering wages, hours, and other standards of employment. This is a valid assumption. But, as already indicated, the signature of an agreement is merely a first step. Then comes the all-important task of implementing it and making it work. There is also the necessity of preparing demands for the next agreement, and negotiating terms when the old one has expired. If these things are not done with a consciousness of the responsibilities involved, there can be no hope for harmony in the industrial world.

CHAPTER II

ADJUSTMENT MACHINERY: NEW AGREEMENTS

In handling controversies over the application of agreements, unions and employers are generally ready to follow certain prearranged procedures. These steps are incorporated in the agreements, forming what is known as adjustment or grievance machinery, and providing for a series of conferences between the two parties in case of dispute. Both sides, of course, promise to submit all such disputes to the grievance machinery. In establishing this machinery the two parties act on the assumption that there is a clear-cut distinction between matters concerning the interpretation of existing agreements and matters involving the terms of prospective agreements. Where bargaining relations have existed for many years this assumption is almost always well founded. But under newly established systems, controversies over the interpretation of an agreement are often little different from controversies over the original terms of the agreement. First agreements are usually framed in general and rather vague terms, leaving many important issues to be decided later. Then, too, parties to first agreements are often unfamiliar with collective bargaining procedures. Most important of all, perhaps, considerations of power politics frequently arise even after the original agreement is signed. One side or the other may conclude that the new agreement has not substantially altered conditions or that its terms do not accurately reflect the true balance of power.

Under these circumstances, even a dispute during the life of the agreement becomes a test of the relative strength of the two sides. The union may disregard the grievance procedure and take the "law into its own hands." The employer or employers may refuse to negotiate grievances in good faith. An open break may ensue, even leading to the termination of the agreement. When these conditions exist, grievance procedures and other provisions of the agreement have little effect. No longer are arguments treated on individual merit. No longer are the facts of each case carefully examined. If such a spirit prevails, disputes are approached with the intent not of settling them but of keeping them unsettled. Each dispute becomes part of a broad strategy to strengthen one party and weaken the other. Controversies no longer concern particular cases, except incidentally. The real issue is a struggle for power.

Where long-established systems exist, the agreement is more likely to be an accurate reflection of the relative bargaining strength of the two parties. Both the union and the employer have become accustomed to discussion and conference rather than to trial by combat. It is in such cases that the grievance machinery may make a valuable contribution to the orderly handling of controversial issues. Even under newly established agreements, circumstances may quickly change so that grievance procedures become of greater importance. Indeed, a well-planned grievance apparatus may spell the difference between constructive dealings and open conflict.

GENERAL CHARACTERISTICS

Under most agreements, the machinery for adjusting grievances proceeds in the following manner. When a dispute occurs, various representatives of the two parties meet in a series of conferences until a settlement is reached. If they fail to reach a solution they resort to an appeal, usually provided for, to some outside third party. In this event both sides are committed in advance to accept the impartial spokesman's findings, for refusal would mean repudiation of the agreement. When responsibility has been fixed—by direct dealings between the disputants or by the decision of an arbitrator—redress is made under the agreements. In some cases penalties also are specified.

Cases usually begin as grievances raised by individual employees. A worker, for example, may charge that he has not been paid overtime at the rate provided in the agreement. According to some agreements, he could personally complain to his immediate superior; under most agreements, however, he would take the grievance to his union spokesman (variously referred to as steward, delegate, or representative). The unions prefer the latter method since workers are sometimes hesitant about making direct protests to management. Moreover, unions can thereby claim credit for any gains won. On the other hand, employers feel that controversy would be reduced and that decisions would be more "reasonable" if the former procedure were observed.

The union spokesman, himself an employee of the firm, accepts the complaint if it is a justifiable one and if there is some hope of getting a favorable decision. If he fails to settle the matter properly, it is referred to the next ranking union official. This official may or may not be an employee of the firm, depending chiefly on its size; in the building trades, for example, the second spokesman is a full-time employee of the union, while in the automobile industry he is an employee of the company. At some step in the procedure, however, a union spokesman whose livelihood is in no way dependent on the employer enters the proceedings. If successive negotiations fail to produce a satisfactory settlement, the case may go to the highest officials of the company and the union.

In a number of industries such as coal mining, clothing manufacture, and building construction, agreements are generally signed, not by single employers, but by employers' associations acting on behalf of their individual members. In these fields the union representatives eventually deal with a committee representing the whole employers' group. If negotiations with this committee fail, the dispute is referred to an impartial outside person for settlement. Sometimes the arbitrator holds office for the duration of the agreement; more frequently provision is made for his appointment only when a deadlock arises. It is worth noting that permanent arbitrators are to be found almost exclusively in fields where agreements are signed with employers' associations. This is true of the clothing, hosiery, fur, and millinery industries, the longshoring industry on the Pacific Coast, and the hotel and laundry industries in New York City.[1] Agreements between the anthracite coal association and the United Mine Workers of America have provided for an Anthracite Board of Conciliation since 1902. This board consists of three employer and three union spokesmen who, in case of a deadlock, refer the dispute to an outside umpire. Beginning in 1929 the umpire has served on a full-time basis. In recent years disputes referred to the umpire have averaged about fifteen a month.[2] On the other hand, agreements between the Building Trades Employers' Association and the New York City building unions do not provide for permanent arbitrators. Controversies are referred to joint trade boards, and umpires are appointed only when necessary. Jurisdictional disputes in the New York City building trades are settled by the Executive Committee of the Building Trades Employers' Association, composed entirely of employers. The great majority of agreements in American industry, however, provide for appeal to some sort of arbitration tribunal if other efforts to settle a controversy fail.[3]

Typical of the procedure for handling disputes under agreements

---

[1] Other New York City industries in which there are permanent arbitrators are: restaurant, cleaning and dyeing, publishers and newspapers, scrap iron and steel, trucking, garage, wholesale grocers, retail grocers and sales clerks, luggage and leather, painting and decorating, machine manufacturing, shoe manufacturing, dry goods, and furniture. In most of these latter industries, employers' associations have been formed, but only in a few do permanent arbitrators have jurisdiction over a majority of the industry's employers.

[2] *New York Times*, June 21, 1941, p. 27. The anthracite coal agreements cover 300 operators and 91,000 workers in the five anthracite-producing counties in northeastern Pennsylvania. At present the umpire is Thomas E. Larkin.

[3] For a discussion of these points, see "Grievance Settlement under Union Agreements," *Monthly Labor Review* (U. S. Department of Labor, Bureau of Labor Statistics), vol. 50, no. 2 (February 1940), pp. 286-311. The article was written by Helen S. Hoeber. The union agreements cited in this chapter are on file in the Industrial Relations Division of the U. S. Bureau of Labor Statistics. These agreements are not available to the public. The writer was given access to them with the understanding that the specific firms covered by the agreements would not be identified.

is this clause taken from an agreement signed by a painters' local in Terre Haute, Indiana:

> In the case of a dispute between the union and the company on any matter pertaining to rates of pay, wages, hours of employment or grievances of employees, all reasonable efforts to settle such disputes shall be made by the shop committee and the company. Such efforts failing, an arbitration board of three shall be chosen, one by the shop committee, one by the company, and a third by the first two selected. The decision of such board on all disputes shall be final and binding. Under no circumstances shall a strike or lock-out be called on account of any such dispute.[4]

Most agreements specify in some detail what steps the unions can take to check on possible violations, investigate grievances, and carry cases to designated company officials. To facilitate the presentation and discussion of claims, relatively few agreements require that grievances be reduced to writing. A good many set time limits on the period of negotiation, particularly with regard to the later steps in the procedure. Some agreements grant representatives of the union access to the plant or shop for the purpose of ascertaining possible violations; others specify that the union may examine payrolls and personnel records. Thus, an agreement of an automobile workers' local provides that "Shop payroll records and all records bearing on seniority and payrolls will be open for inspection by the shop grievance committee, or other representative of the union authorized to make such inspection."[5] In some cases the union is given opportunity to investigate the propriety of an action before it is undertaken. Thus, one agreement provides as follows:

> The employer has the right to discharge or suspend employees for good cause. In the interest of proper procedure, the shop chairman shall be notified of the proposed discharge or suspension of a worker twenty-four (24) hours in advance, and the union shall be given an opportunity to discuss the proposed discharge or suspension with the management before it occurs, and the union will give the management a decision on the case before the 24th hour expires.[6]

Under union agreements a settlement at any stage of the proceedings is final and binding. If the charge of violation is sustained, agreements usually provide redress only for the loss incurred; thus, if there has been an underpayment of wages, the employer is merely directed to pay the amount due; or if certain employees have not worked the prescribed number of hours during a given period, they are simply required to make up for the time lost. In a few cases additional penalties are provided. These are designed to serve as deterrents rather than to furnish redress for past wrongs. Here is a typical example:

---

[4] National Brotherhood of Painters, Decorators, and Paperhangers of America, Local 1123, Terre Haute, Indiana (1939).

[5] International Union, United Automobile Workers of America, C. I. O., Local 241, Duluth, Minnesota (1939).

[6] United Electrical, Radio and Machine Workers of America, Local 1121, Chicago, Illinois (1939).

The parties hereto hereby agree that the following sums are fair and just in liquidation of damages because of violation of this agreement: Violations by individual members of the parties hereto, $50.00 to $250.00 for each violation. Violation by either party hereto, or its officers or representatives, $250.00 to $1,500.00 for each violation. Each of the parties hereby agrees for itself and its members to pay to the other, within 30 days, any sum or sums so assessed because of violations of the agreement by itself, its officers or representatives, or its member or members.

Should either party to this agreement fail to pay the amount so assessed within 30 days of its assessment, the party so failing to pay shall be deprived of all benefits of this agreement until such time as the matter will have been adjusted to the satisfaction of the joint conference board.[7]

Another agreement provides as follows:

Neither party to this agreement shall declare a lock-out or strike without five days' written notice to the other party, but no such notice shall be given by either party until the arbitration committee . . . has acted upon the grievances and disputes in question. For any violation of this provision by the employer, the employer shall forfeit and pay to the union the sum of one dollar per day for each union employee in his service at the time of such lock-out; and for any violation of this provision by the union, the union shall forfeit and pay to the employer the sum of one dollar per day for each union employee in the service of the employer who engages in such strike, to be paid during the said five-day period and thereafter at the rate of one dollar per day.[8]

RECENTLY ESTABLISHED SYSTEMS

In light of the general characteristics just described it is instructive to compare enforcement procedures established under two groups of agreements. The first group, covering the automobile industry, the maritime industry (in relation to its sea-going personnel), and the steel industry, were established only recently. The second group of agreements, discussed in the next chapter, cover bituminous coal mining, railroad transportation, and the women's garment industries; these have been in existence for a long time. Grievance procedure for the first group usually consists of five or more steps. As outlined in typical agreements of the three unions concerned, the procedure is illustrated by the charts below:[9]

---

[7] Carpenters' District Council, United Brotherhood of Carpenters and Joiners of America, Chicago, Illinois (1939).

[8] Hotel and Restaurant Employees' International Alliance and Bartenders' International League of America, Local 389, Uniontown, Pennsylvania (1939).

[9] Data for these charts were taken from Agreement between the Carnegie-Illinois Steel Corporation and the Steel Workers' Organizing Committee, on behalf of the Amalgamated Association of Iron, Steel and Tin Workers of North America (March 1937, renewed February 1938), Section 7 (hereinafter referred to as the Carnegie-Illinois Steel Corporation Agreement); from Agreement between the Chrysler Corporation and the International Union, United Automobile Workers of America, C. I. O. (November 1939), Article I (hereinafter referred to as the Chrysler Corporation Agreement); from Agreement between member companies of the American Merchant Marine Institute, Inc., and the National Maritime Union (1938), Articles II, XII (hereinafter referred to as the Merchant Marine Institute Agreement). Each of these agreements is typical of others signed by the unions mentioned.

STEEL WORKERS' ORGANIZING COMMITTEE

(1) Worker	(1) Foreman of department
(2) Representative(s) of local union grievance committee	(2) Foreman and superintendent of department
(3) Local union grievance committee	(3) General superintendent of plant
(4) Representatives of national union	(4) Representatives of top corporation management
(5) Impartial chairman (*ad hoc*)	

UNITED AUTOMOBILE WORKERS, C. I. O.

(1) Worker	(1) Foreman of department
(2) Representative of local union shop committee	(2) Foreman of department
(3) Representative of local union shop committee	(3) Superintendent of department
(4) Local union shop committee	(4) Labor relations supervisor of plant
(5) Local union shop committee	(5) Superintendent of plant
(6) Officer(s) of local union	(6) Superintendent of plant
(7) Officer(s) of national union	(7) Director of industrial relations of corporation

NATIONAL MARITIME UNION

(1) Worker	(1) Immediate superior
(2) Spokesman of ship delegate	(2) Immediate superior
(3) Ship delegate	(3) Head of department
(4) Ship delegate(s)	(4) Master of ship
(5) Representative of national union	(5) Representative of top corporation management
(6) Representative(s) of national union on port committee	(6) Representatives of corporations on port committee
(7) Impartial chairman (*ad hoc*)	

Grievance procedure under agreements of the three unions does not in every instance follow the steps shown in the charts. Variations are numerous, due chiefly to diversities in the size of firms or bargaining units. The essentials, however, remain the same. The really important differences arise not because of variations in the terms of agreements, but because of differences between the written word of an agreement and the way it is administered in actual practice. A striking illustration of this fact is the agreement between the National Maritime Union and the American Merchant Marine Institute (as spokesman for its member firms). If a dispute cannot be settled either by shipboard or shoreside delegates of the union, the agreement provides that the union and company shall appoint a port committee, which, if necessary, is to choose an impartial member. Actually, unsettled disputes go directly from the shoreside spokesmen of the union to the Merchant Marine Institute. After deliberation by the Institute's committee in charge of agreement negotiations, this body issues a decision on the dispute. Should either party refuse to accept the ruling, further negotiations are held between the union spokesmen and the Institute's negotiating committee. If an agreement cannot be reached, the matter is supposed to be referred to arbitration. During the life of the 1938 agreement, however, no cases were brought to arbitration;[10] consequently, a few disputes have remained unsettled.

Nevertheless the procedure for handling grievances is generally similar in all three industries. Each step provides an additional opportunity to secure a settlement. As a particular grievance moves from one level of negotiations to another, different spokesmen make an effort to settle the controversy. On the union's side, negotiations progress from worker, to union departmental representative, to union grievance committee, and finally to officials of the local and national union. On the employer's side, negotiations are handled successively by department foreman, department superintendent, plant superintendent, and finally by top officials of the company or their representatives. There are modifications in this procedure, largely due to differences in the type of work performed and in the way supervision is exercised,[11] but, as already indicated, the basic steps are essentially the same.

It is pertinent, at this point, to express some doubt whether all of these stages of negotiation are necessary or desirable. Of course, it is important that every opportunity be given to settle grievances by those immediately concerned. At the same time, it is clear that if there are too many steps in the procedure, there is the possibility of serious delay before reaching final decisions, during which charges of "bad faith" are likely to arise and an atmosphere of mutual suspicion may develop. Just where the line should be drawn cannot be determined without a careful investigation of the facts of each situation. One rule, however, can be laid down quite categorically: each step in the procedure should be on a genuinely different level than the preceding step. If the spokesmen at any one stage in the negotiations possess only the same authority and point of view as those who acted before, a likely result is the waste of valuable time and a growth of distrust in the whole procedure. Some such difficulty seems to be present in the relations between the large automobile manufacturers and the C. I. O. automobile workers' union. Their agreements call for no less than seven different steps in the handling of grievances.[12] The third step provides that, for the company, the superintendent of the department take over from the foreman, but, for the union, the same spokesman remains. In the fifth step, the superintendent of the plant carries on where the plant's labor relations supervisor leaves off; the union representative is identical at both levels. Such roundabout procedures readily arouse suspicion. As a result, the union has frequently charged that the large automobile manufacturers do not

---

10 *Report to the President and to the Congress* (Maritime Labor Board), March 1, 1940, pp. 196-197.

11 The widest departures from this method of handling grievances are found under agreements of the National Maritime Union.

12 See Chart, p. 17.

handle grievances in good faith.[13] This source of suspicion and unrest has been less important in the steel and maritime industries.

Setting time limits on deliberations at various stages of the procedure helps to expedite the handling of grievances. In most of the agreements of the U. A. W.-C. I. O. and of the National Maritime Union, time limits are set on the final stage of the procedure. Under the Chrysler agreement the board of final appeal, which consists of two executives of the company and two representatives of the international union, must dispose of any grievance within thirty days after the case is submitted.[14] The agreement signed with the General Motors Corporation on June 27, 1940, also imposes time limits on earlier steps in the grievance procedure. In the agreements of the National Maritime Union and member concerns of the American Merchant Marine Institute, three days is the maximum allowed for the deliberations of the board of final appeal. In this instance the board consists of three representatives of the union and three representatives of the company, plus a seventh member chosen at the time the board is convened.[15] No such time limits are provided in the agreements between the Steel Workers' Organizing Committee and the steel manufacturers. With regard to discharge cases, however, the agreements of this union as well as those of the U. A. W.-C. I. O., require that such matters be disposed of within five days of the date of dismissal.[16]

In their dealings with one another the authority of employer and union spokesmen in these industries is of varying scope. In theory, under all three of the agreements, there are certain matters which are not to be taken up under the grievance procedures. Each agreement, according to usual practice, prohibits grievances which involve questions of general wage policy, plant discipline, and other broad managerial functions. For example, a clause in the 1940 agreement between the General Motors Corporation and the U. A. W.-C. I. O. provides that:

> The right to hire; promote; discharge or discipline for cause; and to maintain discipline and efficiency of employees, is the sole responsibility of the Corporation except that union members shall not be discriminated against as such. In addition, the products to be manufactured, the location of plants, the sched-

---

[13] These charges do not come from the C. I. O. union alone. Responsible spokesmen for the A. F. of L. union in this industry have made similar charges. During the past year accusations of this sort have become less frequent. As late as the fall of 1940, however, the general secretary of the Mechanics Educational Society of America, Matthew Smith, had occasion to charge the General Motors Corporation with "deliberate stalling" in the handling of grievances. *New York Times*, October 3, 1940, p. 22.

[14] Chrysler Corporation Agreement (1939), Article I, Section 9. It is worth noting that time limits were not included in the first Chrysler Corporation Agreement, signed in April 1937.

[15] Merchant Marine Institute Agreement (1938), Article XII, Section 2.

[16] Carnegie-Illinois Steel Corporation Agreement (1937, renewed 1938), Section 9. Chrysler Corporation Agreement (1939), Article 2 (Discharge).

ules of production, the methods, processes and means of manufacturing are solely and exclusively the responsibility of the Corporation.[17]

Actually, the zone in which management has exclusive authority seems to vary considerably from company to company and, in some cases, from plant to plant within the same concern. The question of managerial authority is one of the most important aspects of the problem of union-employer responsibilities. This question is discussed at some length in Chapter VI in connection with the automobile industry.

Another rule (albeit unwritten) excludes grievances which would occasion a change in the original terms of agreements. This rule is not contained in any one provision of the agreements and is subject to even more varied interpretation than the rule just noted. The fact that both of these provisions are so vague makes for two unfortunate results: First, it encourages representatives of the unions to bring up complaints which have no rightful place in the grievance procedure; second, it makes it easy for representatives of the employers to rule out of consideration certain grievances which, though embarrassing to the management, may be legitimate issues for deliberation. The former difficulty has thus far proved to be the more important. Lesser officials, particularly those in the newer unions, are eager to prove their fighting qualities. To do so they press claims raised by the men whether justifiably or not. In the maritime industry, ship delegates have gone great lengths in this direction. Until recently, numerous strike actions not authorized by the national organization have occurred after men have signed on shipboard. Efforts by national officers and employers have done much to correct this.[18]

Serious difficulties have resulted from this failure to abide by the rule requiring both parties to distinguish between disputes over the interpretation of agreements, on the one hand, and, on the other, disputes over changes in the agreements or over issues not covered by the agreements. It has meant that disputes in the first category are frequently approached in the same spirit as those in the second. The controlling consideration in both instances becomes the relative strength of the two parties. In such circumstances, decisions are not based on the merits of the case or on methods of persuasion. Emo-

---

[17] Agreement with the General Motors Corporation, signed June 24, 1940, Article 3(c). Similarly, Section 8 of the Carnegie-Illinois Steel Corporation Agreement (1937, renewed 1938) states: "The management of the works and the direction of the working forces, including the right to hire, suspend or discharge for proper cause, or transfer, and the right to relieve employees from duty because of lack of work, or for other legitimate reasons, is vested exclusively in the Corporation . . . ." Agreements signed by the National Maritime Union and the steamship companies in 1938 and 1940 contain no clauses of this sort.

[18] See article by Joseph Curran, President, National Maritime Union, in *The Pilot,* December 10, 1937, p. 20; also letter, dated April 14, 1940, from Frank J. Taylor, President, American Merchant Marine Institute, Inc., to Senator Josiah W. Bailey, Chairman, Senate Committee on Commerce (available at the office of the Institute).

tional rivalries enter the situation, and in the ensuing struggle, the ideal of stable relations is sometimes given short shrift. Under the agreements of the National Maritime Union, for example, many cases have arisen which, in effect, involve demands by the union for a voice in the selection of personnel. Cases under the automobile agreements bearing on the speed of production concern changes of no less importance.[19] This can only mean that disputes are referred to the grievance procedure which it is not designed to handle. The machinery becomes clogged with unsettled cases, engendering impatience, hostility, and mutual distrust.

To a limited extent these circumstances reflect a lack of familiarity with the techniques and obligations of collective bargaining. It should be remembered that union agreements have only recently been established in these industries. It is nevertheless true that the chief difficulties are the result of deliberate measures undertaken by the unions or employers. Indeed, in some instances one or the other side has purposely stirred up unrest and instability in the hope of advancing its special interests during the strife that follows. That is when union strategy is likely to take an overt or extremist form. Employer strategy, resting as it does on the power to hire, fire, and grant or withhold promotions, can assume greater subtlety. In either case, however, the objective is to increase the bargaining strength of one party at the expense of the other. These problems are discussed at some length in later chapters and so are not considered further here.

Another aspect of grievance procedure problems is the authority of union and employer representatives to settle disputes. Under current practice the various spokesmen are empowered to dispose of cases at any step in the procedure. Of course, they must report to their superiors and, particularly in regard to the more important issues, care is taken to conform to the general policies of the organization. Union delegates must be prepared to answer the criticisms of the membership at the next meeting of the local. The tenure of office of national union officials is relatively secure, but turnover among shop delegates in these unions is high. Similarly, employer representatives must answer to the top management and, ultimately, to the board of directors. Nonetheless, considerable latitude is left to the spokesmen of each side, even in the early stages of negotiations, and the particular abilities and personal characteristics of these men play a correspondingly important part in the whole procedure.

Spokesmen for the companies, of course, are chosen by the top management. The union representatives who handle the first steps of the negotiations are elected by the men in their plant unit or district; later proceedings are entrusted to officials of the national union assigned to this type of work by the national executive board. The

---

[19]This difficulty has been less widespread in the steel industry.

agreements in these three industries grant certain powers to the union representatives to investigate complaints, discuss grievances with workers, and confer with company officials. In this respect, the agreements of the U. A. W.-C. I. O. and of the Steel Workers' Organizing Committee are somewhat more detailed than those of the National Maritime Union. The agreement with the Chrysler Corporation, for example, permits chief stewards in the various departments to confer with foremen and other company representatives during working hours without loss of time or pay; but it does not specify how or when representatives of the union may confer with the men in regard to their complaints. The Chrysler agreement also provides that the union shop committees in the various plants shall have meetings with the labor relations supervisors of the respective plants once each month; but before any grievance will be discussed by these or higher officials, it must be reduced to writing. Moreover, union committeemen are not to be paid for time spent in meetings of this sort. Finally, union officers and plant committee members enjoy the highest seniority ratings of any workers in the plant. Chief stewards stand next on the seniority lists, although their seniority is figured on a departmental rather than on a plant-wide basis. These safeguards are important since much of the responsibility for handling grievances rests on spokesmen who, themselves, are employees of the concern.[20]

The agreements of the Steel Workers' Organizing Committee are somewhat more specific on this point than those of the U. A. W.-C. I. O. They provide that members of the plant committees shall be given time off—without pay—to attend grievance meetings and to visit other departments in the plant for the purpose of transacting any legitimate business. As in the case of the automobile agreements, the members of the plant committees must be employees of the company involved. Meetings with plant superintendents are held at specified periods, but in the case of the steel union agreements, grievances do not have to be reduced to writing.[21]

With regard to the powers of union delegates to investigate complaints and to confer with workers, the agreements of the National Maritime Union are singularly non-committal. The only provision touching directly on these points lays down rules for the distribution of passes. A typical agreement specifies that representatives of the union may board vessels for the purpose of transacting union business with the unlicensed personnel (who make up the membership of the National Maritime Union), provided they do not interfere with or retard the work of the ship or violate any provisions of the agreement.[22] This marks out a rather vague zone of activity. Day-to-day

[20] Chrysler Corporation Agreement (1939), Article I, Sections 1-7.

[21] See, for example, Carnegie-Illinois Steel Corporation Agreement (1937, renewed 1938), Section 7.

[22] Merchant Marine Institute Agreement (1938), Article I, Section 5.

dealings, of course, will make the grant of authority more explicit, but at present this issue is a potent source of controversy. Neither the maritime, automobile, or steel agreements grant union representatives the right to check payrolls, investigate cost figures, or study company earnings. If confidence between unions and employers can be increased, this feature of the agreements may be changed.

The position and authority of employer representatives who deal with these problems is an equally important consideration. Generally speaking, the relation between the under-officials and top management of business organizations in these industries is a close one. However, there is always a possibility of lesser officials taking responsibility into their own hands. At one time plant foremen enjoyed considerable latitude in their dealings with employees, sometimes even violating written company rules. During the 1920s, for example, foremen in the automobile industry had considerable influence over questions of hiring, firing, and promotion. Today much of the foremen's independence with regard to these matters is gone, although there are still occasions when foremen disregard the official labor policies of their companies. In this connection, the maritime industry, of course, presents distinct difficulties. The tradition of the sea requires unquestioning obedience of every man on board. The captain of a ship is therefore pretty much his own master. The way he deals with complaints may or may not coincide with the policies of the company's top management or, for that matter, with the formal provisions of the union agreement. The union has attempted to deal with this problem by securing specific commitments from the corporation's management before the men put out to sea; in some conspicuous instances, they have gone to extreme lengths to achieve this end. The requirements of genuine collective bargaining as opposed to the traditional authority of shipmasters present a contradiction which probably will not be resolved for a long time. Perhaps the best course for the union to follow is to become fully informed as to conditions on shipboard and then bring pressure on uncooperative captains through company officials. It would hardly be advisable for the union to try to exert pressure directly on the shipmasters themselves.

The provision for the final disposition of grievance cases raises complicated questions. When unions lose confidence in the methods by which final appeals are handled, they tend to become distrustful of all prior steps in the procedure. Decisions which would otherwise be accepted in good grace are viewed with suspicion or are bitterly opposed. This is why the manner of settlement is so important. Provision for ultimate appeal to some impartial outside party is at least an indication that the agreement has been accepted in good faith by both sides. Most agreements of the Steel Workers' Organizing Committee and of the National Maritime Union contain such a provision.

In steel disputes the appointment of an umpire by mutual consent of the union and company officials is called for when a deadlock in the final step of the negotiations occurs.[23] In National Maritime Union cases the impartial member is chosen at the outset of the deliberations of the port committees. If these port committees (which are made up of three representatives from the union and three from the company involved in the dispute) cannot decide on the seventh member, he is designated by the Mediation and Conciliation Service of the United States Department of Labor.[24] In actual practice, arbitrators have only rarely been appointed in these two industries. But the very fact that this step can be taken increases confidence in the whole procedure.

Agreements between the U. A. W.-C. I. O. and the large automobile manufacturers contain no such provision. The last step in the procedure is simply a conference with two or more officials of the company involved; if both sides remain adamant, there is no recourse to a third party and an open break becomes inevitable.[25] Significantly enough, the agreement with the General Motors Corporation signed in 1940 calls for the appointment of a permanent umpire.[26] Of course, the addition of an extra step in the negotiations may do nothing more than postpone an open break and thus have little effect. It is the spirit in which cases are handled rather than the mechanics of grievance machinery that really counts. There is little reason to believe, for example, that developments under the Chrysler agreement, which contains no arbitration clause, will prove to be very different from developments under the General Motors agreement.

Finally, even if both parties concede that a violation of the agreement has occurred, no formal penalties are invoked under the agreements of these three unions. True, if the union members violate their promise not to strike before they have exhausted the grievance procedures outlined above, the managements may discipline the men as they see fit and can terminate the agreements at once.[27] In the agreements between the National Maritime Union and the member companies of the American Merchant Marine Institute, such action would be a cause for discharge.[28] On the other hand, if an employee has been unfairly dismissed and is reinstated to his position, according to customary practice he would receive full back-pay.[29] But there are

[23] Carnegie-Illinois Steel Corporation Agreement (1937, renewed 1938), Section 7.

[24] Merchant Marine Institute Agreement (1938), Article XII, Section 2.

[25] See, for example, Chrysler Corporation Agreement (1939), Article I, Section 9.

[26] Dr. George W. Taylor is now permanent umpire under the General Motors agreement. He succeeds Dr. Harry A. Millis.

[27] See, for example, Chrysler Corporation Agreement (1939), Section 4, p. 1.

[28] Merchant Marine Institute Agreement (1938), Article I, Section 2.

[29] There is no such provision, however, in the agreement with the Merchant Marine Institute (1938).

no penalties as such for violating the agreements. The upshot is that deterrents to violations tend either toward mildness and ineffectiveness or toward action of an extreme sort. An example of the latter may occur when a union calls a strike to enforce an agreement or where the employer dismisses workers for disregarding an agreement. Obviously, such measures tend to aggravate rather than settle difficulties. If these agreements are worth enforcing, probably some system of financial penalties should be established. This assumes that both parties would consent to the fines prior to imposition; it would be manifestly unwise to let employers or unions set the amount *ex post facto.* The advantage of money penalties is that such a system places deterrents on violations; at the same time it is much less serious than threats by the union to call a strike or threats by the employer to dismiss all "troublemakers." In short, the method would seem to be a compromise between too lenient and too severe a policy.

It is worth noting, in passing, that there have been fewer disturbances under the steel agreements than under the automobile agreements. Various reasons have been advanced to explain this difference. The officials of the steel union have had a background of many years of responsible union leadership. Most of them were drawn from important posts in the United Mine Workers of America. On the other hand, the leaders of the automobile unions were generally untried and inexperienced. Moreover, factional disputes have not plagued the Steel Workers' organization; in contrast, such disputes have figured prominently in the automobile industry since the advent of unionism. Then, too, extremist groups have played a more conspicuous part in the automobile unions, where charges of Communism and radicalism have been frequent. Seldom have such accusations been brought against the Steel Workers' Organizing Committee. Finally, and probably most important, the first agreements in the automobile industry were won after hard-fought battles. These struggles left a deep mark on union-employer relations. No such bitter struggles preceded the original agreements with the United States Steel Corporation and with most of the other steel mills. The only companies which refused to grant recognition were those of the "Little Steel" group. Inasmuch as bargaining relations were established peacefully in most of the steel companies, both sides felt more ready to administer the agreements in good faith. In its dealings with the United States Steel Corporation, for example, the union made no important demands between 1937 and 1940. This policy of moderation is hardly surprising since at the time the first agreement was signed, the union's membership in that company was not very large.

CHAPTER III

ADJUSTMENT MACHINERY: OLD AGREEMENTS

In contrast with the comparatively recent agreements just reviewed, it is illuminating to examine the grievance and enforcement procedure in three industries where union agreements have existed for many years—bituminous coal mining, women's clothing, and railroad transportation. Unionism is well established in each of these fields; in all three, likewise, employers' associations play an important part in the scheme of industrial relations.[1] In bituminous coal and women's clothing, closed shop agreements are commonly accepted. These three industries have had machinery for handling grievances and enforcing agreements long enough to show that it possesses considerable survival value. Their apparatus therefore indicates the lines along which similar devices may develop in newly organized industries.

The steps in the grievance procedures established under union agreements in these three industries are shown in the charts below. As in the charts of the previous chapter, each stage of the negotiations presents an additional opportunity to reach a settlement. In the present instances, however, every step represents a definite advance in the negotiations, with the result that each spokesman expresses a greater degree of authority or a broader point of view than the one who acted before.[2]

---

[1] In some ports of the maritime industry, employers' associations figure in negotiations over new agreements; but in contrast to current practice in the coal, women's clothing, and railroad industries, they play a very minor part in the settlement of grievance cases. In the automobile and steel industries, employers' associations do not participate, directly at least, in either type of negotiations.

[2] Data for these charts were taken from Agreement between the Central Pennsylvania Coal Producers' Association, etc., and the International Union, United Mine Workers of America and Districts 2, 3, etc. (1939), article entitled *Settlement of Disputes* (hereinafter referred to as the Appalachian Agreement); from Agreement between the Merchants' Ladies' Garment Association, Inc., and the International Ladies' Garment Workers' Union and the Joint Board of Cloak, Suit, Skirt and Reefer Makers' Union of the I. L. G. W. U. (1937-1940), Article 16 (hereinafter referred to as the Merchants' Garment Agreement); from Agreement between the Boston and Albany Railroad Company and the Order of Railroad Telegraphers (1939), Rule 30 (hereinafter referred to as the Boston and Albany Agreement). Each of these agreements is typical of others signed by the three unions mentioned.

UNITED MINE WORKERS OF AMERICA

(1) Worker	(1) Mine management
(2) Pit committee	(2) Mine management
(3) Bi-partisan board made up of two members from each side with a fifth member if necessary	

INTERNATIONAL LADIES' GARMENT WORKERS' UNION

(1) Worker	(1) Employer
(2) Local union shop chairman	(2) Employer
(3) Manager of local union or his deputy	(3) Manager of employers' association or his deputy
(4) Impartial chairman	

ORDER OF RAILROAD TELEGRAPHERS

(1) Worker and union representative(s)	(1) Immediate superior
(2) Worker and union representative(s)	(2) Next higher official(s)
(3) Worker and union representative(s)	(3) Highest official designated by company
(4) National Railroad Adjustment Board	

Among the mine workers, an aggrieved worker first goes to the management. If a settlement cannot be secured, negotiations then begin between the pit committee (generally consisting of three employees of the mine elected by their fellow-workers to adjust disputes) and the management. Should this step fail, the dispute is referred to a joint board made up of two representatives chosen by the employers' association and two by the union. Lack of success here brings the matter before an umpire selected by the board.[3] The decision of the umpire is final.[4]

In the ladies' garment field, if a worker cannot settle with his employer, the case is referred first to his shop chairman and then to the manager of his local union. If the local union manager (or his deputy) cannot effect a settlement with the employer, he next negotiates with the manager of the employers' association. If they also fail to agree, the matter is referred to the impartial chairman for final action.[5]

As for grievance procedure in the railroad industry, cases first pass through a hierarchy of company officials. Thus, under the agreement of the Railroad Telegraphers and the Boston and Albany Railroad Company, a worker starts with a complaint to his immediate superior, then to the next ranking official, then to the next, until he has reached "the highest official designated by the company to whom ap-

[3] If the joint board cannot agree upon the selection of an umpire, he is designated by the International President of the United Mine Workers of America and by the president of the operators' association involved.

[4] Appalachian Agreement (1939), articles entitled *Mine Committee* and *Settlement of Disputes.*

[5] Merchants' Garment Agreement (1937), Article 16. The agreement provides for a permanent arbitrator to hold office as long as the agreement is in effect, to be chosen by the parties who draft and sign the agreement.

peals may be made . . . ." At every stage of the negotiations, including the first, the worker "may be assisted by a committee of employees or by one or more duly accredited representatives."[6] If these efforts are unsuccessful, the two parties are bound by existing legislation to refer the case to the appropriate division of the National Railroad Adjustment Board.[7] Cases involving the Order of Railroad Telegraphers, for example, are referred to Division Three of the board. This board, created in 1934 by amendment of the Railway Labor Act of 1926, consists of eighteen members selected by the carriers and eighteen chosen by such labor organizations as have been "freely and independently organized by the employees themselves." The board is made up of four divisions, each organized on a bi-partisan basis and each having jurisdiction over designated categories of railroad employees. If the members of a division cannot reach a settlement, the law provides that they are to appoint a neutral person, or referee, who shall sit with the division and make an award. If they cannot agree on a neutral person, the responsibility for his selection falls upon the National Mediation Board.[8]

Under each of these three long-established systems of collective bargaining a fairly sharp line of demarcation has developed between controversies over new agreements and controversies over the interpretation or enforcement of existing agreements. The legislation already mentioned, which covers labor relations in the railroad industry, is explicit on that point. In addition to the National Railroad Adjustment Board, the same legislation created the National Mediation Board, which consists of three members appointed by the President of the United States. Broadly speaking, this board has mediatory powers over disputes concerning changes in rates of pay, rules, or working conditions.[9] Furthermore, it has the power to conduct elec-

---

[6] Boston and Albany Railroad Agreement (1939), Rule 30. Workers usually act alone when first presenting grievances to their foreman or immediate superiors.

[7] Railway Labor Act, 44 Stat. 577 (1926), as amended, 48 Stat. 1185 (1934), 45 U. S. C. A., ¶¶ 151-188 (Supp. 1940). Cases are referred to the board by petition of either party.

[8] At least up to the present time the National Mediation Board has been obliged to appoint referees in the great majority of cases in which the services of third parties have been required. William H. Spencer, "The National Railroad Adjustment Board," *The Journal of Business of the University of Chicago*, vol. XI, no. 2, part II (April 1938), p. 23.

[9] Section 5, Railway Labor Act, 44 Stat. 580 (1926), as amended, 48 Stat. 1195 (1934), 45 U. S. C. A., ¶ 155 (Supp. 1940). The board may intervene in disputes of this sort only on the request of one of the parties involved. However, it can proffer its services on its own initiative at any time that it finds that a "labor emergency" exists. In either case, it can exercise only mediatory powers. If it is unsuccessful in securing a settlement, the National Mediation Board is instructed to try to induce both parties to submit their controversy to arbitration. If they refuse, the board may call upon the President to appoint an emergency fact-finding board. For thirty days after the Mediation Board has notified the parties that its mediatory efforts have failed, and for a similar period after the emergency board has made its report to the President, neither side is to make any change in the conditions out of which the controversy arose.

tions among employees in order to settle disputes over the selection of employee bargaining representatives. The National Railroad Adjustment Board, on the other hand, has jurisdiction only over disputes "growing out of grievances or out of the interpretation or application of agreements . . . ."[10] While it is not always clear in every case, a line has thus been drawn between disputes involving basic issues and matters concerning interpretation; more specifically, between the formulation of the new terms of agreements or the modification of existing ones, on the one hand, and the interpretation or application of agreements, on the other.[11] If an issue has not been covered by the terms of an agreement, the National Railroad Adjustment Board has hesitated to accept jurisdiction even when the case has seemed rather unimportant. For example, in the case of *American Train Dispatchers' Association v. C. & O. Ry. Co.*, the referee refused to take jurisdiction over a dispute bearing on the abolition of the jobs of two train dispatchers. He found that the agreement did not specify how many positions of this sort should be maintained nor did it expressly or by implication prohibit the carrier from discontinuing regularly established positions. He concluded that "The making of working rules, establishing working conditions or agreements upon wages . . . are basic matters and left to the processes of the Mediation Board."[12]

In effect, a similar distinction exists in bituminous coal mining and women's clothing. Here, however, no legislation has specified what the respective areas of jurisdiction shall be. The line of demarcation has emerged only as a by-product of years of actual dealings between the unions and the employers. During this period innumerable rules have received general acceptance, even though many have not been specifically incorporated in the basic agreements. Usually, unwritten rules have been established as the result of pressure by local union groups on individual employers, and some of these rules have gradually come to be accepted as part of the common law of the trade. Disputes growing out of the interpretation and application of these written and unwritten rules are handled by the grievance machinery described above. But disputes involving matters which have not yet been agreed upon or matters which would constitute a change in the existing agreements are generally deferred until negotiations for a new agreement are commenced.

---

10 Section 3(i), Railway Labor Act, 44 Stat. 578 (1926), as amended, 48 Stat. 1189 (1934), 45 U. S. C. A. ¶ 153 (Supp. 1940).

11 This does not mean that the work of the National Railroad Adjustment Board is simply an extension of the grievance procedure of the agreements. To some extent this is true, since the board's personnel consists half of union and half of employer representatives. But the board's work goes beyond mere adjustment of grievances when a referee enters a case. At this point, at least, the board's work becomes adjudication.

12 N. R. A. B. (3rd Division), Award 42 (1935), cited in Spencer, *op. cit.*, p. 30.

As already remarked, these methods stand in sharp contrast to current practice in the three fields examined earlier. As time goes on the contrast will doubtless become less conspicuous. Under the new agreements today there is little effort to distinguish between disputes over the terms of existing agreements and disputes over basic changes in employment conditions. The unions try to utilize both to strengthen their positions in the plants. The employers, on the other hand, endeavor to checkmate any such moves by the unions.[13] Perhaps tactics of this sort are always characteristic of situations in which power politics dominate. Nevertheless, the goal toward which each side should work is clear. Cases involving basic changes in agreements should be deferred until the time for drafting new agreements has arrived. If the issues are so pressing that they cannot be postponed, the cases still should not follow the regular grievance procedure. Instead, they should go directly to the parties who drafted the agreements, for they are the only persons possessing proper authority to alter the terms. Only in this way can the grievance machinery perform the function for which it was designed.

Another interesting point of comparison is the number of steps in the grievance procedures of the three "old" as against the three "new" collective bargaining systems, although there is little reason to believe that grievance procedures become simpler as bargaining systems grow older. True, there are relatively few steps in the procedure adopted by bituminous coal and women's clothing. But the likelihood is that the contrast with the steel, automobile, and maritime industries is chiefly due to the fact that in coal and clothing the employing units are usually small. In the railroad industry where employing units are large, there are many steps in the grievance procedure. Moreover, in railroads, government and arbitration agencies play an important part in handling disputes. Consequently, litigation over grievance cases, particularly in connection with the National Railroad Adjustment Board, is sometimes prolonged.

In the railroad industry, however, time limits are placed on all early steps in the procedure. This helps to speed up the process of adjustment and partly offsets the delays encountered at later stages. An employee who feels that he has been unjustly treated may have an impartial hearing, but only if he presents a written request within ten days of its occurrence to his immediate superior. Hearings are held and a decision rendered before two weeks have elapsed. If the case is appealed to the next higher official, similar time limits are operative, and likewise if the case is carried still further.[14] No time

---

13 These comments are less applicable to the steel industry than to the automobile and sea-going branch of the maritime industry. For a discussion of these issues see Chapter VI.

14 See, for example, Boston and Albany Railroad Agreement (1939), Rule 30.

limits are prescribed by agreements in the women's garment industry, except in connection with discharge cases, which must be settled within two days after the union asks the employers' association for an investigation.[15] The same thing is true of bituminous coal, where discharge cases must be settled within five days;[16] no other time limits are specified. Presumably such provisions are less important when the steps in grievance procedure are few. Where the steps are numerous as in automobiles and steel, time limits might well be established.

Another point of contrast between the three new and three old systems of collective bargaining is the type of representative which each calls for. On paper, at least, the difference is rather striking. Under agreements of the automobile industry, for example, spokesmen who are not employees of the firm enter negotiations rather late in the procedure. Actually, there is reason to believe that union spokesmen have been given considerable latitude on this score. Agreements in the bituminous coal industry, however, explicitly provide that "outside" spokesmen take over negotiations at the third step in the procedure. In the women's garment industry an outside representative may participate in the negotiations from the start. The same holds true in the railroad industry. The result is that, from the very outset, both parties approach each issue more nearly as equals, and the danger of exploiting employees in their dealings with company spokesmen is reduced. Another not unimportant consequence is that the union officials keep better informed as to the problems which are troubling their members and can therefore function more adequately as leaders of their organizations. It needs to be pointed out, however, that care should be taken not to exclude the union spokesmen most familiar with a particular case too soon in the negotiations. They should be allowed to participate in the proceedings whenever a fresh examination of the facts is required.

As in the three recently organized industries, agreements in the coal, women's clothing, and railroad industries prescribe certain zones in which management is to be free from any union interference. Thus, agreements of the United Mine Workers provide that the "management, direction of the working force and the right to hire and discharge are vested exclusively in the Operator."[17] In actual practice, the lines marking off the exclusive province of managerial control are more narrow than this would imply. Frequently miners and their spokesmen raise issues which fall within the generally accepted sphere of employer authority. In some instances union locals even have gained control over the distribution of the available jobs and

---

[15] See Merchants' Garment Agreement (1937), Article 21.

[16] Appalachian Agreement (1939), article entitled *Disputes.*

[17] *Ibid.*, article entitled *Management of Mines.*

have taken steps to improve the efficiency of mine operations.[18] According to one employer spokesman, controversy over this issue is becoming rare.[19] Nonetheless, cases still arise in which employers charge the union with usurping the functions of management. Agreements in the fields of women's clothing and railroad transportation are more specific in this regard. For example, both prescribe the circumstances under which a worker can be discharged. Likewise, both lay down rules governing the reclassification of jobs, shifts in personnel, and other changes in work schedules. Agreements of the I. L. G. W. U. are quite explicit in this regard. They specify the conditions under which an employer may reorganize his business, or enter into another partnership, or send materials to other firms for fabrication, or introduce a week-work as opposed to a piece-work basis of wage payments.[20] These are substantial encroachments upon what have always been deemed the prerogatives of management. They widen the area of negotiations between union and management considerably and give powers to the union which are hardly mentioned in the automobile, steel, and maritime agreements.

Similarly, union representatives in bituminous coal, railroad transportation, and women's clothing are allowed greater freedom to investigate complaints, check on alleged evasions of agreements, and confer with workers about their grievances. Most striking in this regard are the agreements of the I. L. G. W. U. They provide that union representatives may visit all firms once each season to determine the union standing of the workers; moreover, in company with represenatives of the employers' association, they may investigate any books and records of an employer to ascertain whether he is dealing with non-union shops; the union also has access to the weekly reports which employers file with the impartial chairman, showing the number of garments being made, the piece rates agreed to, and the actual money received by the workers who fabricated them.[21] On such issues as the distribution of available work and the speed of production schedules, the I. L. G. W. U., in effect, enjoys the privilege of joint supervision with management. The task of ferreting out violations of employment standards largely falls on the shoulders of a staff of union investigators, who are continuously checking on day-to-day operations in the shops. This is a concession on the part of management which has hardly reached the discussion stage in the automobile and steel industries.

Representatives of the employers also hold a different position in

---

18 For a good discussion of this problem, see Carter L. Goodrich, *The Miner's Freedom* (Boston: Marshall Jones Company, 1925), Chapter 3.

19 Interview on July 10, 1939, with Byron H. Cannon, Executive Secretary, Western Pennsylvania Coal Operators' Association, Pittsburgh, Pennsylvania.

20 Merchants' Garment Agreement (1937), Articles 6, 10, 25, and 29.

21 *Ibid.*, Articles 3, 4, 41, and 42.

fields where collective bargaining has been long established. This is chiefly due to the fact that, in these industries, employers' associations play an important part in the grievance procedure. Thus, difficult disputes come to the attention of employer spokesmen who, since they are not acting solely for the company immediately involved, are less apt to take a narrow or vindictive view of the situation. In the railroad industry the benefits of this procedure are secured, not through the work of employers' associations, but through the National Railroad Adjustment Board. The personnel of this board represents a broad cross-section of railroad employers and unions.[22] In the other two industries, direct spokesmen for the various employers' associations take charge of negotiations. Moreover, they intervene at the third or fourth step in the proceedings, which means that the influence of other employers is brought to bear on grievances much sooner than in the railroad industry. This circumstance tends to remove disputes from the immediate area of controversy and makes it possible to approach issues from a more detached point of view, thus increasing the chances of reaching a peaceful and satisfactory settlement. A not unimportant result is that the confidence of the union in the whole grievance procedure is strengthened.

An additional factor contributing to stable labor relations in these three industries is the impartial arbitration machinery which their agreements provide. If, in the railroad industry, the National Adjustment Board cannot reach a decision in any particular case, the law requires that a referee be chosen and that the matter be submitted to him. No judicial review of his decision can be secured except by the party in whose favor the award is made—a fact which, to all intents and purposes, renders the referee's decision final.[23] Under agreements of the I. L. G. W. U., the parties who draft the agreements choose permanent arbitrators or impartial chairmen; all unsettled disputes involving the interpretation or application of any clause of the agreements, or involving any acts "between the parties or their respective members, directly or indirectly," are referred to these third parties for final action.[24] In both industries, the employers and unions agree that there shall be no interruption of production through strikes or lock-outs until the entire procedure for handling grievances has been exhausted. In bituminous coal mining, the joint boards choose umpires if deadlocks occur. As in the other two industries, their decisions are final.

---

[22] Employer representatives on the board, however, almost always vote the same way on a case, as do the union representatives. Nonetheless, viewpoints taken towards controversies are probably somewhat broader than would otherwise prevail.

[23] Section 3 (p), Railway Labor Act, 44 Stat. 578 (1926), as amended, 48 Stat. 1189 (1934), 45 U. S. C. A., ¶ 153 (Supp. 1940). Employers in the railroad industry have criticized this restriction on judicial review.

[24] Merchants' Garment Agreement (1937), Article 16.

There seems to be little doubt that disputes have been settled through the impartial machinery provided by these agreements which otherwise would have led to open breaks. But it is hard to say whether the permanent arbitration apparatus existing in the women's garment industry is superior to the *ad hoc* type prevailing in bituminous coal.[25] No evidence was developed in the course of the present study which might decide the point. Against the *ad hoc* method it could be argued that if spokesmen for the two sides cannot adjust a controversy, it would prove just as difficult to agree on the designation of an outside arbitrator, with the result that another issue may be injected into an already thorny question. Under a permanent arbitration system this would not occur. Moreover, it is on the whole advantageous to have arbitrators who are thoroughly familiar with the industry in which they are working, a requirement more likely to be fulfilled by permanent arbitrators than by those appointed for single cases.[26] Finally, the very presence of a permanent arbitrator may serve as a restraining influence on employers and unions. Both parties would tend to have greater confidence in the whole grievance procedure than if cases ultimately come to some person whose identity is not know in advance.

On the other hand, some permanent systems have probably served to increase the amount of litigation, and therefore the cost of handling disputes. Under these systems there is a tendency for both parties to submit matters to arbitrators which they would otherwise have decided by themselves; possibly the differences are thereby multiplied rather than lessened. However, the cost must be considered small if the permanent systems provide a means for disposing of issues which would cause open rupture unless settled. Moreover, under some of these systems, the number of disputes has been reduced. The experience of the men's clothing industry seems to be a case in point. Another danger is that permanent arbitrators cannot be quickly dislodged if they prove to be inept, unfair, or corrupt. True, their period in office ends with the expiration dates of the agreements,

---

[25] Arbitration machinery existing in the railroad industry is somewhat different from both of these types. As already noted, referees are not appointed unless the National Railroad Adjustment Board fails to reach a settlement. Under these circumstances, however, the selection of a third party is required by law and his decision can be enforced by court action.

[26] This feature of the arbitration machinery in the railroad industry has recently been criticized by railroad companies. The charge has been made that the referees who have been chosen know little or nothing about the technicalities of railroad operations and working rules. The carriers, therefore, suggest certain changes in the board's procedure, such as providing referees with a transcript of all board hearings in a case, providing him with all the relevant facts, and requiring referees to make written decisions, giving reasons for their conclusions. See *Reply Brief of Class I Railroads before the Attorney General's Committee on Administrative Procedure, in Re: National Railroad Adjustment Board,* September 6, 1940, pp. 20-24. Copies are available at the office of counsel for the Class I Railroads, Investment Building, Washington, D. C.

usually within one or two years, but much harm may be done in that time. More important, a permanent arbitrator may try to entrench himself by supporting certain powerful elements and neglecting the interests of the industry as a whole. Under the permanent systems a measure of "political" favoritism is probably inescapable. It should be pointed out, however, that the problem does not seem to have become serious under any of the permanent arbitration systems now in effect.

A final aspect of the comparison between the new and the old is the scheme of liquidated damages and penalties which has been set up under the agreements of two of the long-established unions. Agreements in the railroad industry make no specific provision for such a system, though certain by-laws of the unions have much the same effect. It must be borne in mind that both the railroad unions and employers are closely restricted in their freedom of action because they are responsible for the transportation service of the nation. Should either side cause a serious disruption of rail traffic, the Federal government, under its power to regulate interstate commerce, could undoubtedly secure authority from Congress to maintain adequate service. As for bituminous coal mining, agreements there provide definite money penalties if strikes and lock-outs occur before the regular procedure for handling grievances has been completed. It is specified that if there is an illegal stoppage, no further discussions between employer and union can take place; moreover, every worker who participates in such an act is fined one dollar for each day that he remains idle. On the other hand, if an employer locks his men out, he is fined one dollar per mine worker for each day that the mine is shut down.[27]

The agreements of the I. L. G. W. U. have created a system of liquidated damages and penalties applicable only to employers. No money damages can be collected from the union under the agreements; nor can any money penalties be placed on employees who violate the terms of agreements. The question of fining individual workers is thus left to the union to decide. If the employees of a firm cause a stoppage or shop strike during the life of an agreement, the union obligates itself to return the men to work within twenty-four hours. If the union fails to do so and the impartial chairman finds that there has been a "substantial violation" of the no-strike clause, the employers' association can terminate the agreement. On the other hand, if an employer violates the no lock-out clause of the agreement, he is subject to damages. The same is true if he pays his workers less than the established rate, in which case the damages are added to the

---

[27] These penalties were not included in the Appalachian Agreement signed in 1939, but they appear in almost all of the current district agreements. The money collected in this way is generally put into a joint fund and used for charitable purposes.

amounts owed on back-wages. An employer is also open to damages if he violates the hours provision of the agreement. With regard to jobbers, employers found dealing with non-union firms or with firms not on the "designated" list of jobbers are required to pay a fine sufficiently high to offset any advantage gained through such transactions; if the offense is repeated the guilty employer may be expelled from the employers' association and lose all rights and privileges under the agreement.[28] It would seem proper to suggest that, despite the obvious difficulties in the way of enforcement, some system of penalties against the union and its members might well be instituted.

Except for purposes of introducing the problem posed by this study, the bare outline of grievance procedures given above is of secondary value. The more important objective sought in the present investigation is to discover how the adjustment machinery established under union agreements is administered in actual practice, what obstacles are being encountered, and to what extent they are being overcome. Later chapters, therefore, deal with a number of situations in which enforcement problems have been particularly difficult to handle—so much so that in some cases union-employer relations have, in fact, been terminated. The remainder of this chapter deals with the enforcement question in the fields of railroads and bituminous coal.

THE NATIONAL RAILROAD ADJUSTMENT BOARD

It would be wrong to infer from the preceding observations that the enforcement and interpretation machinery in the railroad industry has proved satisfactory to all concerned. At the present time considerable criticism is coming from the employers. They charge that the unions have used the National Railroad Adjustment Board machinery as a device to secure changes in working rules which have long been part of union-employer relations. Under existing board procedure, a union can protest against the application of these rules simply by starting an action before the board. In doing so, the union in question has everything to gain and nothing to lose. The upshot, according to the employers, is that the board is deluged with thousands of cases having little or no real merit. A report to the Attorney General's Committee on Administrative Procedure written under the direction of Professor Walter Gellhorn lends substance to this contention. Says this report:

> Approximately two-thirds of the decisions without referees, and approximately two-thirds of the decisions with referees are in favor of labor. The labor members of the board frankly recognize that they can control these percentages by choosing the cases that are brought to the board, and they admit that they bring some cases which they have no hope of winning, in order that the percentage of

---

[28] Merchants' Garment Agreement (1937), Articles 5, 6, 8, 22, and 37.

favorable decisions will not be too high. They allege that the carriers resort to the same tactics.[29]

It is not surprising, then, that a great many cases finally go to the referees for settlement. This is true in about half of all the cases coming before the board.[30]

The carriers contend, further, that board decisions are frequently unjust. For example, they allege that the board has ruled that particular jobs belong to certain employees even though the amount of work to be done is small and even though the ruling is not in accord with customary practice or is not required by provisions of the agreements.[31] Similarly, the board has ruled that if employees do work belonging to other employees, both must be paid even though the latter do not participate and the work is incidental to other tasks. In one case the members of a road crew changed a caboose themselves as it was Sunday and no yardmen were on hand. The board nevertheless ordered that the yardmen as well as the road crew be paid.[32] The board has also ruled that no positions can be abolished so long as any of the work remains to be performed. Years after the cessation of certain jobs, men have continued to receive back pay for the work that they lost. In one case the positions of hostler and hostler helper were eliminated because an additional yard engine was available to do their work. The board ruled that they should be reinstated and given back pay for the five years since their positions had been terminated.[33] The way in which the board has interpreted "starting-time" and "yard-road" rules has worked particular hardships on the carriers. If starting time is eight o'clock and the crew is supposed to work eight hours, the crew may get paid for twenty hours if it starts at seven-thirty and puts in eight hours. The period between seven-thirty and eight is considered to be part of a different working day; inasmuch as an eight-hour day is guaranteed, the extra half-hour calls for eight hours' pay. Moreover, all of the work is within a twenty-four hour period; therefore, one of the eight-hour periods calls for pay at the rate of time and a-half, or twelve hours, which, added to the other eight, make a total of twenty hours.[34]

---

[29] *Railway Labor* (The Attorney General's Committee on Administrative Procedure, U. S. Department of Justice, Monograph No. 17, April 1940), p. 37. This report is available at the office of the Attorney General, Department of Justice, Washington, D. C.

[30] *Ibid.*, p. 11.

[31] See National Railroad Adjustment Board, Third Division, Awards 1024 and 1113, First Division, Award 929, cited in *Statement and Recommendations of Class I Railroads to the Attorney General's Committee on Administrative Procedure Re: The National Railroad Adjustment Board,* June 26, 1940, pp. 45-48.

[32] First Division, Award 1849, cited in *ibid.*, pp. 44-45. In this connection another decision of the First Division, Award 1947, was cited—*ibid.*, pp. 49-50.

[33] First Division, Award 1930, cited in *ibid.*, p. 54.

[34] *Railway Labor* (Attorney General's Committee on Administrative Procedure), p. 6.

The employers assert that certain changes in the board's procedures would remove the difficulties. Their recommendations are as follows:[35]

1. Each submission should be required to contain a full statement of the claim with opportunity for reply.
2. Time limits should be placed on claims for retroactive awards.
3. Proper means of proof should be provided for determining disputed issues of fact.
4. Persons whose rights may be adversely affected should be given notice, with right of intervention.
5. Interested parties should be allowed to appear before the referee.
6. Procedure in the several divisions of the board should be uniform.
7. Opinions should be prepared and published.
8. Board decisions should be subject to judicial review by the losing party.

In a brief filed with the Attorney General's Committee on Administrative Procedure, the railway unions stated their objections to several of these proposed steps.[36] Their arguments reflect a general approval of the board's work and an apprehension that the carriers are trying to hamstring the board. The brief pointed out that if carriers were allowed to conduct oral hearings before referees, so many would be held that the board's work would be disrupted. It also contended that if rules of evidence were established, board proceedings would lose much of their informal, conference-room atmosphere. Again, it insisted that if notice had to be given to all interested employees, the board would be confronted with very difficult administrative problems. The other proposals advanced by the carriers were not considered in the brief.

On the whole, the objections made by the unions do not seem well taken. The procedural changes suggested by the carriers could probably be instituted without undermining the effective operation of the board. Even the proposals which would allow hearings before referees or which would permit the exercise of rules of evidence in board proceedings could be adopted without impairing the soundness of the board's work. In one important respect, however, the union argument does seem valid. The procedural changes advocated by the carriers will certainly do little to alter the decisions of the board; and the decisions of the board (notably, of course, those rendered by referees) are the real source of the carriers' criticisms.[37] The truth is

---

[35] *Statement and Recommendations of Class I Railroads to the Attorney General's Committee on Administrative Procedure*, June 26, 1940.

[36] *Memorandum filed in behalf of Railway Labor Executives' Association before the Attorney General's Committee on Administrative Procedure in Re: The National Railroad Adjustment Board*, July 11, 1940. Copies are available at the office of counsel for the unions, Nicholas Building, Toledo, Ohio.

[37] On procedural grounds the most serious criticism is that Division I of the board, which handles about eighty per cent of the cases, is three years behind in its work. The other is that the board can deadlock on procedural questions such as those just discussed and no action may be taken one way or another. See *Railway Labor* (Attorney General's Committee on Administrative Procedure), pp. 23-25 and 36-40.

that the real issues at stake are the rules and regulations which the railway unions have been able to establish, and which have imposed such heavy economic burdens on the industry. Admittedly, the National Railroad Adjustment Board has not eliminated these rules nor apparently made them any less harsh from the carriers' point of view. In fact, there is reason to believe that the board has sometimes provided a convenient means for creating additional restrictions. Nevertheless, mere changes in the board's procedure will not attack these basic problems. Negotiations at the time agreements expire are much more important than actions before the board. If the employers and unions could agree to remove some of the rules and regulations, the board would act accordingly. But so long as the two parties refuse to do so, the board can hardly be criticized for following their lead.

These observations concerning the administration of union agreements in the railroad industry raise important questions relating to collective bargaining. Apparently the problem of responsibility is no less acute under long-established systems than under more recent ones. It simply takes a different form in the two situations. In the new systems, power relationships are at stake. In the old systems, economic problems of the industry are uppermost. As bargaining relations become better organized, the problem of responsibility or lack of responsibility chiefly involves economic rather than "political" issues. If unions and employers, in their dealings with one another, pursue policies which are economically disadvantageous to their industry, their policies can rightly be termed irresponsible. That is what seems to have occurred in the railroad industry. The unions have constructed an elaborate system of rules and regulations which have put the industry under a serious economic handicap. Both the government and the employers have pursued a policy of timidity and drift in the face of this tendency, and the absence of firm leadership allows it to proceed unchecked. Unless such leadership asserts itself, the industry's system of collective bargaining will be seriously endangered. Violations of union standards may occur, and there may even be open breaks between the carriers and the unions. The problem of economic responsibility deserves strong emphasis, for it arises in every industry where collective bargaining has long existed.

THE BITUMINOUS COAL INDUSTRY

In connection with current grievance procedures in bituminous coal the present study uncovered no criticism of the kind encountered in the railroad industry. It is important, therefore, to examine the operations of this machinery in some detail. Actual practice in the handling of grievance cases in the bituminous coal industry varies widely. Sometimes the pit committee brings a complaint to the foreman or "mine-boss" first; sometimes it goes directly to the mine superintendent. In some cases representatives of the district union office enter negotiations with the mine management before action is taken by the joint board; in others this step is omitted. In some districts there are labor commissioners who speak for the employers' associations in dealings with the union, and frequently they intervene before cases come to the joint boards. In some instances, too, spokesmen for the international union try to effect settlements with the employers.

Much of the variety in current practice stems from the traditional independence of the mine-worker.[38] Despite striking changes in mining operations, the men are still left pretty much to themselves. True, such innovations as the mechanical cutting and loading machines have increased management supervision of their work; certain improvements in managerial methods have had the same result. But the men "at the face" still work in isolated rooms, payment for at least two-thirds of all the men in the mines is on a piece-work basis, and contact with the "mine-boss" more than once or twice a day is still the exception rather than the rule. All these circumstances make for individualism, as well as for variety, in the miner's relations with his employer.

The absence of uniformity is also rooted in countless differences in the conditions of employment. The miner's earnings do not depend alone on the rate established for his job classification in the district agreement or on the number of days that he receives work during the week. They also depend to some degree on the particular circumstances under which he works from day to day. Part of the roof of the room in which he is working may collapse; the "bottom" may lift and upset the track; water may seep in; the seam of coal on which he is working may narrow or disappear altogether in a fault; the number of cars available for loading may be insufficient.[39] These variations give rise to what is known as yardage and deadwork. The innumerable adjustments which they occasion cannot all be settled in advance at the bi-annual negotiations; in particular situations, considerable responsibility falls on the parties immediately concerned—the worker, pit committee, or district union representative, on the one hand, and the mine superintendent or company official, on the other. In the initial stages of a case the worker himself takes up issues of this sort with the "mine boss," and the workers themselves sometimes play a prominent role in the process. They usually handle initial negotiations in a case; they help to check on violations of the agreements and carry a share of the burden of securing compliance. If a superinten-

[38] The best discussion of this phase of labor relations in the soft-coal industry is contained in Goodrich, *The Miner's Freedom*, pp. 15, *passim*.

[39] For good discussions on this phase of the problem, see Goodrich, *ibid.;* Isador Lubin, *Miners' Wages and the Cost of Coal* (New York: McGraw-Hill Book Co., 1924); and Heber L. Blankenhorn, "The Conquest of Isolation," *Survey*, vol. XLVII (March 25, 1922), pp. 1006-1008.

dent is not making a fair distribution of cars within the mine in accordance with the well-established custom of the "square turn," the duty of protesting devolves on the miners and their pit committees; if wages for a certain type of work are not paid at the rate agreed upon, it is first up to the aggrieved worker to seek an adjustment; if the men believe that the fire boss in their mine is too inexperienced to determine whether there is gas "at the face," they cannot afford to let the matter wait. Of course, on many issues, they can request the assistance of the district representative, but at least part of the task of protest and enforcement falls on their shoulders.

Since the men play such an important part in the day-to-day administration of the agreements, flare-ups are almost sure to occur. True, the agreements specify that strikes and lock-outs are not to be called so long as the agreements are in effect, but the employer who continues to "cut corners" under the agreements and the local union leader who wants "his day in the sun" seem to be indigenous to the industry. The surprising thing is that disruptions during the life of agreements are not more frequent and more serious than they have been. Since the union's return to power in 1933, relations under agreements between the United Mine Workers and the employers have been generally amicable. Concerning their dealings with one another during the N. R. A. code period (between the summers of 1933 and 1935), one observer has remarked:

> One of the outstanding achievements of operation under the code was the high degree of industrial peace that prevailed. . . . In terms of the industry as a whole and compared with previous labor disputes, the code period compares favorably with any in the history of the industry. Wage contracts entered into were remarkably well observed throughout their life.[40]

In more recent years strikes and lock-outs during the life of agreements have also been relatively few. According to figures computed by the writer from data secured from the records of the United States Department of Labor, only twenty-five strikes and lock-outs occurred in the area covered by the Appalachian Agreement between March 1937 and April 1939.[41] These strikes and lock-outs involved about 17,000 men. Most of them lasted less than a week and only four in-

---

[40] Fred E. Berquist and associates, *Economic Survey of the Bituminous Coal Industry under Free Competition and Code Regulation* (National Recovery Administration, Division of Review, Work Materials No. 69), vol. I, pp. 6-7.

[41] There were brief "national" strikes in the bituminous coal industry at the time of the expiration of the Appalachian Agreement in 1939 and 1941; these strikes, however, did not occur while the agreement was still in effect. The Appalachian Agreement covers the bituminous coal fields of Ohio, Pennsylvania, Michigan, West Virginia, Maryland, Virginia, northern Tennessee, and eastern Kentucky. These fields produce about two-thirds of the nation's annual tonnage. The figures do not include strikes or lock-outs which involved less than six workers or lasted less than one day. For a discussion of the reliability and interpretation of these figures, see the Preface.

volved more than 1,000 workers each. The total of man-days-idle during these twenty-five strikes numbered about 100,000.[42] For an area in which there are some three hundred thousand coal miners these figures seem surprisingly small, especially when it is remembered that in 1937 the number of strikes in industry as a whole was unusually large.[43]

Most of the issues involved in these disputes were personal differences between individual workers and the mine managements. Typical of the immediate causes were charges of wage under-payment or defaults, objections to the collection of penalties for dirty coal, installation of double-shifts, and demands for earlier shifts or for no work on Saturdays. In only a few cases were basic issues involved.[44] In one case, however, the men tried to secure a closed shop, even though there was no such provision in the existing agreement. John L. Lewis, President of the United Mine Workers, wired the men to return to work immediately and then ". . . in the manner set forth in the contract, proceed to take up any grievances with the company."[45] The stoppage lasted only two days and involved about 1,300 workers. In some of the other cases, local leaders betrayed an eagerness to show their fighting spirit. In one case, the men quit when the company refused to alter the working-time of the men; in another, a group of workers demanded higher pay; in still another, they demanded a more equitable distribution of available work. In all cases of this sort, the district or international office ordered the men to return to work immediately, pending settlements in accordance with established procedure.[46]

In well over a majority of the disputes occurring during the life of the 1937-1939 Appalachian Agreement, employers had taken some step which gave definite provocation to the workers. In some instances, it was patent that they sought to evade their obligations under the agreements. An operator in southern Tennessee, for example, refused to pay the union scale of $4.96 for seven hours' work, estab-

---

[42] This is not the same as working-days-lost, since in many cases there was slack work anyway.

[43] In 1937 there were 4,740 strikes in the United States, the highest number for any year in the country's history. "Analysis of Strikes in 1938," *Monthly Labor Review* (U. S. Department of Labor, Bureau of Labor Statistics), vol. 48, no. 5 (May 1939), p. 1110.

[44] See, for example, strike reports to the U. S. Bureau of Labor Statistics, dated April 5, 1937; May 3, 1937; May 7, 1937; July 6, 1937; and July 9, 1937. Because of the confidential nature of these reports, further identification is not possible.

[45] Statement of John Saxton, President, District 28, quoting telegram signed by John L. Lewis, in *Times-Dispatch* (Richmond, Virginia), April 24, 1937. This strike, as reported to the U. S. Bureau of Labor Statistics, began on April 21, 1937. A copy of Mr. Saxton's statement is included in the report of the strike.

[46] Strike reports to the U. S. Bureau of Labor Statistics, dated April 5, 1937, October 5, 1937, and March 16, 1938.

lished in accordance with the settlement at New York a little while before. He asserted that he could not afford to pay more than $4.46. "We cannot run this mine," he declared, "until there are some adjustments made, either the men will go back at the old scale, or else the price of coal must be increased."[47] The dispute dragged on for over two months, but at the end the old rate was still in effect. In another case, the employer apparently had violated the agreement in a number of ways; for example, he had failed to collect death benefits and dues as required by the agreement, and he had also violated various "prior custom" clauses of the wage section of the agreement. When the district office of the union ordered the men to stop work, this employer soon altered his policies.[48] In still another case, an employer was allegedly undercutting wage rates established by the agreement; in addition he was accused of unfairly discharging two of his men. A compromise solution was finally worked out.[49] In cases of this character the district and international officials rarely ordered the men back to work. If the union was likewise charged with violating its agreements, the officers replied that the companies had already abrogated them so that the agreements were no longer in effect; therefore, the union was free to use what measures it could in order to regain its bargaining status. More important, the union officials knew that unless vigorous pressure were brought immediately, they would lose their status in these companies altogether.

A few of these disputes were closely related to basic difficulties and changes confronting the industry. An interesting example of this was a strike in the Central Pennsylvania coal field in the fall of 1938. One company had just gone through receivership, and another company had agreed to operate it on the assumption that modern machinery would be installed and the concentrated method of mining introduced. Under this system of operation the management was to perform certain advance services such as drilling, shooting, and furnishing powder; in return, the rate for loading was to be reduced to 57 cents a ton in contrast to the previous rate of 76 cents under "straight loading." The union protested that it had not been consulted about the introduction of the new method and that some of its features were inequitable. The company retorted that the system had been discussed with the union and that the agreement with the Central Pennsylvania Coal Producers' Association (signed April 1937) specifically provided for its introduction. The company also pointed out that unless the innovations were made, it could not hope

---

[47] Letter dated May 25, 1937, from the president of the firm to Isador Lubin, Commissioner of the U. S. Bureau of Labor Statistics. This letter is in the files of the bureau.

[48] Strike reports to the U. S. Bureau of Labor Statistics, dated June 9, 1937.

[49] Strike reports to the U. S. Bureau of Labor Statistics, dated December 18, 1937.

to compete with firms in West Virginia and Ohio.[50] The union then called the men out on strike. At the end of two days the company and union agreed to refer the dispute to an arbitration board; the new system of operations was meanwhile withdrawn.[51]

The work of the joint boards gives a good picture of the variety of disputes which occur during the life of agreements in the coal industry. In the preparation of this study, a review was made of the decisions of the joint board of the Western Pennsylvania Coal Operators' Association and of District 5 of the United Mine Workers of America,[52] between October 30, 1933, and January 11, 1939. During this period of five years and two months the board dealt with 112 cases. The table below shows the principal issues involved in these disputes in the order of their frequency.

CASES OF WESTERN PENNSYLVANIA JOINT BOARD (1933-1939)

Issues	*Frequency*
Union appeals from application of strike fines	46
Payment for deadwork	14
Discharge of employee	10
Wage payments per agreement	8
Payment for overtime, work on idle days, etc.	5
Discrimination in distribution of work	5
Miscellaneous (bosses working, dockage, payment for lost time, etc.)	24
Total	112

Source: Joint Board of Western Pennsylvania Coal Operators' Association and District 5, United Mine Workers of America (October 30, 1933, to January 11, 1939).

The board rendered written decisions in eighty-eight of these cases; fifty of them were adverse to the workers, twenty-six were in their favor, and twelve could be called compromises. The large number of rulings against the workers was due to the fact that the great majority of cases came to the board in the form of employee appeals from decisions already made by employers. In fact, only nine of the cases were brought by employers and of these, six came from the management of a single mine. Forty-six cases were appeals brought by workers against fines which employers had levied against them for illegal stoppages of work. The board was particularly firm in dealing with these disruptions. In one case, the mere threat of a stoppage was held to be a violation of the agreement;[53] in another, the board

[50] Article in the *Democrat* (Johnstown, Pennsylvania), September 14, 1938. A copy of this news article is in the report of the strike filed with the U. S. Bureau of Labor Statistics. The strike began September 12, 1938.

[51] The arbitration board allowed the company to introduce the new methods with some modifications.

[52] This board, consisting of two representatives from each side, is located in Pittsburgh, Pennsylvania.

[53] Case No. 5-003, February 9, 1934, Joint Board of the Western Pennsylvania Coal Operators' Association and District 5, United Mine Workers of America. The decisions of this board are available at the offices of the employers' association and of the district union in Pittsburgh, Pennsylvania.

was unmoved by the union's plea that although some of the men refused to enter the mine, they "soon afterwards" changed their minds;[54] in still another, a stoppage to vote in a union election was held to be a violation.[55] In all of these cases, fines were collected from the workers in accordance with the provisions of the Appalachian Agreement discussed above. Nor did the board hesitate to impose fines on men not immediately involved in the dispute. For example, when certain key men held up operations of the entire mine by their refusal to work, the board approved fines assessed against all members of the local.[56] However, cases relating to discharges found the board[57] rather lenient. Thus, when a man was dismissed for serving as a ringleader in an illegal stoppage, the board merely ordered a temporary suspension from work. A similar decision was given in a case in which the men had disregarded disciplinary rules inside the mines.[58] In cases alleging discrimination on the part of management against employees, either in the distribution of work or in laying off or rehiring men, the board seemed more inclined to accept the employer's view.[59]

Many of the cases coming before the board concerned wage standards and payment for yardage and deadwork. Here the board took particular pains to learn all the details of each situation. In many of the wage disputes, issues were raised which were not covered by any provisions of the agreements. If the board found that the practice in question did not conflict with the terms of the agreement, it was guided in its ruling by the traditional custom of the locality in which the matter arose. In a case where the workers were paid "by the wagon" for loading slate in the mines, the board found that this was a prior practice not in conflict with the agreement; however, since earnings for this work were found not to be comparable with wage-rates for other types of work, the board ordered the company to pay $2.26 to each man for every shift that he worked on such a basis.[60] In many instances of this sort the board referred the matter back for settlement to the local groups involved, at the same time ordering them to bring up the issue again if they failed to reach an agreement a second time.[61]

Third parties play a very limited role in the conduct of bituminous coal disputes. Of the 112 cases coming before the Western

---

54 Case No. 5-019, August 16, 1934.
55 Case No. 5-043, August 29, 1935.
56 Case No. 5-088, July 19, 1937.
57 Or umpire, as the case may be.
58 Case No. 5-070, October 1, 1936, and Case No. 5-079, February 15, 1937.
59 See, for example, Case No. 5-108, January 14, 1939 (decision by an umpire).
60 Case No. 5-069, October 16, 1936.
61 See, for example, Cases No. 5-053, No. 5-055, and No. 5-095, decided in 1936 and 1937.

Pennsylvania Joint Board only four were referred to an umpire. This conforms to current practice in other districts as well.[62] The only exception is Illinois where umpires have been serving for many years on a permanent, rather than on an *ad hoc*, basis. There a tendency exists for employers and unions to refer troublesome cases to the umpire. A similar condition is found in certain branches of the clothing trades. As remarked earlier, apparently such a result is caused by the very fact that permanent arbitration machinery is in effect.

CONCLUSIONS

On the whole, the machinery for interpretation and enforcement of agreements in the six industries described seems adequate for the work it is expected to perform. The problem of union-employer responsibility does not have its roots in questions of adjustment procedure. The troubles besetting the railroad unions and employers, for example, do not seem to be due primarily to the type of grievance apparatus found in that industry. By the same token, the fact that few criticisms are voiced against the grievance procedure in bituminous coal can not be attributed to the particular kind of set-up existing in that field. Actually, almost any type of machinery will prove satisfactory if the contracting parties are determined to make it work. Difficulties encountered under collective bargaining systems are almost always due to other causes.

It remains true, however, that certain kinds of procedure make it easier to achieve stable relations. In this connection, the review of grievance machinery in the three older systems of collective bargaining suggests several improvements for the steel, automobile, and maritime industries: Steps in the grievance procedure might be reduced in number, or time limits placed on certain stages of the negotiations; representatives of the workers, not employed by the firm involved, might enter negotiations earlier than they do at the present time; so might employer representatives who speak directly for the top management; moreover, at some stage of the proceedings, spokesmen for other employers, in addition to the one immediately concerned, might well be given a part in the deliberations—a move which is already current practice under some agreements of the National Maritime Union. It would also be helpful if more latitude were given to representatives of the union to confer with workers about grievances and to investigate alleged evasions of agreements. Similarly, greater emphasis should be placed on impartial outside agencies as a court of last resort for dead-

---

62 Mr. A. D. Lewis, brother of John L. Lewis, in an interview (June 27, 1939), stated that not one dispute "in a thousand" ever gets to a joint board and that of the few which reach a joint board, only rare ones are referred to an umpire.

locked cases. Likewise, the introduction of a system of money penalties and liquidated damages merits serious consideration.

These recommendations are offered in general and tentative terms because the circumstances of particular situations may require important modifications. There are two principles of grievance procedure, however, which need no qualification: First, each step in the procedure should constitute a genuine change (or advance) in the negotiations; second, disputes over issues not covered by the agreement or over demands for alteration of the agreement should be deferred until negotiations are started on the next agreement, or they should be sent directly to the parties who drafted the agreement. These two principles deserve explicit recognition in all industries where collective bargaining is practiced.

CHAPTER IV

THE LAW OF UNION AGREEMENTS

In addition to the adjustment procedures incorporated in collective agreements by the contracting parties themselves, there is opportunity for appeal to the courts. Even though action of this nature is relatively infrequent, the possibility of litigation cannot be ignored. The wording of the statutes and, even more important, the way in which they are interpreted constitute the framework within which collective agreements are administered. For this reason a summary discussion of the legal aspects of the problem belongs in the present study.

In the United States far-reaching changes have occurred in the law of union agreements since the turn of the century. Forty years ago labor cases chiefly concerned the methods which unions could pursue in extending their membership and winning agreements. Twenty years later the courts had begun to ask whether the terms of these agreements were enforceable. It is this phase of labor law which is of interest here. The courts have attempted to distinguish between union agreements that are valid and those that are not. Today valid agreements are generally enforceable; that is, judicial remedy will be forthcoming when a simple breach occurs. The fact that unincorporated associations may be involved presents no serious barriers, for the methods whereby the contracting parties can sue and be sued are now well established. Court debate on this topic at present is not so much concerned with enforceability as such as with the questions of how, by whom, and to what effect union agreements shall be enforced.[1]

There is less unanimity, however, on the prior question of what constitutes a valid agreement. Court argument on this question is colored by the distrust with which union organizations themselves were viewed under common law doctrine of the nineteenth century. Judges have long since ceased to apply the terms conspiracy and restraint of trade to unions themselves, but on occasion these terms are still applied to union agreements. The Sherman anti-trust law, for example, has sometimes been interpreted in this way. The crux of

[1] T. Richard Witmer, "Collective Labor Agreements in the Courts" (1938) 48 *Yale Law Journal* 195, 197, 199.

the matter is that some union agreements place serious restrictions on the movement of trade—a fact demonstrated by the data gathered in the United States Attorney General's current efforts to enforce the anti-trust law. The difficulty lies in separating the wheat from the chaff. There are no well-defined differences between "good" and "bad" agreements. Judges are thus given wide latitude. Indeed, it would not be very difficult for them to conclude that all union agreements are in restraint of trade. If sought, the stigma could be found in the methods employed in winning the agreements, or in the provisions they contain, or in the circumstances surrounding their application. On the other hand, there are those judges who take as their starting point the fact that trade unions have won the right to legal existence and that union agreements are essential to that existence. The presumption is, therefore, that such agreements are valid. From that point of view, the application of the prohibitions of common law doctrine and anti-trust legislation to union agreements is the exception rather than the rule.[2]

THE CLOSED SHOP

The second school of thought has made substantial headway in recent years. Today the issue is rarely raised in connection with union agreements that are voluntarily signed by the contracting parties. But with regard to closed shop agreements, even though voluntarily signed, the conflict in viewpoint still persists. Despite its longevity the question of the legality of the closed shop remains very much alive. Lawyers have had ample opportunity to refine their arguments and discover a wide variety of distinctions. The result is something of a labyrinth.

The courts have approached closed shop agreements in terms of their intent or their effect. When written primarily with a view to benefiting a union organization and to securing the advantages of collective bargaining, they have been held valid. When the primary aim has been to injure workers outside the union by excluding them from employment opportunities, closed shop agreements have been

[2] This difference in viewpoint bears on the question whether the Sherman Act applies to union agreements. The first sentence of the first section of that law reads [26 Stat. 209 (1890), 15 U. S. C. A., ¶ 1 (1927)]: "Every contract, combination in the form of trust or otherwise, or conspiracy, in restraint of trade or commerce among the several states or with foreign nations, is hereby declared to be illegal." If a judge inclines to the view that the Sherman Act prohibits most union agreements, he underlines the word "every"; if he inclines to the opposite view, he underlines the entire phrase "every contract . . . in restraint of trade." The first allows for a broad construction; the second for a narrow construction. See Louis Boudin, "The Sherman Act and Labor Disputes" (1939) 39 *Columbia Law Review* 1283 and (1940) 40 *Columbia Law Review* 14.

held invalid.[3] But when is the aim to injure non-union workers primary and when is it merely incidental? The answer has frequently turned on whether measures were taken against particular workers to force them into the union. This element of compulsion was found in the cases of *Plant v. Woods* and *Berry v. Donovan,* and the agreements were held to be an unjustifiable interference with the individual's right to dispose of his labor as he chooses.[4] In *Plant v. Woods* two unions sought jurisdiction over all painters in the city of Springfield, Massachusetts. The defendant union made it clear to employers that if they retained men who belonged to the other organization they would experience trouble in the form of strikes or boycotts. Finding that the strikes which did occur had this purpose, the court held such an aim to be illegal. In *Berry v. Donovan* a worker who refused to join the Boot and Shoe Workers' Union was discharged because of a closed shop agreement which covered most of the shoe-manufacturing firms in the vicinity and was signed after the worker had secured employment. Counsel for the employee contended that the agreement was an unjustifiable interference with his contract of employment. The court agreed, concluding:

> The attempt to force all laborers to combine in unions is against the policy of the law, because it aims at monopoly. It therefore does not justify causing the discharge, by his employer, of an individual laborer working under a contract.[5]

In the cases of *Jacobs v. Cohen* and *Shinsky v. O'Neil* the court did not find that the aim of the union was to force certain workers into its membership, and the contracts were upheld. In the latter case a shoe worker in Lynn, Massachusetts, brought suit against the United Shoe Workers of America. He refused to become a member of the union and for that reason a number of firms rejected his application for employment. The court distinguished the case from the two discussed above on the ground that in this instance no steps were taken to make certain workers join the union. Rather, the union was merely trying to secure closed shop agreements in an effort to secure the

---

[3] See, for example, the statement of the court's position in the case of *Pickett v. Walsh,* 192 Mass. 572, 582, 78 N. E. 753, 757, 758 (1906): ". . . it is not legal (even where he wishes to do so) for an employer to agree with a union to discharge a non-union workman for an arbitrary cause at the request of the union. . . . *A fortiori,* the members of a labor union cannot by a strike refuse to work with another workman for an arbitrary cause."

[4] *Plant v. Woods,* 176 Mass. 492, 57 N. E. 1011 (1900); strike threats had been made in connection with attempts to induce workers in another union to join their organization. *Berry v. Donovan,* 188 Mass. 353, 74 N. E. 603 (1905); the union had secured discharge of a non-union worker. See also *Walker v. Cronin,* 107 Mass. 555, 562 (1871) and *Rhoades v. Malta Vita Pure Food Co.,* 149 Mich. 235, 112 N. W. 940 (1907).

[5] *Berry v. Donovan,* 188 Mass. 353, 359, 74 N. E. 603, 606 (1905). See also *Curran v. Galen,* 152 N. Y. 33, 46 N. E. 297 (1897); the union forced a firm to discharge a non-union worker under a closed shop agreement and brought the worker into general ill-repute by circulating false and malicious reports; the worker's suit for damages against union was sustained.

advantages of collective bargaining for the common benefit. In this connection, the court took particular pains to point out that membership in the union was open to all employees "qualified to perform the work done by members of the union in question."[6] In the case of *Jacobs v. Cohen* the Tailors' and Pressers' Union brought suit to recover liquidated damages against a clothing shop. The firm had agreed to employ only members of the union and later declined to do so. The court held that the agreement was not oppressive since it did not operate in the community generally to prevent qualified workers from securing employment. Moreover, the employer voluntarily accepted the agreement, only later charging that it was illegal. The New York Court of Appeals concluded:

> That, incidentally, it might result in the discharge of some of those employed, for failure to come into affiliation with their fellow workmen's organization, or that it might prevent others from being engaged upon the work, is neither something of which the employers may complain, nor something with which public policy is concerned.[7]

Besides inquiring whether there has been "intent to injure," some courts have asked whether there has been "intent to monopolize." Both of these criteria have been applied to closed shop agreements. Both have been found equally vague. The latter has grown out of the restraint of trade doctrine of the common law and the Sherman anti-trust Act. The courts have usually found such an intent to monopolize where the contract is signed by an employers' association representing most of the employers in a given trade. Under these circumstances, a non-union worker would have little chance of securing employment, while an employer not a member of the association would have difficulty in recruiting a labor force.[8] On the other hand, the courts have almost always held "that a closed shop in a single factory is consonant with public policy and lawful."[9] In applica-

---

[6] *Shinsky v. O'Neil*, 232 Mass. 99, 104, 121 N. E. 790, 792 (1919).

[7] *Jacobs v. Cohen*, 183 N. Y. 207, 215, 76 N. E. 5, 8 (1905); see also *Kissam v. U. S. Printing Co.*, 199 N. Y. 76, 92 N. E. 214 (1910); *Harper v. Local Union No. 520*, 48 S. W. (2d) 1033 (Tex. Civ. App. 1932); and *Hoban v. Dempsey*, 217 Mass. 166, 104 N. E. 717 (1914).

[8] *McCord v. Thompson-Starrett Co.*, 129 App. Div. 130, 113 N. Y. Supp. 385 (1st Dept. 1908); the employer association ordered members to hire only union carpenters. *Brescia Construction Co. v. Stone Masons' Contractors' Association*, 195 App. Div. 647, 187 N. Y. Supp. 77 (1st Dept. 1921); under the agreement the union could not work for anyone in debt to a member of the association. In neither case was the agreement upheld. Since most of the state anti-trust laws exempt labor unions, state courts have looked with more favor than federal courts on closed shop agreements with employers' associations; see *American Fur Manufacturers' Association, Inc. v. Associated Fur Coat and Trimming Manufacturers, Inc.*, 161 Misc. 246, 291 N. Y. Supp. 610 (Sup. Ct. N. Y. County 1936), aff'd., 251 App. Div. 708, 296 N. Y. Supp. 1000 (1st Dept. 1937).

[9] *Four Plating Co. v. Mako*, 122 N. J. Eq. 298, 300, 194 Atl. 53, 55 (Ch. 1937); but see *Jordan's Wearing Apparel, Inc., v. Retail Sales Clerk Union*, 193 Atl. 806 (N. J. Ch. 1937).

tion, then, the two criteria seem to have had substantially the same results.

These criteria are hardly exact, but many courts have made confusion worse confounded by introducing others. Nearly all the courts (at least those outside of Connecticut)[10] have inquired whether the non-union plaintiff lost a job he *already had* because of a closed shop agreement or whether he was seeking employment he *could not find* because of such an agreement. In the former circumstance, the plaintiff has been permitted to recover damages from the union, but not in the latter.[11] Other courts have attempted to treat closed shop agreements in terms of the "right" of the employer to run his open-shop plant as he pleases and the "right" of union members to refuse to work except under such conditions as they choose. This approach has led to findings which more often than not appear to beg the question.[12]

It seems reasonable to suppose that, in this important phase of the law of collective bargaining, the courts' own confusion has contributed to the general uncertainty in the field of industrial relations. A first step toward stability would be taken if the position of the courts regarding closed shop agreements were clarified. On the other hand, there is no simple rule-of-thumb by which the courts may tell where there is primary intent to injure or primary intent to monopolize. The distinction between agreements that exclude non-union employees from a particular job, on the one hand, and from all jobs in their trade, on the other, is certainly not satisfactory in every case. The worker who refuses to join a union and loses his job as a result is being coerced either way. The only sure means for a court to determine in a specific situation whether there has been primary intent to injure or monopolize would be to inquire into a wide range of facts surrounding the case. First, the court would have to discover the terms of the agreement and the onerousness of the obligations assumed by the employer or employers, union, and employees; for example, the effects on competitive conditions would have to be considered. Second, the court would have to learn the circumstances under which the agreement was secured and the manner in which it was subsequently administered. Third, the court would have to

---

[10] *Connors v. Connolly*, 86 Conn. 641, 86 Atl. 600 (1913), the court indicates that if the question were before it, the contract would be held valid unless it affected a large sector of an industry or an entire locality.

[11] *Berry v. Donovan*, 188 Mass. 353, 74 N. E. 603 (1905); *Fairbanks v. McDonald*, 219 Mass. 291, 106 N. E. 1000 (1914); the defendant union raised membership fees when plaintiffs who had belonged to a rival union applied for membership; the defendant was enjoined from interfering "with the employment of the plaintiffs."

[12] *Kemp v. Division No. 241*, 255 Ill. 213, 99 N. E. 389 (1912), judgment for defendant union; *Alfred W. Booth v. Burgess*, 72 N. J. Eq. 181, 65 Atl. 226 (Ch. 1906), judgment for plaintiff employer. The foregoing discussion of the status of closed shop agreements follows that of Witmer, *op. cit.*, pp. 212-215.

ascertain the conditions under which workers were allowed to join the union, the provisions regarding dues and special assessments, and the voting privileges of individual members. Finally, the court would have to inquire whether the attack on the closed shop agreement was a genuine expression of worker protest or part of a broader attack by the employer on the union itself.[13] If the evidence on the whole showed that the closed shop agreement was a defensive measure, designed to prevent the employer or employers from undermining the union by discharging union members, the agreement would presumably be held valid. If, on the other hand, the evidence showed that the agreement was designed to give certain individuals virtually complete and unchecked power to determine what firms would be allowed to operate and what workers could get jobs, the agreement would be held invalid.

This approach to the problem would place burdens on the courts which they are not in a position to assume. Much discretion would rest with the individual judge. A simpler view would be to hold closed shop agreements invalid only under exceptional circumstances —where, for example, there is unmistakable evidence of fraud or of malicious design to injure or damage. At the present time closed shop agreements are an integral part of a number of collective bargaining systems. Their destruction by court action would prove just as serious to certain employer groups as to union organizations themselves. It may be that agreements of this sort are frequently not in the best interests of working people, employers, or the general public. But this is not for the courts to decide; it is up to Congress and the state legislatures. In commenting on the distinction which some courts have made between primary intent and incidental effect, the New York Court of Appeals recently declared with laudable restraint:

> We think that this distinction is not justified, and that if there be an evil in the monopoly of the labor market in a particular industry by labor organizations it is a matter to be considered by legislatures and not by the courts, for the reason that there are two sides to the question—the other side being that the labor organizations, through this means of contracting and negotiating, are enabled to strengthen their representative bodies and to effectuate collective bargaining.[14]

Judges in other courts, in passing on closed shop agreements, have too often taken the opportunity presented by vague legal concepts to read their own social philosophies into the law.

---

13 Presumably, even if a group of non-union workmen showed that all avenues of employment had been closed to them, the court would not be moved if their protests were "employer-inspired" or resulted from any other unfair labor practice within the meaning of the National Labor Relations Act or of state labor relations laws in jurisdictions covered by such legislation.

14 *Williams v. Quill*, 277 N. Y. 1, 9, 10, 12 N. E. (2d) 547, 551 (1938), affirming 165 Misc. 99, 300 N. Y. Supp. 166 (1937), certioriari denied, 303 U. S. 621, 58 Sup. Ct. 650 (1938).

THE NATIONAL LABOR RELATIONS ACT

The National Labor Relations Act and the state labor relations laws also contain grounds on which courts may find union agreements invalid. The prohibitions of these laws, moreover, may fall not only on closed shop agreements but on other types of union agreements as well.[15] In this connection there are two changes in the law of union agreements which are worth noting here. First, the National Labor Relations Board has interpreted this legislation as outlawing agreements with "employer-dominated" labor organizations. Accordingly, the board orders employers, in unfair labor practice cases, to repudiate such agreements. In representation cases the board simply disregards them. The importance of these cases for the present study is that an "employer-dominated" (or, more strictly, an "employer-favored") labor organization may even be a nationally affiliated union. In the National Electric Products Corporation case, for example, the board outlawed an agreement with the International Brotherhood of Electrical Workers despite a decree issued by the United States District Court for Western Pennsylvania ordering specific enforcement of the agreement.[16] In cases of this sort it is the employer's relation to the union, not the agreement itself, that is found to be contrary to the act; the same agreement between the same parties may be valid when this relation is corrected.[17] So long as the employer favors or assists a labor organization by any of the unfair labor practices specified in the act, an agreement with the organization is also in violation of the act.

However, in view of the Supreme Court's decision in the *Consolidated Edison Company* case, the conditions under which board orders of this sort are lawful are not altogether clear. The Supreme Court overthrew the section of the board's order directed against the

---

[15] Care was taken when these statutes were drafted not to illegalize closed shop agreements as such. The 1939 Wisconsin law, however, has this qualification: "all-union" agreements are valid so far as the act is concerned if the "employee [affected by the agreement] is eligible to membership" in the union. The 1939 law also provides that an employer can enter an all-union agreement "where three-quarters or more of the employees in such collective bargaining unit shall have voted affirmatively by secret ballot in favor of such all-union agreement in a referendum conducted by the Board." Wis. Stat. (1939) ¶¶ 111.06 and 111.08. (Chapter 111 is known as the Employment Peace Act.)

[16] *The Matter of National Electric Products Corp.*, 3 N. L. R. B. 475 (1937); the board held that the court decree could not foreclose the board from invalidating the agreement. See also board's decisions, *The Matter of Consolidated Edison Co.*, 4 N. L. R. B. 71 (1937), order reversed by the Supreme Court in *Consolidated Edison Co. v. N. L. R. B.*, 305 U. S. 197, 59 Sup. Ct. 206 (1938); *The Matter of Lenox Shoe Co.*, 4 N. L. R. B. 372 (1937); *The Matter of Zenite Metal Corp.*, 5 N. L. R. B. 509 (1938); *The Matter of Jacob A. Hunkele*, 7 N. L. R. B. 1276 (1938); *The Matter of The Serrick Corp.*, 8 N. L. R. B. 621 (1938).

[17] *Consolidated Edison Co. v. N. L. R. B.*, 305 U. S. 197, 59 Sup. Ct. 206 (1938); see also N. L. R. B. order, *The Matter of The Serrick Corp.*, 8 N. L. R. B. 621 (1938).

agreement, apparently on an accumulation of objections. Aside from procedural points, the court's chief reason was that invalidation of the agreement did not constitute such action as would "effectuate the policies of the act"—this because (1) some of the employees of the concern wanted to be represented by the union, while for those who did not, coercion would be removed by other provisions of the board's order; (2) the agreement was made by the union not as the exclusive representative of all the workers but only as representative of its own members; (3) the agreement was "highly protective to interstate commerce and foreign commerce"; (4) even though the agreement may have been made after the board's original complaint had issued, it still may have been "fair" under the meaning of the National Labor Relations Act. According to one authority, the Supreme Court probably would have sustained the board if the agreement had purported to cover all of the workers[18]—especially if it had been a closed shop agreement, or an agreement where there was no spontaneous union membership among the workers of the concern. For, under these circumstances, evidence would probably have been found of discrimination by the employer against workers who refused to join the union.[19]

The National Labor Relations Act has occasioned a second change in the law of collective bargaining. It is now an unfair labor practice to hire only workers who belong to a particular union if another union has the support of a majority of the workers. This situation can occur under closed shop agreements. Such a policy would involve discrimination against the majority group within the meaning of the act. To date, this second change has been of less moment than the one discussed first. Under just what conditions the board will invalidate agreements with minority groups is not altogether clear. Of course, it will approve genuine bargaining with groups of this sort if no one union has the support of a majority of the workers and no efforts by rival organizations are being made to win such a majority. An agreement confined to members of the minority group only, would not be the result of employer favoritism or preference. On the other hand, if another union has the support of a majority of the workers, the agreement with the minority group would not be allowed to stand. However, a situation in which there are two competing groups (say a

---

[18] William G. Rice, "The Legal Significance of Labor Contracts under the National Labor Relations Act" (1939) 37 *Michigan Law Review* 693, 706-707. At least the board concluded its order would have had a firmer basis if this had been true. *The Matter of Consolidated Edison Co.*, 4 N. L. R. B. 71, 94 (1937). Thus, in the Greyhound Company court case the contract was invalidated where the union professed to have the support of the majority but actually did not. *N. L .R. B. v. Pennsylvania Greyhound Lines, Inc.*, 303 U. S. 261, 58 Sup. Ct. 571 (1938).

[19] For criticisms of the Supreme Court's decision in the *Consolidated Edison Co.* case, see Joseph Rosenfarb, *The National Labor Policy* (New York: Harper and Brothers, 1940), pp. 254-256.

C. I. O. union and an A. F. of L. union) and where the issue of majority rule has not yet been decided is not so easily classified. Under these circumstances, the union that secures the agreement wins an important advantage over its rival. This might be deemed an act of favoritism on the part of the employer even if no other preferential sign were shown. If, on the other hand, agreements were declared invalid under these circumstances simply because a union did not at the moment have majority support, large numbers of workers would be deprived of the benefits of collective bargaining. The board has not yet made its position plain on this point. The Supreme Court touched only briefly on the issue in the Consolidated Edison Company case when it declared:

> The continued operation [of agreements with minority groups] . . . is necessarily subject to the provision of the law by which representatives of the employees for the purpose of collective bargaining can be ascertained.[20]

Even though an employer and union sign an agreement which, at the time of signing, was valid under the National Labor Relations Act, changes may meanwhile have occurred which would render it invalid. This would be true of a situation in which a majority of the workers have shifted their allegiance from one union to another. In handling cases of this sort the board has been chary of upsetting contractual relations. Considerable weight has been given to the time factor. If an agreement with a union still has a long time to run, the board has usually called for an election to determine the majority will; if the time period is short, say six months or less, the board has left the contractual relationship undisturbed.[21] In one case the members of a local union affiliated with the A. F. of L. changed their affiliation to a C. I. O. union during the life of a closed shop agreement. Representatives of the A. F. of L. group tried to reorganize the local, insisting that the employer discharge the men for violating the closed shop agreement. The board concluded that the local had withdrawn from the A. F. of L. union and that its identity had not been altered. The board decided therefore that the employer had no right to require membership in the reorganized A. F. of L. local as a condition of employment.[22] However, the Circuit Court of Appeals reversed the

---

[20] *Consolidated Edison Co. v. N. L. R. B.*, 305 U. S. 197, 59 Sup. Ct. 206 (1938).

[21] *The Matter of M. and J. Tracy, Inc.*, 12 N. L. R. B. 916 (1939); since the agreement had more than a year to run there was no bar to an election. But see *The Matter of Superior Electrical Products Co.*, 6 N. L. R. B. 19 (1938); agreement which had more than a year to run was nevertheless a bar to holding an election inasmuch as the unexpired portion of the agreement was "not for such a long period as to be contrary to the policies or purposes of the Act" and because a majority of the unit whom the rival union "claims to represent, favored the execution of the contract and participated in negotiations for it." See Rosenfarb, *op. cit.*, p. 266.

[22] *The Matter of M. and M. Wood Working Co.*, 6 N. L. R. B. 372 (1938).

board's decision, ruling that the local's withdrawal from the A. F. of L. union had not been in accordance with the union's constitution and that therefore the closed shop agreement with the A. F. of L. local was still in effect.[23] Needless to say, the board's decision in this case and others like it have incurred the opposition of union organizations which have been deprived of their contractual privileges. Since the C. I. O. has been more active than the A. F. of L. in setting up new unions, the latter has been injured more greatly by such board actions. Indeed, in only one case has the board invalidated an agreement held by a C. I. O. union (United Mine Workers of America).[24] Consequently, one of the amendments to the National Labor Relations Act sponsored by the A. F. of L. would take power away from the board to cancel agreements. But it seems clear that, if this were done, a large measure of protection now afforded workers by the act would be removed.

REMEDIES AGAINST EMPLOYERS

The validity of a union agreement once established, the courts usually extend legal remedy to a union in the event of a simple breach on the part of an employer. This has not always been the practice. An important turning-point, at least in New York, came in *Schlesinger v. Quinto.*[25] In 1921 the women's garment industry had fallen on evil days and the employers' association was negotiating with the International Ladies' Garment Workers' Union for a modification of the terms of the 1919 agreement. Before the matter was settled the association attempted to reduce wages and increase hours, despite the fact that the earlier agreement had not expired. Besides calling a strike the union turned to the courts for help and was successful in its appeal for an injunction. The employers' association relied on the familiar defense that the injunction would amount to an order of specific performance of a contract calling for personal services. The reply given by the Appellate Division could be construed as justifying an injunction against almost any breach of a union contract. The court said the contract was not one for personal services at all. Rather it was a contract between two organizations, each of which had disciplinary powers over its members. The injunction order, therefore, only required that that disciplinary authority be exercised.

This decision, according to Professor Witmer, was followed by a number of injunctions against simple breaches by employers in the lower New York courts. He estimates there were at least fifteen successful suits of this sort brought by unions in the New York courts

---

23 *M. and M. Wood Working Co. v. N. L. R. B.*, 101 F. (2d) 938 (C. C. A. 9th, 1939).

24 *The Matter of Mine B Coal Co.*, 4 N. L. R. B. 316 (1937); despite agreement with the U. M. W. A., the board held an election and the Progressive Miners' union won majority.

25 201 App. Div. 487, 194 N. Y. Supp. 401 (1st Dept. 1922).

between 1928 and 1938.[26] This case also had a marked influence in such widely diverse jurisdictions as California, Georgia, Massachusetts, Mississippi, New Jersey, Ohio, and Texas.[27]

In a few jurisdictions, such as Iowa, Michigan, and West Virginia, the objections to enforcement of union agreements inherited from an earlier day still carry weight.[28] These objections are pretty well standardized by this time and are stated in rather formal terms. Some courts find union agreements unenforceable because of a lack of consideration to support them. Others come to the same conclusion on the ground that there is an absence of mutuality of performance or of remedy under the terms of union agreements. It should be pointed out that these two objections generally arise from a misconception of the nature of union agreements. Under these agreements, the employer promises to meet certain standards of employment; the union, for its part, agrees that its members will perform the work under the prescribed conditions. There is consideration on both sides, although perhaps not always in the technical sense that some courts require. Similarly, there is mutuality of performance. The employer agrees to fulfill certain requirements if he offers employment; the union agrees to accept the offer, assuming the requirements are fulfilled. It is difficult to see how a court could hold a union agreement unenforceable on these grounds. The view that there is no mutuality of remedy warrants more attention. As a matter of fact, the employer is correct who contends that he could not get an injunction to force a striking employee to return to work. But neither could a union or employee secure an injunction to compel an employer to provide work; he is only under obligation to meet certain standards of employment if he has work to offer. Only in a limited sense, then,

---

[26] Witmer, *op. cit.*, pp. 201-202. The most important are: *Farulla v. Freundlich*, 152 Misc. 761, 274 N. Y. Supp. 70 (Sup. Ct. N. Y. County 1934), 153 Misc. 738, 277 N. Y. Supp. 47 (Sup. Ct. 1934), 155 Misc. 262, 279 N. Y. Supp. 228 (Sup. Ct. 1935); *The Matter of Ralph A. Freundlich, Inc.*, 2 N. L. R. B. 802 (1937), a successive stage in the fight; *Maisel v. Sigman*, 123 Misc. 714, 205 N. Y. Supp. 807 (Sup. Ct. 1924); *Dubinsky v. Blue Dale Dress Co.*, 162 Misc. 177, 292 N. Y. Supp. 898 (Sup. Ct. N. Y. County 1936). For a discussion of the runaway shop as it bears on this problem, see Note, 36 *Columbia Law Review* (1936) 776.

[27] Some of these cases are: *Weber v. Masser*, 286 Pac. 1074 (Cal. App. 1930); the appeal was dismissed (question moot), 210 Cal. 607, 292 Pac. 637 (1930). *Mississippi Theatres Corp. v. Hattiesburg Local Union No. 615*, 174 Miss. 439, 164 So. 887 (1936); *Harper v. Local Union No. 520*, 48 S. W. (2d) 1033 (Tex. Civ. App. 1932).

[28] *Wilson v. Airline Coal Co.*, 215 Iowa 855, 246 N. W. 753 (1933); *Schwartz v. Cigar Makers International Union*, 219 Mich. 589, 189 N. W. 55 (1922); *Berkhammer v. The Cleveland and Morgantown Coal Co.* (W. Va. C. C. 1926), discussed in 8 *Law and Labor* 217; *Hudson v. C. N. O. and T. P. Ry. Co.*, 152 Ky. 711, 154 S. W. 47 (1913); *Burnetta v. Marceline Coal Co.*, 180 Mo. 241, 79 S. W. 136 (1904). The soundness of the court's position in the last two cases is questioned in *McCoy v. St. Joseph Belt Ry. Co.*, 77 S. W. (2d) 175, 181 (Kansas City Court of Appeals 1934).

is there no mutuality of remedy. Most courts, moreover, are satisfied if there is mutuality of performance alone.

The foregoing discussion bears on a rule of law which in the past has been more important than any other in protecting employers against actions to enforce union agreements—the rule that makes agreements for personal services unenforceable. Union agreements, so employers have frequently argued, call for personal services by particular workers; making these agreements enforceable would mean requiring specific performance of personal service agreements. This would violate a well-established rule of the common law. Courts at the present time, however, generally recognize that this rule has little bearing on most legal actions to enforce union agreements. An action to secure enforcement does not mean that a specific employee must perform a specific service but only that the work must be done by the *group* of employees covered by the agreement. More important, perhaps, such an argument could conceivably be justified if raised by employees, but hardly by employers. In agreeing to certain conditions of employment if he has work to offer, an employer is certainly not promising to render any "personal services" within the usual meaning of the term.[29]

A circumstance which may prove to be a serious limitation on equitable actions brought by either employers or unions to secure compliance with union agreements arises where the plaintiff charging the breach has himself breached the agreement. Frequently this is the case, or so it can be alleged. On this issue, however, the courts are sharply divided—so divided, in fact, that there is probably no unanimity even within a single jurisdiction. Certain courts in Wisconsin, for example, have insisted that the plaintiff, in order to secure equitable remedy, must have "clean hands";[30] courts in Massachusetts and Oregon have held otherwise.[31] The New York lower courts are about

[29] For a discussion of this rule as it applies to actions against individual workers who have violated agreements, as opposed to actions against unions or employers, see pp. 70-75, *infra*. The question has been raised whether orders by the National Labor Relations Board may not sometimes run athwart this rule. A board order to reinstate a particular employee who has been laid off in violation of the seniority provision of an agreement would be an instance in point. But it is at least arguable whether the employer is asked to perform a specific service even under these circumstances. In some board reinstatement orders the employer is told to rehire certain workers only if employment conditions permit. Those who cannot be re-employed are simply placed on a preferred list. This problem only arises where a plant is shut down or a department is discontinued. The employee who is ordered reinstated is, of course, not required to perform a service which he does not want to perform.

[30] *David Adler & Sons Co. v. Maglio*, 200 Wis. 153, 228 N. W. 123 (1929).

[31] *Samuel Hertzig Corp. v. Gibbs*, 295 Mass. 229, 3 N. E. (2d) 831 (1936); *Greenfield v. Central Labor Council*, 104 Ore. 236, 192 Pac. 783 (1920), modified on appeal, 207 Pac. 168 (1922). But the "clean hands" doctrine was applied against an employee in a Massachusetts case, although the action was not brought to secure enforcement of a union agreement. *Cornellier v. Haverhill Shoe Manufacturers' Association*, 221 Mass. 554, 109 N. E. 643 (1915).

equally divided.[32] This same problem arises under slightly different circumstances where one party to an agreement seeks release from its terms on the ground that the other party has already violated its provisions. However, that phase of the problem has not been discussed in the cases.

Under both circumstances, probably the most reasonable view would be to distinguish between violations that are trivial and those that are so serious that they undermine the very basis of the contractual relationship. Union agreements cover a wide variety of issues, some of little significance, others of great importance. It would hardly be fair to refuse equitable remedy merely because the aggrieved party had himself committed some slight breach. Nor, on the other hand, would the aggrieved party be justified in considering the bargain off no matter how small the violation. Sometimes unions resort to this tactic. Rather than exhaust all steps in the grievance procedure they allege that the employer has violated the agreement and that they are therefore free to strike immediately. There is a great difference, however, between violating some substantive provision of an agreement and disregarding the procedure for handling disputes. The former is anticipated under agreements; that is why machinery for adjusting disputes is established. But the latter step destroys the foundation upon which continuing bargaining relations rest. At the same time, there is an important difference between a violation which is settled in accordance with the terms of the agreement and one that is not. If certain workers strike in violation of an agreement but the union quickly orders them to return to their jobs in compliance with its terms, the employer is not thereby justified in abrogating the agreement at some later date. In a run-away shop case where this situation was involved, the New York court pointed out:

> The important difference between the methods adopted by the two sides is that the plaintiffs continued content with the collective agreement, while the defendants . . . took the law into their own hands through the radical and conclusive step of [moving away].[33]

THE NORRIS-LA GUARDIA ACT

Another restriction on the right to secure judicial redress for violation of a union agreement comes from a different and rather unexpected source. Where an aggrieved party brings suit for breach of a union agreement he usually asks the court for an injunction.

---

[32] Pro-Wisconsin: *Segenfeld and Kalin v. Friedman,* 117 Misc. 731, 193 N. Y. Supp. 128 (Sup. Ct. 1922); also *Burickson v. Kleen Laundry Service, Inc.,* 242 App. Div. 701, 272 N. Y. Supp. 866 (2d Dept. 1934); injunction denied where plaintiff had violated existing contract with defendant. Pro-Massachusetts: *Bolivian Panama Hat Co., Inc. v. Finkelstein,* 127 Misc. 337, 215 N. Y. Supp. 399 (Sup. Ct. 1925).

[33] *Dubinsky v. Blue Dale Dress Co., Inc.,* 162 Misc. 177, 182, 292 N. Y. Supp. 898, 904-905 (Sup. Ct. N. Y. County 1936).

This is so chiefly because the time element is extremely important in labor disputes and the problem of measuring and collecting damages is a difficult one. However, the right to injunctive relief in controversies "involving or growing out of a labor dispute" has been sharply restricted by recent federal and state statutes.[34] A controversy over the application of a union agreement is a "labor dispute" within the meaning of these laws;[35] so before injunctive relief can be granted in controversies of this sort the requirements of the statutes must be fulfilled.

Unions, however, will probably not encounter many difficulties in meeting these requirements in actions to secure enforcement of union agreements. The only restrictive terms of the Norris-La Guardia Act that could be applied to union actions of this sort are contained in Section 7 and Section 8 of the law. To secure an injunction it must be shown under Section 7 "(a) That unlawful acts have been threatened and will be committed unless restrained . . . . (b) That substantial and irreparable injury to complainant's property will follow . . . . (e) That the public officers charged with the duty to protect complainant's property are unable or unwilling to furnish adequate protection . . . ."[36] Where an employer breaches an agreement it seems safe to assume that the courts will usually consider these conditions fulfilled by the employees or union, particularly in view of the dominant purpose of the legislation.[37] In a New York case, for example, an employer who had violated his agreement with the union argued that no injunction should issue because there was no allegation in the union's complaint that public officers had failed to furnish protection. Justice Poletti, however, found that the complaint complied with all the conditions precedent and that this particular allegation was unnecessary since the action arose out of contract and not out of tort or crime.[38] Under Section 8 of the law, on the other hand, in-

---

[34] Norris-La Guardia Act, 47 Stat. 70 (1932), 29 U. S. C. A. ¶¶ 101-115 (Supp. 1940). The state statutes, patterned after the Federal law, are collected and discussed in Osmond K. Fraenkel, "Recent Statutes Affecting Labor Injunctions and Yellow Dog Contracts" (1936) 30 *Illinois Law Review* 854.

[35] Comment (1937) 50 *Harvard Law Review* 1295; but see *United Electric Coal Cos. v. Rice*, 80 F. (2d) 1 (C. C. A. 7th, 1935) certiorari denied, 297 U. S. 714, 56 Sup. Ct. 590 (1936). In this case the court held that a jurisdictional dispute between a union which had an agreement and its rival was not a "labor dispute" within the meaning of sub-section C, section 113 of the Norris-La Guardia Act. The court made a similar decision in a case where a railroad company abrogated an agreement without notice to the union and made an agreement with another union on the grounds that it represented the majority of the employees. *Railway Employees Cooperative Assn. v. Atlanta B. and C. Ry. Co.*, 22 F. Supp. 510 (D. C. Ga. 1938); *Assd. Flour Haulers, etc. v. Sullivan, etc.*, 168 Misc. 315, 5 N. Y. S. (2d) 982 (Sup. Ct. 1938).

[36] Section 7, Norris La Guardia Act, 47 Stat. 71 (1932), 29 U. S. C. A., ¶ 107 (Supp. 1940).

[37] Comment (1938) 51 *Harvard Law Review* 520, 531-532.

[38] *Murphy v. Ralph*, 165 Misc. 335, 299 N. Y. Supp. 270 (Sup. Ct. N. Y. County 1937).

junctions are not to be granted to anyone (union representative as well as employer) "who has failed to comply with any obligation imposed by law which is involved in the labor dispute in question or who has failed to make every reasonable effort to settle such dispute" either by negotiation, mediation, or voluntary arbitration.[39] This provision may limit union requests for injunctions more frequently than Section 7 of the law.

Where employers seek enforcement of agreements against unions the anti-injunction statutes may present serious obstacles. In addition to the limiting provisions cited above, the courts are prohibited from enjoining a long list of activities in which workers engage, so long as these activities involve or grow out of a labor dispute. This list of activities includes ceasing work, joining any labor organization, paying strike benefits, publicizing the facts of a labor dispute, and advising or notifying any person of an intention to do, or not to do, any of these things.[40] The scope of these prohibitions depends chiefly on how the courts interpret the phrase "labor dispute" as defined in the anti-injunction laws. The definition contained in these laws is extremely broad. It includes all disputes concerning the conditions of employment which either involve workers engaged in the same industry or workers who have direct or indirect interests therein. This definition would seem to be comprehensive enough to cover disputes where strikes or other types of union action occur in violation of union agreements.[41] In any event, the anti-injunction acts (with but a few exceptions) do not specifically exclude such situations from the safeguards of these laws; consequently, employers may now frequently find it difficult to secure restraining orders against unions even where the latter have disregarded their agreements and threaten to do so again.

The law in Pennsylvania is an exception; an amendment passed in 1939 provides that the state anti-injunction act does not apply to a labor dispute "which is in disregard, breach or violation of . . . . a valid subsisting labor agreement . . . ."[42] Legislation passed in the

---

[39] Section 8, Norris-La Guardia Act, 47 Stat. 72 (1932), 29 U. S. C. A. ¶ 108 (Supp. 1940). The courts to date have held that a plaintiff who has not complied with Section 8 can get no relief, even though the defendants are committing fraud or violence. *Cinderella Theater Co. v. Sign Writers' Local Union*, 6 F. Supp. 164 (E. D. Mich. 1934); *Dean v. Mayo*, 8 F. Supp. 73 (W. D. La. 1934), 9 F. Supp. 459 (W. D. La. 1934), aff'd., 82 F. (2d) 554 (C. C. A. 5th, 1936). In reference to a similar provision in the Pennsylvania state anti-injunction law (prior to its amendment in 1939), see *Bulkin v. Sacks*, 31 D. and C. 501 (Pa. 1938) and *Tobin v. Shapiro*, 32 D. and C. 291 (Pa. 1938).

[40] Section 4, Norris-La Guardia Act, 47 Stat. 70 (1932), 29 U. S. C. A. ¶ 104 (Supp. 1940).

[41] But see *Greater City Master Plumbers Association, Inc. v. Kahme*, 6 N. Y. S. (2d) 589 (Sup. Ct. N. Y. County 1937).

[42] Amendment to Pennsylvania Anti-Injunction Act, Act of 1937, P. L. 1198 as amended by Act of 1939, P. L. 302, Pa. Stat. Ann. (Purdon, 1941) tit. 43 ¶ 206d.

same year in Minnesota and Wisconsin has much the same effect, since it provides that a strike called in violation of a union agreement constitutes an unfair labor practice.[43] Finally, in Oregon in 1938 the coverage of the state anti-injunction law was substantially narrowed by a re-definition of the term "labor dispute" to include only controversies "in which the disputants stand in proximate relation of the employer and the majority of its employees and which directly concerns matters directly pertaining to wages, hours or working conditions of the employees of the particular employer directly involved in such controversy."[44] No provision in the Oregon law, however, specifically excludes strikes in violation of union agreements from the safeguards provided against the use of injunctions.

In the author's view it would be unfortunate if anti-injunction legislation proved to be a barrier to effective enforcement of union agreements. On the side of union actions against employers there is little to fear; but employer actions against unions may be blocked. If the amendments could be carefully and explicitly drawn, the anti-injunction laws should be so altered as not to apply to strikes in violation of valid agreements. The trouble is that such amendments might be used as a means of weakening many protections afforded by the legislation. Unless definite guarantees were given against this eventuality, the change would not be worth the risk involved.

REMEDIES AGAINST UNIONS

Obstacles also confront the employer who attempts to serve a process on a union or to seek damages for breach of contract. The difficulties in this connection relate to the fact that generally unions are not incorporated. This issue has received wide attention but its importance has been unduly magnified. True, under the common law, there could be no proceedings against an unincorporated association like a trade union, as such.[45] Suit could be brought only against the individual officers and the members committing the unlawful act. There is no doubt that if this doctrine prevailed today unincorporated labor unions would be adequately protected from destruction by damage suits; important limitations to actions in equity brought against labor unions would also exist. However, the Supreme Court's decision in the celebrated *Coronado Coal Company* case made unincorpo-

---

[43] Section 11 of Minnesota Labor Relations Act, Laws of 1939, Ch. 440 ¶ 11, Minn. Stat. (Mason, Supp. 1940) 4254-31; Employment Peace Act, Wis. Stat. (1939) ¶ 111.06 as amended by Laws of 1939, Ch. 57.

[44] See Ore. Comp. Laws Ann. (1940) ¶¶ 102-196.

[45] See, for example, *Karges Furniture Co. v. Amalgamated Woodworkers L. Union*, 165 Ind. 421, 75 N. E. 877 (1905); *Pickett v. Walsh*, 192 Mass. 572, 78 N. E. 753 (1906); *Citizens' Co. v. Asheville Typographical Union*, 187 N. C. 42, 121 S. E. 31 (1924).

rated associations suable as such in federal jurisdictions.[46] In this case the plaintiff company sought payment from the union treasury for damages allegedly committed by representatives and members of the United Mine Workers of America in the course of an organizing strike. In passing on the issue whether unions are suable, the Supreme Court declared that Congress had recognized the legal existence of trade unions in various federal statutes, citing Section 8 of the Sherman Act in confirmation of this view.[47] The state courts, with apparently only one exception,[48] have not followed the rule laid down in the *Coronado Coal Company* case. But in almost half the states, unincorporated associations have been made suable by express statutory authorization.[49] Elsewhere, the courts are still disposed to deny such associations the right to sue and be sued.[50]

Actually, the fact that few damage suits are brought against unions for breach of agreements is due not so much to any legal characteristics of labor organizations; the explanation lies rather in the nature of the disputes in which unions become involved. The normal remedy against a union for breach of an agreement is the injunction. In disputes of this sort, the employer's primary objective—if not his only one—is immediate resumption of operations on his terms of employment. It is the injunction instead of the suit for damages which will most likely secure this end. This is true chiefly because restraining orders can be secured quickly, and also because injunctions prevent the occurrence of damages. Moreover, there are fewer legal obstacles in obtaining an injunction against a union than in bringing a damage suit. The extent to which unions are held to be legal entities, separate and apart from their members, has already been noted. In addition, thanks to the device of the representative suit, the entire membership of a union can be brought before the court in injunction proceedings simply by naming a few of its members. Then, too, injunctions obviate the difficulty of calculating money damages and the usually greater difficulty of collecting them.[51] Thus it is not surpris-

---

[46] *U. M. W. A. v. Coronado Coal Co.*, 259 U. S. 344, 391, 42 Sup. Ct. 570, 576 (1922). Three years later, after retrial, this same case was brought to the Supreme Court again. *Coronado Coal Co. v. U. M. W. A.*, 268 U. S. 295, 45 Sup. Ct. 551 (1925).

[47] 26 Stat. 210 (1890), 15 U. S. C. A. ¶ 7 (1927).

[48] *Varnado v. Whitney*, 166 Miss. 663, 147 So. 479 (1933).

[49] Comment (1938) 38 *Columbia Law Review* 454, 456.

[50] But see *St. Germain v. Bakery & Confectionery Workers' Union*, 97 Wash. 282, 166 Pac. 665 (1917). Judgment was brought against the union as such, even though there was no permitting statute, where some of its members were present to defend the action and the membership was too large to summon all of them.

[51] In the ("second") *Coronado Coal Co.* case, for example, there was a settlement for damages after a lapse of many years at a fraction of the amount originally set by the court. The amount was first set at $600,000, but the case was finally settled out of court for $27,500. *Coronado Coal Co. v. United Mine Workers of America*, 268 U. S. 295, 45 Sup. Ct. 551 (1925). See Edwin E. Witte, *The Government in Labor Disputes* (New York: McGraw-Hill Book Co., 1932), p. 70, footnote 2.

ing that there are relatively few cases in which damages have been sought by employers against labor unions. One authority found that in all jurisdictions between 1922 and 1932, there were only 314 cases in which damages were claimed, and many of these were actions brought by non-unionists or expelled union members. In at least sixty-six of these cases damages were recovered.[52]

Another barrier to legal action against a union for breach of an agreement applies to injunctive relief as well as to damage suits. Violations of union agreements on the workers' side of the agreement are almost always committed by certain members or officers of the union or by some sub-division of the organization. Before legal action will be allowed against a union, however, it must be shown that it is responsible for the acts which constitute the breach.[53] The courts have found that such responsibility existed when the union has authorized the acts violating the agreement. In a great many instances, however, it is not clear whether the individual members or the local union actually committing the breach acted with the knowledge and approval of the parent organization. It is under these circumstances that judges who are reluctant to make union agreements enforceable against labor organizations find their opportunity. They can simply resort to a very strict interpretation of what they consider the requisite authorization.

The courts for the most part have not done so. In a case where the breach was committed by officers of the union, the court held that the union organization as such violated the agreement and that no inquiry into the attitude of the membership was necessary.[54] In another case, the judge declared that the union was not necessarily free from liability for its officers' behavior even though the membership had made vigorous protests.[55] In still another case—where a group of individual members committed the breach without authorization from the officers of the union or from the rest of the membership—the court held the union liable on the ground that a considerable proportion of the membership was involved; in addition, the court found that while the union (at its meetings and through its officials) had not encouraged the breach it had made no great effort to get the men to return to work.[56] The latter point touches on a consideration to which many courts attach decisive importance. If the union organization takes disciplinary action against those committing the violation, the

---

[52] Witte, *op. cit.*, pp. 138-139.

[53] The same thing would be true if an employers' association were involved.

[54] *Meltzer v. Kaminer*, 131 Misc. 813, 227 N. Y. Supp. 459 (Sup. Ct. 1927). See also *Clarkson v. Laiblau*, 202 Mo. App. 682, 216 S. W. 1029 (1919).

[55] *Ill. Central Ry. Co. v. International Association of Machinists,* 190 Fed. 910 (C. C. E. D. Ill. 1911).

[56] *Nederlandsch Amerikaansche Stoomvaart v. Stevedores' and Longshoremen's Benevolent Society,* 265 Fed. 397 (E. D. La. 1920).

court has held the union not liable for the breach; but if the union fails to do so, the court has been disposed to hold the organization as such liable.[57] Even though a majority of the union's membership opposes the violation, the courts have found the union liable if no disciplinary action is taken against the offending members.[58] The same rule has been applied to make the union officials liable as well.[59]

The courts have been criticized for attempting to make this distinction, on the ground that mere failure to penalize offending members does not necessarily mean that the union has granted even tacit approval to their acts. According to this view, union officials generally hesitate to risk the internal dissension which such penalties would be likely to involve.[60] For the same reason, criticism has been levelled against decisions holding unions liable merely on a showing that the members, although disapproving the wrongful acts, knew of their occurrence; or merely on a showing that the union received some benefit from such acts.[61] For the most part, these criticisms do not square with the facts. As a rule, in their dealings with employers, unions follow a predetermined program, of which any acts committed by their representatives and members are but a part. This may not apply so generally to relations between officials of national and local union organizations, especially where the unions have only recently been established. It is more particularly applicable to the acts of local union spokesmen (either officers or members) in relation to their local organization. This is hardly surprising since individuals would hesitate to incur the risks of committing illegal acts without some organizational backing.

If the courts follow the path marked out by the Norris-La Guardia Act, however, the opposite viewpoint will prevail. This law provides that:

---

[57] *Moran v. Lasette*, 221 App. Div. 118, 223 N. Y. Supp. 283 (1st Dept. 1927); refusal to order men back to work was held to be a direct participation in the strike.

[58] *United Traction Co. v. Droogan*, 115 Misc. 672, 189 N. Y. Supp. 39 (Sup. Ct. Albany County 1921). See *Alaska S. S. Co. v. International Longshoremen's Assn.*, 236 Fed. 964 (W. D. Wash. 1916); *Herket and Meisel Trunk Co. v. United Leatherworkers International Union*, 268 Fed. 662 (E. D. Mo. 1920), decision holding strike in restraint of trade, reversed, 265 U. S. 457, 44 Sup. Ct. 623 (1924); but see *Tannenbaum v. Hofbauer*, 142 Misc. 120, 253 N. Y. Supp. 90 (Sup. Ct. 1931).

[59] In one case the court said that the officers of a union were liable for contempt of a restraining order where the actual violation had been committed by the rank and file members of the organization, on the grounds that the officers did not prevent the violation when they could have done so. *Phillips S. and T. P. Co. v. Amalgamated Assn., etc.*, 208 Fed. 335 (S. D. Ohio 1913).

[60] Comment (1938) 38 *Columbia Law Review* 454, 465.

[61] *Jones v. Maher*, 62 Misc. 388, 116 N. Y. Supp. 180 (Sup. Ct. 1909), aff'd., 141 App. Div. 919, 125 N. Y. Supp. 1126 (2d Dept. 1910); *Industrial Council v. Sigman, N. Y. L. J.*, Sept. 30, 1926, p. 2238, col. 1 (N. Y. Sup. Ct. 1926).

No . . . association or organization . . . participating or interested in a labor dispute shall be held responsible or liable in any court of the United States for the unlawful acts of individual officers, members, or agents, except upon clear proof of actual participation in, or actual authorization of, such acts, or the ratification of such acts after actual knowledge thereof.[62]

Following the enactment of this law, a case occurred in which an injunction order was requested against a union because of the lawless acts of some "unknown stench bombers and poster vandals," the court refusing to grant the request for lack of "clear proof of actual participation in, actual authorization of, or ratification of, such acts, by any of the defendants."[63] In this case, the union sought the discharge of a theater signwriter because he was not a member of its organization, although no agreement was in effect. Union pickets patrolled the theater carrying placards and distributing cards charging "unfair" treatment. Stench bombs were discharged in the theater on two occasions, followed by the tearing down of the advertising posters in front of the theater. However, the court found no evidence that the acts of violence were committed by representatives of the union. Appearances are frequently deceiving in cases of this sort, and it is extremely important for the courts to go behind the outward scene to discover the parties really responsible for the unlawful conduct. Otherwise victims of lawless acts will be deprived of adequate protection.

Finally, there is the question of the liability of the international union for acts in violation of an agreement committed or sanctioned by its locals. In this connection, the courts tend to require more definite authorization than in the situations just discussed. In the "first" *Coronado Coal Company* case the court refused to accept as conclusive the facts which purported to show that the International Union, United Mine Workers of America, had approved the conduct of the local union.[64] These facts indicated that the officers of the international knew of the local's activities but failed to restrain them; that statements approving these activities appeared in the international journal; that no disciplinary steps were taken; and that the conduct of the local benefitted the international union. The courts are more prone to find the requisite authorization if the international gives financial support to the local in connection with its wrongdoings.[65] Sometimes, however, it is enough for the courts that the local union has acted "in the line and scope of its duties."[66] The courts are jus-

62 Section 6, Norris-La Guardia Act, 47 Stat. 71 (1932), 29 U. S. C. A. ¶ 106 (Supp. 1940).

63 *Cinderella Theater Co., Inc. v. Sign Writers' Union,* 6 F. Supp. 164, 171 (E. D. Mich. 1934). Whether this view will be adopted by the courts in reference to damage suits, as opposed to requests for injunctions, remains to be seen.

64 *U. M. W. A. v. Coronado Coal Co.,* 259 U. S. 344, 42 Sup. Ct. 570 (1922).

65 *Hillenbrand v. Bldg. Trades Council,* 14 Ohio, Dec. 628 (1904).

66 *Great International Brotherhood, etc. v. Green,* 210 Ala. 496, 98 So. 569 (1923), app. dismissed, 265 U. S. 576, 44 Sup. Ct. 636 (1924).

tified in requiring proof of definite authorization. Local organizations not infrequently chart their own course, sometimes in defiance of sound national leadership, sometimes in the face of corrupt or ineffective leadership. Because of these circumstances, proof of authorization is warranted, even though in most instances the policies of national and local unions are in close conformity.

The barriers to enforcement in actions brought by employers do not bear on the enforceability of the terms of union agreements as such, but rather on the method by which they are to be enforced. As already indicated, union agreements are enforceable in most courts of the country. Indeed, one authority believes that judges have been more ready to grant relief in actions brought by employers than by unions.[67] The cases brought against unions for breach of agreement have been almost exclusively concerned with but two clauses in the agreements: promises to submit disputes to arbitration and promises not to strike during the life of an agreement. With regard to the former, some states have enacted general arbitration laws which exclude union agreements as well as "personal service" contracts. In these jurisdictions, therefore, promises to arbitrate future disputes are unenforceable.[68] Elsewhere, such promises are legally binding if they relate to disputes over a union agreement still unexpired. If the dispute involves the negotiation of a new agreement, there seems to be some doubt whether a promise to arbitrate will be held enforceable. In the only case bearing on this point, the court declared that the arbitration clause was not enforceable since the arbitration law of the state [of New York] was not intended to assist in the making of new agreements.[69] A court following the lead of this decision would be warranted in holding that either party could withdraw at any time from a promise to arbitrate (at least up to the moment when a dispute is actually submitted to the arbitrators for final settlement).[70] In the field of commercial arbitration, at least twelve states, including New York, Pennsylvania, and Ohio, have passed laws providing that an agreement to arbitrate all existing or future disputes shall be valid, irrevocable, and enforceable. One authority declares, however, that even in these states arbitration has not become more generally used as a method of settling commercial disputes.[71] In the field of industrial relations, an attempt to establish the enforceability of agreements to arbitrate all prospective disputes would probably have even less ef-

---

67 Witmer, *op. cit.*, p. 199.

68 Osmond K. Fraenkel, "Legal Enforceability of Agreements to Arbitrate Labor Disputes" (1937) 1 *Arbitration Journal* 360, 361.

69 *Matter of Buffalo Erie Railway Co. v. Amalgamated Association of Street and Electric Railway Workers of America*, 250 N. Y. 275, 165 N. E. 291 (1929).

70 Fraenkel, *op. cit.*, p. 364.

71 Philip G. Phillips, "The Paradox in Arbitration Law" (1933) 46 *Harvard Law Review* 1258, 1263.

fect on prevailing practice. For neither unions nor employers are generally prepared to go that far in turning over control to third parties.

Most court actions against unions to secure the enforcement of agreements concern strikes or "stoppages" occurring during the life of an agreement. A promise not to strike while an agreement exists is the most important commitment made by a union to an employer. It is, of course, a vital matter to a company not to have operations disrupted by strikes. As a result, employers have resorted to a wide variety of devices and strategies, including court action, in the attempt to prevent such interruptions.[72]

The courts have not been backward in fashioning remedies to fit the particular circumstances of any given case. They have enjoined actions preliminary to the calling of the strike; they have enjoined actions attendant upon the strike, such as picketing or appeals to the workers for support; they have enjoined the strike itself. In the case of *Grassi Contracting Company, Inc. v. Bennett*, for example, the court took a clear-cut position:

> Where a strike, or other action, is threatened by a labor union in violation of its contract, or of the contract of its members with their employers, the jurisdiction of a court of equity to issue an injunction is well recognized.[73]

To what extent anti-injunction legislation may alter the courts' position on this issue was discussed above. But there is one type of situation concerning strikes in violation of agreements in which equitable relief has not been granted. These are cases where, according to the court, the workers left their employment not as a single union group but as individual employees. The courts held that injunctive relief would subject such workers to involuntary servitude.[74] Actually, the issue turns on whether the individual workers, as distinguished from the union members as a group, are to be bound by agreements

---

[72] Recent state legislation, as already indicated, seeks to prevent strikes of this sort. In Minnesota the list of unfair labor practices contained in the state labor relations law had previously pertained to certain employer activities only. In 1939 this list was extended to certain activities on the part of labor organizations as well; among these activities was the calling of a strike in violation of any valid collective agreement if "the employer is, at the time, in good faith complying with the provisions of the agreement." Section 11, Minnesota Labor Relations Act, Laws of 1939, Ch. 440 ¶ 11, Minn. Stat. (Mason, Supp. 1940) ¶¶ 4254-31. A similar provision was put into the Wisconsin Employment Peace Act, Wis. Stat. (1939) ¶ 111.06, as amended by Laws of 1939, Ch. 57. In Pennsylvania, the state anti-injunction law was altered in such a way that it would not henceforth apply to a labor dispute which was "in disregard, breach or violation of . . . a valid subsisting labor agreement . . . ." Amendment to Pennsylvania Anti-Injunction Act, Act of 1937, P. L. 1198, as amended by Act of 1939, P. L. 302, Pa. Stat. Ann. (Purdon, 1941) tit. 43 ¶ 206d. The restrictions placed on unions in other states did not deal directly with strikes which violated union agreements.

[73] 174 App. Div. 244, 248, 160 N. Y. Supp. 279, 283 (1st Dept. 1916).

[74] *Arthur v. Oakes*, 63 Fed. 310 (C. C. A. 7th, 1894); *Preble v. Architectural Iron Workers' Union of Chicago*, 260 Ill. App. 435, 439 (1931).

entered into by their union organizations. It is one of the most perplexing questions in the field of labor law today, and the courts have yet to find a satisfactory answer.[75]

INDIVIDUAL MEMBERS

There have been few cases involving this vexatious problem, but in those instances courts have almost always held that the individual members are bound by the union agreement unless there is express provision to the contrary in the member's contract with his employer. In one case where the court found that the members of the union knew the terms of the agreement, it was ruled that they were to be bound by them.[76] The way in which a judge frames his answer to this question, however, depends chiefly on his attitude toward the relation between the union's agreement and the individual worker's contract of employment. There are several schools of thought on that point. The first believes in the usage or custom theory which holds that a union agreement becomes a part of every existing or subsequent employment contract in the absence of any agreement to the contrary. This view goes further than any other in placing duties on the individual union member under an agreement. However, the courts have restricted its application since it creates no obligations between the employer and union organization and thereby renders uncertain the validity of the union agreement as such.[77]

The second attitude considers the union organization to be the agent of its individual members. According to this view, the union agreement becomes the individual member's contract of employment and, in this sense, the individual member is bound by it. But this position, in avoiding the deficiency of the usage theory noted above, encounters difficulties of its own. For it must be shown that the individual members have authorized or ratified the union as their agent in negotiating the agreement. As already noted, this is not always easy, for workers seeking escape from the terms of an agreement can claim they gave their supposed spokesmen no such warrant. The courts, however, have been quick to find the authorization. In some instances, it has been inferred from the organizational relationship alone. In others, the courts have held that express authorization or ratification is not a necessary requirement.[78] A more serious weakness affects the employee who becomes a member of the union after the signing of the agreement. It would be hard to argue that the

---

75 There is no "law of union agreements" in the sense of a body of doctrine, as it applies to the individual employee. There are, perhaps, 100 cases bearing on this problem. Witmer, *op. cit.*, p. 238.

76 *Leading Cleaners v. Senate* (Sup. Ct. Kings Co., N. Y. 1937).

77 Comment (1932) 41 *Yale Law Journal* 1221, 1223.

78 *Whiting Milk Co. v. Grondin*, 282 Mass. 41, 184 N. E. 379 (1933), individual union member bound by provision in union agreement.

union was acting as an agent for the employee under these circumstances.[79] Similarly, it would seem impossible under this view to hold an individual employee not a member of the union to be bound by the terms of its agreement.[80] Perhaps these difficulties explain why there have been comparatively few decisions based on the agency theory alone.

There is still another theory which treats the individual employee as a third-party beneficiary under the union agreement. According to this view, therefore, there is no contract of employment between the employer and the individual worker which embodies the terms of the union agreement. The benefits of the agreement are extended to him as a third party to the arrangement. In terms of this theory, it can be argued that union agreements are framed with an intent to benefit not only the unionized workers but also the non-union workers of an employer. To this extent it is more realistic than the agency theory noted above. But though it permits the individual worker to recover from the employer as a third party beneficiary of the agreement, it seems to throw doubt on the right of the employer to bring suit against the individual worker who violates the agreement. Except in the Mississippi courts this theory has had limited application.[81]

When the relation just discussed is reversed, the question arises whether the individual employee can sue his employer for violating the agreement with the union. Here again the answer is, generally speaking, an affirmative one. It should be noted, in this connection, that some courts have attempted to square their decisions with the various theories already outlined. Most of the courts, however, have simply required the employee to show that he was a member of the union and that the employer violated the agreement between the firm and the union.[82] A minority, it is true, have held that something more than mere membership—for example, ''acceptance'' or ''ratification'' of the agreement—must be shown.[83]

Where the courts have confronted complicated situations and relationships of this character, the attempt to conform their findings

---

[79] This same problem arises on the employer's side when an employer joins an employers' association after the latter has signed an agreement with a union.

[80] *Gregg v. Starks*, 188 Ky. 834, 224 S. W. 459 (1920), non-union worker entitled to benefits of agreement applicable to all the workers.

[81] *Yazoo & Miss. Valley Railroad v. Webb*, 64 F. (2d) 902, 903 (C. C. A. 5th, 1933). Indeed, in some states the third party beneficiary doctrine has never been accepted in regard to contracts generally.

[82] *Bell v. Western Ry. of Alabama*, 228 Ala. 328, 331, 335, 153 So. 434, 436, 439 (1934), collective bargain in issue partly as employer's defense; *Mastell v. Salo*, 140 Ark. 408, 215 S. W. 583 (1919); *Beatty v. Chicago, Burlington and Quincy Railroad Co.*, 49 Wyo. 22, 32, 52 P. (2d) 404, 407 (1935).

[83] *Burnetta v. Marceline Coal Co.*, 180 Mo. 241, 79 S. W. 136 (1904), defendant employer used union agreement as a defense against the plaintiff's claim; *Ahlquist v. Alaska-Portland Packers' Association*, 39 F. (2d) 348 (C. C. A. 9th, 1930).

with legal theories has often produced rather strained results. If a non-union worker, for example, sues on a union agreement, his position would be defensible under the custom and third-party beneficiary theories, but hardly so under the theory of agency.[84] If, in another instance, the employer abrogates the agreement after the union has violated its terms, the individual union member may contend that the provisions of the agreement are separable, some running to the individual and some to the union. Under the custom theory a court would not find it so difficult to accept this contention. On the other hand, if the court views the union as the agent of the individual employee, the complications multiply, for here the agent has violated the agreement while the principal has not. Under the third-party beneficiary view the position of the plaintiff employee is even more precarious. According to this theory, he is an outside third party to the agreement between the union and the employer; but if the basic bargain has been broken, how is it to be argued that he is to continue to receive benefits from an instrument which no longer exists?

In dealing with the relation between the union's agreement and the individual worker's contract of employment, judges seem to be more concerned with verbal niceties than with the realities of the problems confronting them. Perhaps this is an instance where theories underlying the general law of contracts have been applied too mechanically to the law of union agreements. It is one thing to inquire whether union agreements are enforceable as between employers and union organizations as such; it is quite another thing to ask whether they are enforceable as between employers and individual employees. The two questions involve different considerations. The answer to the latter in specific situations, for example, should certainly take into account the various types of labor disputes that occur, the sort of union organizations involved, and the customary practices prevailing in the industry affected. The attempt, therefore, to join both aspects of the problem and deal with them in terms of a single theory is likely to lead to unfortunate results.

According to the view reached in the preparation of this study, individual members of a union should be legally bound by their organization's agreements as long as they are members; in turn, they should have the right to secure legal redress for agreement violations. Union agreements establish standards of employment which apply to specific workers for a particular time. If union members can disregard these standards with impunity, the agreements might just as well not have been written. The realities of union-employer relations do not permit any other interpretation. If certain members refuse

---

84 *Yazoo & Miss. Valley Railroad v. Webb*, 64 F. (2d) 902, 903 (C. C. A. 5th, 1933), action sustained on third party beneficiary theory; *Young v. Canadian Northern Ry.* (1931) I. D. L. R. 645 (P. C.), action not sustained.

to be bound by the agreement, they are, in effect, no longer members of the union. It is their privilege to withdraw, and no court can deny it; but the court should prevent workers from being half-in and half-out of a union. This is an important distinction. It means that if union members refuse to comply with their organization's agreements, they are not to receive any of the benefits of membership. In some industries, particularly where closed shop agreements are in effect, loss of membership is a serious matter.

The exact purpose of the terms of union agreements—just what they do and do not say—must be understood in applying them to individual employees. Workers can still protest any decision of their employer; they can demand a different job, a higher wage-classification, another timekeeper, and any number of other changes. They can make similar objections to the policies of their union officials. But if such methods are ineffective, the root of the problem will not be reached by limiting the scope of agreements. The only adequate remedy would be to render it easier for workers to make their objections effective. The one important thing which individual workers cannot do, however, is walk off the job until the regular procedure for handling disputes has been exhausted. The foregoing analysis draws a clear distinction between union members and non-members, sharper perhaps than the facts of some situations justify. On the other hand, unless non-members definitely agree to be bound, or unless prevailing practice points to the same conclusion, it would certainly be arbitrary to hold them to an agreement just as though they were members of the union.

Also defying easy solution are legal questions arising from another aspect of the relationship between the individual member and his union organization.[85] Sometimes a union confronts situations where dissident groups within its membership violate the terms of agreements, particularly by strike actions—conduct which is usually an infraction of their organization's constitution and by-laws as well. It is an important point whether the union can take legal action against the rebellious members on the basis of their obligations to the organization. But even in this connection disciplinary measures rarely involve resort to the courts, although on the occasions when that was done, the union has generally been sustained. Indeed, the courts have granted unions a wide area of discretion over their internal affairs. Some courts have held that the relation between union and member is a "contractual" one and that, so long as the union stays within its written rules, its disciplinary actions are not subject

---

85 These comments also bear on the relationship between the individual employer member and his employers' association.

to judicial review.[86] Other courts have asked whether the analogy to the law of contracts is persuasive or complete. Nevertheless, there is general agreement that unions have the power to expel individual workers or locals from membership[87] and to impose a wide variety of other penalties where violations of the rules of membership occur.[88]

Assuming that unions have the legal prerogative to discipline unruly members, the further question is presented whether they *must* do so when such groups or individuals violate the union's agreement with an employer. As noted above, the courts regard such agreements, if valid, as enforceable against unions. Does this mean that unions can be made to take disciplinary steps against members who violate the provisions of the agreement? It could probably be argued, for example, that where a minority within a union strikes in violation of an agreement, any legal action brought against the union must provide for such disciplinary measures in order to be effective. The courts, however, have not yet answered this question. Some lower New York courts have suggested, in dicta, that unions may be required to enforce decrees by disciplining their members.[89] But in Ohio such a requirement has been held to involve involuntary servitude.[90] Here again an important contribution would be made if the position of the courts were clarified. The feasibility of this requirement would most likely be determined by the stage of development that had been reached by the particular union affected. It would be workable only if the union were a well-knit, highly centralized organi-

---

[86] Comment (1936) 45 *Yale Law Journal* 1248, 1263-1264; see also Comment (1934) 12 *New York University Law Quarterly Review* 291; Zechariah Chafee, Jr. "The Internal Affairs of Associations Not for Profit" (1930) 43 *Harvard Law Review* 993; Note (1930) 30 *Columbia Law Review* 847.

[87] *Commonwealth v. Hunt*, 45 Mass. 111 (1842), disciplinary penalty upheld despite charge union constituted a criminal conspiracy; *Thomas v. Cincinnati, N. O. and T. P. Ry. Co.*, 62 Fed. 803, 817 (C. C. S. D. Ohio 1894), wide area of permissible union disciplinary action outlined.

[88] Where the reverse of this relationship is under consideration the question becomes one of the legal rights of union members against their officials and organizations, in case they violate their obligations to the membership. Its bearing on the subject of this study is too remote to warrant consideration here. In general, the courts hesitate to give redress under these circumstances unless the union members can show that all methods provided under the by-laws of the union for settling disputes have been exhausted and that property rights have been injured. See *Jennings v. Lee*, 295 Fed. 561 (W. D. N. Y. 1923), expelled local union member denied relief because of failure to use transfer opportunities available within the union. Court actions brought by union members against their officials, usually in the form of requests for injunctions, are much more frequent than actions where the positions of the two parties are reversed.

[89] See, for example, *Schlesinger v. Quinto*, 201 App. Div. 487, 499, 194 N. Y. Supp. 401, 410 (1st Dept. 1922).

[90] *Lundoff-Bicknell Co. v. Smith*, 24 Ohio App. 294, 303-304, 156 N. E. 243, 245-246 (1927).

zation. This circumstance suggests that no such requirement should be established unless the union and employer agree to include it as a provision in the agreement.

CONCLUSIONS

The foregoing review of the legal aspects of the problem of union agreement violations has brought out the important points at which controversy still exists. Clarification of the courts' position on these issues would mark a real advance in the field of labor relations. The lines along which agreement might well be reached have been suggested. On the whole, however, the courts are now prepared to give judicial remedy where violations of union agreements occur. This is true whether the breach has been committed by the employer or the union. A different result might obtain if the aggrieved party has himself broken the agreement, although this very important matter has not yet been thrashed out in the courts. Moreover, labor relations laws and anti-injunction legislation place restrictions on requests for judicial remedies, particularly if the requests come from the employer. But difficulties attaching to the unincorporated association and to questions of a union's responsibility for the acts of its individual members do not constitute very serious barriers.

Yet despite the fact that judicial remedies are available, neither employers nor unions have frequent resort to the courts to secure observance of the terms of agreements. This suggests that disputes regarding the application and interpretation of union agreements do not lend themselves to court adjudication. The issues involved are frequently too technical, the time element too important, and the cost of legal action too great to recommend resort to the courts. In industries where collective bargaining has been long established and widely practiced, both parties are likely to conclude that they are in a better position than any court to deal with agreement violations. In industries where collective bargaining has made little headway, the stronger party is likely to feel that litigation is unnecessary to gain the results desired. By contrast, the weaker party is likely to be in straitened circumstances or to be fearful of retaliation if he starts legal proceedings. These two type-situations cover most of the field of industrial relations in this country.

At the same time, the employer has other and more effective legal strategies available for use in labor controversies; court relief can be secured for a wide variety of acts involving coercion, violence, and damage to property. Labor, however, is usually reluctant to seek court aid to obtain enforcement of union agreements. The following statement by John L. Lewis, in reference to violations of the terms of the Jacksonville Agreement by coal operators during the period 1924-1927, is still fairly typical of the union point of view:

> . . . if we had sought to enjoin these coal companies to prevent them from using their mines except under the scale in the Jacksonville Agreement, we would have been compelled to file an enormous bond, beyond our means to file, to guarantee the coal company against loss in the event that our position was not sustained. That was one practical reason. On the other hand, there were diverse opinions among our attorneys as to the practicability of filing a suit for civil damages . . . we have been reluctant to engage in a long battle in the courts that might take years to decide. We preferred to determine whether or not there was some manner in which the thing could be adjusted and the obligations of the contract come to be recognized.[91]

Of course, as the number of union agreements multiply and their coverage widens, litigation involving agreement violations will increase. Nevertheless, it seems unlikely that both employers and unions will soon lose their unwillingness to place main reliance on intervention by the courts.

These considerations indicate that the problem of responsibility under union agreements is not due to imperfections in the law. Adequate legal machinery is already in existence to secure observance of agreements. Yet the problem persists. In earlier chapters it was shown that grievance machinery was a relatively unimportant part of the problem of responsibility. The same conclusion, it appears, applies to the law of union agreements. The analysis will have to follow quite different lines if causal circumstances surrounding this problem are to be uncovered.

Nevertheless, some changes in the law of union agreements along the lines indicated should undoubtedly be made. But in doing so, whether by legislative enactment or judicial interpretation, it is extremely important to take account of the varying circumstances surrounding the administration of union agreements. Some agreements, like those in certain parts of the building industry, are but a phase of a program to restrict the number of workers entering the trade or to allocate the available business among a certain group of employers. Others, like those in the bituminous coal industry, are designed primarily to prevent competition in the setting of wage-rates and other employment standards. Agreements elsewhere also offer significant variations. First, there are differences in leadership on the side of both unions and employers. Sometimes the spokesmen are men of restraint and integrity; sometimes they are ruthless and unscrupulous. Second, agreements differ in the degree of unanimity which they achieve. Some, particularly in industries where collective bargaining has been long established, are accepted in good faith by both parties.

---

[91] *Conditions in the Coal Fields of Pennsylvania, West Virginia and Ohio*, Hearings before the Committee of Interstate Commerce, U. S. Senate, 70th Cong., 1st Sess., pursuant to S. Res. 105 (1928), p. 385.

Others merely mark a truce before the struggle starts again. Third, there are differences in the attitudes of the workers themselves toward the agreements and toward their leaders. In some cases the workers are in close accord with the policies of the union; in others they have lost interest or are in active opposition. Finally, the economic conditions under which agreements operate vary to a marked extent. Sometimes economic circumstances make compliance easy; sometimes they make it virtually impossible. These differences are not clear-cut; they are matters only of degree. Be that as it may, those who formulate public policy should keep such distinctions in mind. Otherwise, the legislatures and the courts may find that they are aggravating rather than alleviating the conditions of industrial unrest.

CHAPTER V

DISINTEGRATION WITHIN

When an employer first signs an agreement with a union there is often little immediate change in the basic conditions of employment. The principles accepted by both parties are usually phrased in vague language and subject to widely varying interpretations. Upon application of the agreement, the union may find that its objectives are little nearer realization than before: many employees may still be outside the union's fold; a promise to re-study piece-rate classifications or establish a seniority system may not be carried out; wage-rates established under the agreement may be no different than those already in effect; the employer may even remain as "anti-union" as ever, fully prepared to resort to extreme tactics to rid himself of the union altogether. Needless to say, responsibilities assumed in this uncooperative spirit are more nominal than genuine. Consider, for instance, a promise by a union not to strike during the life of an agreement. If an agreement brings no real improvement in the standards of employment, it is likely that the leaders of the union will conclude that organizing tactics are still necessary—one of these tactics, of course, being the strike. Neither is the employer, under these circumstances, likely to view conditions as substantially changed. If ruthlessness has characterized previous efforts to fight the union or restrict its scope, paper pledges will not do much to alter an employer's attitude after an agreement is signed.

It is impossible to determine the extent of these practices under the hundreds of "first agreements" signed since 1933. There is reason to believe that most unions and employers have at one time or another been guilty of this kind of conduct, even though it has probably not usually taken an extremist form. In a few cases, however, there has been a complete disregard of the responsibilities contained in agreements, generally leading to their termination and to the dissolution of the labor organizations signing them. Some of these cases will be examined here, but it must be emphasized that they are not altogether typical of union-employer relations in their early stages of development. They merely present in a clear-cut manner several of the key problems encountered in such situations. In every case to be mentioned, union and employer had recently entered into written agreements but, without exception, all dealings between the two parties were subsequently ended. While the breaking-point was not, in every single case, reached before the formal expiration of the agreement, in each one important provisions were disregarded and the force of the agreements largely undermined before the termination date had arrived. There was a longer period of tranquility in the Louis Hornick case, where the final disruption took place about four years after the first agreement with the Textile Trimming Workers' Union had been signed;[1] in all the others the denouement occurred before two years had elapsed.

These case-situations have been chosen from a wide variety of industries, including shipping, the manufacture of textiles and rubber goods, and the production of machines for industrial and office use. They involve firms large and small, employing labor skilled and common. As for the unions, some were affiliated with well-established international organizations, embracing virtually all workers in the firms as members, but the majority of the unions were newly formed groups, not in very strong positions even after the first agreement had been signed. Although only seven cases are here examined in detail, the investigation covered fifteen—each of which had come before the National Labor Relations Board.[2]

---

[1] *The Matter of Louis Hornick and Co., Inc., and Textile Trimming Workers' Union, Local 2440, United Textile Workers of America,* Case No. C-111, decided June 12, 1937, 2 N. L. R. B. 983.

[2] The seven N. L. R. B. cases chosen for special analysis are:

The Matter of The Firth Carpet Co. and Textile Workers' Organizing Committee, Case No. C-1102, decided January 4, 1939, 10 N. L. R. B. 944.

The Matter of La Favorite Rubber Manufacturing Co., Inc., and United Rubber Workers of America, Case No. C-1220, decided November 20, 1939, 17 N. L. R. B. 955.

The Matter of Louis Hornick and Co., Inc., and Textile Trimming Workers' Union, Local 2440, United Textile Workers of America, Case No. C-111, decided June 12, 1937, 2 N. L. R. B. 983.

The Matter of Ralph A. Freundlich, Inc. and Max Marcus, Tony Armao, et al., Case No. C-78, decided May 19, 1937, 2 N. L. R. B. 802.

The Matter of Remington Rand, Inc. and Remington Rand Joint Protective Board of the District Council Office Equipment Workers, Case No. C-145, decided March 13, 1937, 2 N. L. R. B. 626, aff'd with minor modifications, 94 F. (2d) 862 (C. C. A. 2nd, 1938), certiorari denied, 304 U. S. 576 (Remington Rand), 585 (Employees Association), (1938). Additional charges were brought against this company before the N. L. R. B. in 1939: *The Matter of Remington Rand, Inc. and Remington Rand Joint Protective Board of the District Council Office Equipment Workers,* Case No. C-1588, decided June 28, 1940, 24 N. L. R. B. No. 118.

The Matter of Sands Manufacturing Co. and Mechanics Educational Society of America, Case No. C-33, decided April 17, 1936, 1 N. L. R. B. 546, decision set aside, 96 E. (2d) 721 (C. C. A. 6th, 1938), aff'd., 306 U. S. 332, 59 Sup. Ct. 508 (1939).

The Matter of Wilson Line, Inc. and National Marine Engineers' Beneficial Association, National Organization Masters, Mates and Pilots and Harbor Boatmen's Union, Cases No. C-1277 and C-1278, decided May 27, 1940, 23 N. L. R. B. No. 129.

Eight other N. L. R. B. cases bearing on this problem are:

The Matter of Brown Shoe Co., Inc., etc. and Boot and Shoe Workers' Union, Local No. 655, Case No. C-20, decided May 29, 1936, 1 N. L. R. B. 803; union

One factor contributing to the dissolution of these seven agreements was nothing more than unfamiliarity with the technique and responsibilities of collective bargaining. Moreover, there was evidence that the top officials of the unions and companies had inadequate control over the parties immediately involved. The importance of these two points will become clear as the account is developed. Another factor was the competitive disadvantage to which these firms fell subject when they signed the agreements, although this was apparently not a matter of direct significance. In the first place, the employers did not attach weight to it in their testimony before the National Labor Relations Board trial examiners. Granted that the hearings were not specifically aimed at this issue; still the company lawyers could easily have called attention to the fact of serious economic handicap at some point in the proceedings. Secondly, the agreements did not survive long enough to produce competitive disadvantage. The annual statements of two of the seven companies show no such difficulties; similar data for the other firms are not available.

---

merely had seniority agreement in one of company's seven plants; board supported union's charges.

The Matter of Colonie Fibre Co., and Cohoes Knit Goods Workers' Union No. 21514, Case No. R-1018, decided November 5, 1938, 9 N. L. R. B. 658; board ordered election despite closed shop agreement.

The Matter of Consumer's Power Co. and Local No. 740, United Electrical Radio and Machine Workers of America, Case No. C-790, decided November 8, 1938, 9 N. L. R. B. 701; formation of "independent" organization while agreement was in effect; board ordered it disestablished.

The Matter of Lone Star Gas Co. and Gas Fitters' Auxiliary to Local Union 146, United Association of Journeymen Plumbers and Steam Fitters and Gas Fitters, et al., Case No. C-465, decided December 18, 1939, 18 N. L. R. B. No. 62; employer's refusal to sign new agreement before other expired, not an unfair labor practice.

The Matter of M. and M. Wood Working Co., et al. and Plywood and Veneer Workers' Union, Local No. 102, Case No. C-345, decided April 1, 1938, 6 N. L. R. B. 372, set aside, 101 F. (2d) 938 (C. C. A. 9th, 1939); workers shifted to new organization despite closed shop agreement; board supported new organization.

The Matter of S. and K. Knee Pants Co., Inc. and Amalgamated Clothing Workers of America, Case No. C-106, decided June 9, 1937, 2 N. L. R. B. 940; company shifted operations to another town while agreement was in effect; board supported charges of union.

The Matter of Union Pacific Stages, Inc. and The Amalgamated Association of Street, Electric Railway and Motor Coach Employees of America, Local Division 1055, Case No. C-133, decided December 19, 1936, 2 N. L. R. B. 471, decision set aside except as to posting of notice, 99 F. (2d) 153 (C. C. A. 9th, 1938), rehearing denied, January 9, 1939.

The Matter of Williams Coal Co. and United Mine Workers of America, District No. 23, et. al., Cases No. C-318 to C-322 inclusive, decided February 23, 1939, 9 N. L. R. B. 579; one of the defendants, The Sixth Vein Coal Corp., abrogated its agreement with the union; board supported charges of the union (see 9 N. L. R. B. 642-654).

The original charge in each of the above cases, the complaint, the official proceedings of the hearings before the trial examiner, the intermediate report of the trial examiner, the stipulation and/or decision of the board are available in the Washington office of the N. L. R. B. under the case numbers indicated above.

Covering the period in which agreements were in effect, these are the figures on net earnings by Remington Rand, Inc., and Wilson Line, Inc.[3] For the first, they were as follows: 1935—$1,751,000; 1936—$3,010,000; 1937—$3,517,000; 1938—$4,410,000. For the latter, the figures were: 1935—$36,000; 1936—$34,000; 1937—$190,000; 1938—$175,000.

The one company which apparently suffered serious competitive disadvantages because of its union agreement was Louis Hornick and Company. This firm, manufacturing curtains and trimming for lamp shades, dresses, and upholstery in New York City, ranks about tenth among some 250 manufacturers in the industry throughout the state.[4] The field is a highly competitive one. For nearly four years, beginning in 1932, the firm had a closed shop agreement with the Textile Trimming Workers' Union, Local 2440 (in 1935 the union affiliated with the United Textile Workers of America, A. F. of L.).[5] Throughout this period, its relations with the union were relatively harmonious. However, the industry was only partially unionized and by 1935 competitive pressure on the Hornick Company (as well as on other firms with union agreements) began to make itself felt. In an effort to meet this situation the company introduced a new type of knitting machine in the fall of 1935, which materially increased output per worker. At the outset, each employee operated only two of the new machines, but the gain in efficiency was not enough to overcome the advantage held by non-union producers. Soon thereafter the Hornick firm demanded that each worker operate two and one-half machines. The knitters finally acceded, with the understanding that if any men had to be laid off before Christmas, the shop would return to the former machine-load. This latter guarantee, the company claimed, was not given. The National Labor Relations Board, however, supported the union, concluding that the knitters would not have taken on the extra work unless they had expected additional compensation for it.[6] At any rate, the company continued to operate on the basis of two and one-half machines for each knitter after Christmas despite the fact that some men had been previously laid off. When efforts to reach a settlement failed, a strike occurred, but some of the firm's "extra knitters" took over the vacancies left by the regular workers. The result was that a substantial number of the strikers shortly sur-

---

[3] The figures on net earnings are taken after provision for depreciation and taxes. The information on Wilson Line, Inc., was taken from its annual statement (available in the Scudder Financial Library, Columbia University, New York City); the information on Remington Rand, Inc., was taken from Moody's *Manual of Investments* (*1939*). The writer sent letters to the other companies asking for their annual statements but received no replies.

[4] *The Matter of Louis Hornick and Co., Inc., etc.*, 2 N. L. R. B. 983 (1937).

[5] *Ibid.*, 2 N. L. R. B. 986-987.

[6] *Ibid.*, 2 N. L. R. B. 989.

rendered and returned to work.[7] Eighteen months later, in June 1937, the National Labor Relations Board handed down an order directing the reinstatement of all the strikers. The knitters who had been locked out were to be restored to their jobs and reimbursed for wages lost. The company was further ordered not to interfere with the labor organization of its employees nor to discourage membership in it in any way.[8]

Meanwhile, however, the union had fallen apart and another organizing campaign was begun, this time under the direction of Local 155 of the Knit Goods Workers' Union, affiliated with the International Ladies' Garment Workers' Union. During 1936 the union made substantial gains in membership, and after a strike on January 1, 1937, it finally secured another agreement, which called for a closed shop, equal division of work among the employees, a thirty-seven and one-half hour week, and time and one-half for overtime. Provision was also made for the appointment of an impartial chairman to handle disputes which the contracting parties could not settle themselves. Finally, the employer agreed to operate two machines for each knitter instead of two and one-half as before.[9] These terms were won by the union's own efforts and did not result from any action taken by the National Labor Relations Board. As a matter of fact, when the new union group secured the agreement, it willingly enough waived the back-pay portion of the board's order.[10]

The chief factor leading to the termination of bargaining relations in the Hornick case was undoubtedly competitive pressure on the firm to reduce costs of production. The disruptions in the other six agreements, however, were the result either of a plan by the employers to break the hold of the unions on their employees, or of a deliberate program undertaken by the unions to win gains (and members) at any cost.[11] The agreements, therefore, proved to be merely temporary treaties framed during periods of more or less continuous warfare. They marked a suspension in hostilities, not a permanent peace, and did no more than give both parties an opportunity to strengthen their positions before returning to the field of combat. This is corroborated by the circumstances surrounding the signing of the agreements. In five of the seven cases, hard-fought strikes took place before the agreements were drawn up. In the La Favorite Rubber case, for example, the plant was shut down for more than a month

---

[7] *Ibid.*, 2 N. L. R. B. 991-994.

[8] *Ibid.*, 2 N. L. R. B. 998-999.

[9] Letter to the writer, dated January 2, 1940, from Louis Nelson, Manager, Local 155, Knit Goods Workers' Union, Brooklyn, New York.

[10] *Ibid.*

[11] There were some elements of deliberate attack in the case just discussed, but competitive conditions were chiefly responsible for the breakdown in relations. As already noted, many firms were outside the union's control.

before a written agreement was reached. In the Remington Rand case the employer waged constant resistance. At one point in the fight, the Regional Labor Board for the Western District of New York of the National Labor Board (predecessor of the first National Labor Relations Board) instructed the firm and the union to negotiate an agreement; the company, however, refused to go beyond a "Memorandum of Understanding," signed by James H. Rand, Jr. This document carefully avoided granting recognition to the union as the bargaining agency for the workers. Not until a strike was called and the operations of the firm effectively tied up was an agreement finally signed.[12] In the Wilson Line case there was no strike, but a rival labor organization was formed and the two groups openly contended for the support of the workers.[13] The single instance in which no struggle occurred before an agreement was signed was the Sands case; here the employer readily met with representatives of the union and signed an agreement within a month.[14]

Actually, some of the agreements were of such a nature as to make future battles predictable. Even the Sands agreement contained seeds of dissension. This company, located in Cleveland, Ohio, is a small manufacturer and distributor of gas and kerosene water heaters. In the spring of 1934 a majority of its workers joined the Mechanics Educational Society of America, and an agreement was promptly made. Nevertheless a permanent breach soon developed. The dispute centered around the question whether seniority ratings should apply to a single department or to the whole plant. The latter system had been adopted under the first year's agreement, signed in May 1934; when the agreement for the second year was drawn up the management succeeded in altering the seniority provision to read: "When employees are laid off, seniority rights shall rule *and by departments.*"[15] However, another provision in the same agreement stated that—"*All* new employees [shall] be laid off before *any* old employees, in order to guarantee if possible at least one week's full time before the working week is reduced to three days."[16]

Taken together, these two provisions made it doubtful whether seniority ratings were to apply to each department in turn or to the plant as a whole. The truth is that the union had not accepted the first-mentioned article in good faith. A few months later the company

---

12 *The Matter of Remington Rand, Inc., etc.*, 2 N. L. R. B. 633 (1937).

13 *The Matter of Wilson Line, Inc., etc.*, 23 N. L. R. B. No. 129 (1940).

14 *The Matter of The Sands Manufacturing Co., etc.*, 1 N. L. R. B. 549, 550 (1936).

15 Agreement between The Sands Manufacturing Co. and Mechanics Educational Society of America (June 15, 1935), Article 5 (italics the author's). The union had submitted a draft of this article which omitted the italicized words.

16 *Ibid.*, Article 7 (italics the author's). Both quotations from the agreement are taken from *The Matter of The Sands Manufacturing Co., etc.*, 1 N. L. R. B. 552 (1936).

attempted to hire some new men in the machine shop rather than transfer regular employees from other departments. This move was permissible under a system of departmental seniority, but was actively opposed by workers in other departments who were thereby excluded from the new jobs. The union, therefore, saw that it was to its advantage to insist on plant-wide seniority. Pressing this demand aggressively, a strike (or lock-out) followed and the plant was shut down for about two weeks. During that interim the company approached the International Association of Machinists, signed an agreement with it, and when the plant reopened, almost the entire force was made up of new men.[17] The board ordered that the workers who participated in the strike should be reinstated to their former positions with payment for wages lost. The board also ordered the company to cease and desist from interfering with its employees in the exercise of their rights to self-organization and from refusing to bargain collectively with the Mechanics Educational Society of America.[18] But the board was reversed by the appellate court as well as by the United States Supreme Court on the ground that an impasse had been reached between the employer and the union and that the discharges were not an unfair practice within the meaning of the National Labor Relations Act.[19] In retrospect, it seems clear that the Mechanics Educational Society of America made a serious mistake in its dealings with the Sands Company. The events immediately preceding and following the execution of the agreement showed that the management was entirely willing to recognize and deal with the union. The union subsequently consented to an alteration in the seniority rules and then refused to abide by the change. If the union had been prepared to compromise, it might very well have retained its agreement with this company. Today it has neither an agreement nor the prospect of securing one.

The provisions of the agreement in the Remington Rand case unmistakably foretold the events that were to follow. While the agreement was both fairly detailed and comprehensive, the firm was careful to retain the right to "deal with any individual employee or his or her chosen representative" at the same time that it promised to treat with the union. Moreover, the company secured the union's acquiescence to a supplementary understanding which was not to be disclosed even to the union's own members. This read: "It is understood and

---

[17] Most of the new men were secured through the International Association of Machinists. The agreement with this organization was subsequently cancelled for fear of consequences which might follow the filing of charges under the National Labor Relations Act. *The Matter of The Sands Manufacturing Co., etc.*, 1 N. L. R. B. 554 (1936).

[18] *Ibid.*, 1 N. L. R. B. 560, 561.

[19] *N. L. R. B., Petitioner, v. The Sands Manufacturing Co.*, 96 F. (2d) 721 (C. C. A. 6th, 1938), aff'd., 306 U. S. 332, 59 Sup. Ct. 508 (1939).

agreed that any discrimination or intimidation on the part of any employee toward any other employee shall be just cause for discharge."[20] The union officials felt that the clause went no further than another part of the agreement which called for the cooperation of both parties in restoring "peace and harmony" following the period of strife. Events two years later were to demonstrate that the employer had different motives in asking for this provision.

It is significant that certain key provisions of the other agreements were likewise worded in general or ambiguous terms. Article 7 of the agreement in the La Favorite Rubber Company case, for example, provided that a marking system to determine the quantity of each man's work was "to be put in for the protection of the men as far as possible."[21] Similarly, Article 13 of the agreements with the "associations" in the Wilson Line case provided that work assignments "shall be based on ability, fitness and seniority."[22] In both cases these provisions were subsequently the center of bitter controversy. But it should not be inferred that the vagueness of these agreements was primarily due to careless draftsmanship. Rather their ambiguity simply reflected the failure of the two parties to agree on certain points of controversy.

There is further evidence to show that the agreements under examination were not planned to endure. For in almost every instance rival groups soon sprang up which sought to displace the unions that had signed the agreements. Some of these were clearly the employers' creatures; others were the result of both the employers' efforts and the employees' own activities. Whatever the origin their objective was to erase the agreements then in effect and to wipe out the existing unions as bargaining agencies for the workers. In the Remington Rand case, according to the National Labor Relations Board, rival groups were formed by the employer simply as one part of a broad program to break the strength of the union. In the Wilson Line case a rival labor organization, which the board's trial examiner held to be employer-controlled, was established at about the time that the union organizers began their campaign for members. Although the firm promptly signed up with this allegedly company-sponsored group, it was strange to discover that two months later it also made

---

[20] *The Matter of Remington Rand, Inc., etc.,* Board Exhibit 17, 2 N. L. R. B. 634 (1937).

[21] *The Matter of La Favorite Rubber Manufacturing Co., etc.,* "Official Report of Proceedings before the N. L. R. B." (hearings before the trial examiner), p. 43. In connection with this case references are to these hearings and to the trial examiner's report, since the board's decision simply embodied a stipulation signed by both parties.

[22] *The Matter of Wilson Line, Inc., etc.,* "Intermediate Report of Trial Examiner," dated May 5, 1939, p. 33. In connection with this case references are to this report and to hearings held before the trial examiner. The board's decision is not sufficiently detailed to provide the necessary facts.

agreements with the *bona fide* union organizations. In at least two of the cases the workers themselves were active in weakening the unions' position. In the La Favorite Rubber case a majority of the employees withdrew from the union, while in the Firth Carpet case a large number shifted their allegiance to a rival organization.

Another common characteristic, closely related to those just described, bears directly on the main theme of this study. In each case issues arose which were not settled in accordance with the terms and intent of the agreements. In most instances these issues were of considerable importance; in a few cases they represented an accumulation of many minor grievances and violations. Sometimes the issues were settled by the employer in deliberate disregard of the terms of the agreement and with an eye to breaking the strength of the union. Other times the disputes represented honest differences of opinion over the interpretation of certain provisions of the agreements. At least once the union was chiefly to blame since it insisted on an interpretation of the agreement which the wording did not justify.[23] Particularly noteworthy is the fact that none of these agreements provided definite procedures for hearing and adjusting such disputes.

In tracing the steps which led to dissolution of the agreements, particular attention must be paid to these prior disputes and the methods by which they were handled. It is likewise essential to appraise the measures which were undertaken at the time of final breakdown, with special reference to the part played by the National Labor Relations Board. Thus, the first phase of the analysis will reveal some of the sources of disturbance in union-employer relations; the second will bring out some of the difficulties besetting a government agency like the National Labor Relations Board when it deals with disputes under the circumstances indicated. As already noted, the board's intervention in both the Hornick and Sands cases did not materially affect the final outcome. This was hardly less true of the five remaining cases. In these the disputes leading to the dissolution of the agreements were part of a broader conflict over the very existence of the unions. To that extent they differ from the two already discussed, although the end-results were much the same. But what is distinctly striking is the contrast between the disputes in the following five cases and the controversies under agreements in long-established systems of collective bargaining. The right of unions to existence in industries like bituminous coal and the garment trades is no longer subject to open challenge. But in the situations now to be described the unions were fighting for survival even after agreements had been secured.

---

[23] *The Matter of The Sands Manufacturing Co., etc.;* see pp. 83-84 *supra.*

EMPLOYER ATTACKS

The simplest cases to analyze are those in which the employer deliberately sought to escape union standards. The Ralph A. Freundlich case is of that category. The employer here was ready to go to almost any lengths to escape the terms imposed by his agreement with the union. Although at one point in the proceedings he was obliged to sign an agreement, he apparently had no intention of abiding by its provisions. When this fact became evident the union invoked the aid both of the courts and, later, of the National Labor Relations Board, requesting that the employer be ordered to fulfill his commitments under the agreement and bargain collectively with his workers; however, the intervention of these bodies had little or no effect.

The company, which manufactures dolls, was formerly located in New York City but now operates in Clinton, Massachusetts. In 1933, soon after the National Industrial Recovery Act was passed, an industry-wide strike was called by the Doll and Toy Workers' Union. After a six-week struggle, most of the employers, including the Freundlich company, signed an agreement with the union which was to expire June 1, 1935.[24] The Freundlich agreement provided that only union workers could be hired, specifying certain wages and certain conditions of labor. In June 1934, however, the company moved its plant, taking about fifteen of its four hundred employees to the new location.[25] From the outset the company conducted the Massachusetts factory without regard to its obligations under the agreement with the union. The union appealed to the New York courts for help and a permanent injunction was finally granted, forbidding the firm to function except under conditions specified by the agreement. While the injunction applied only to violations of the agreement that had occurred while the company was still in New York, the court threatened to extend the injunction to the company's operations in Massachusetts. In fact, it even threatened to order the firm to return to New York unless it saw the "error of its ways."[26]

The next step in the proceedings took place in the company's new plant in Massachusetts. In an effort to gain a foothold there the union brought charges against the company in January 1935, for violations of Section 7 (a) of the National Industrial Recovery Act. Hearings were held before the old National Labor Relations Board, which ordered the company to cease and desist from interfering with its employees in the exercise of their rights under Section 7 (a). It further directed the company to reinstate certain discharged workers in their

---

24 Under the agreement Dr. N. I. Stone was appointed impartial chairman.

25 *The Matter of Ralph A. Freundlich, Inc., etc.*, 2 N. L. R. B. 805 (1937).

26 *Farulla v. Ralph A. Freundlich, Inc.*, 155 Misc. 262, 279 N. Y. Supp. 228 (Sup. Ct. 1935). Earlier stages in proceedings are cited on p. 58n, *supra*.

former positions with back pay.[27] The third step was taken by the employer. In March 1935, the company filed a petition in the United States District Court of Massachusetts for reorganization under Section 77 B of the Bankruptcy Act, which the court approved in January 1936. Between March 1935 and January 1936, union efforts to reestablish the standards of the agreement in the company's new plant were unsuccessful. Probably not without some design on the company's part, one of the court's first orders under the reorganization annulled the union agreement,[28] although the plan at the same time provided that $8,250.00 be paid to the Doll and Toy Workers' Union in settlement of its claim. The new company carried on the same business as its predecessor and retained the same name.[29]

The fourth step was taken on the initiative of the union. Blocked in its efforts to organize the company's new plant, the union in October 1935 once again filed charges with the National Labor Relations Board. In hearings held before a trial examiner of the board, it developed that the small group of workers who had been brought from New York to Massachusetts were mostly key men in the firm's organization. They formed the spearhead of efforts to restore collective bargaining in the company. Early in 1935 five of them met with representatives of the company in an attempt to raise wages and reduce working hours. While the company spokesmen did make a few concessions, they were of little importance; moreover, they were made to each worker individually rather than to the group as a whole. Thereupon the workers from New York, together with a few others, decided in the fall of 1935 to start a union at the Clinton plant. As the organization that had existed prior to the removal from New York was a thing of the past, they had to start from the ground up, this time organizing Federal Labor Union 20,090 (A. F. of L.). No sooner was it established than seven of the workers who had been most active in its formation were discharged. The company then proceeded to launch an aggressive program of attack on the new union which included defamatory speeches, the arrest of one of the union's organizers followed a few days' later by physical assault, and intimidation of workers who were active in the union's affairs.[30]

In the hearings before the National Labor Relations Board the company did not deny that these events had occurred, but contended that it was not responsible for the actions taken against the union. The company argued further that the seven men were discharged because of incompetence and not because of their organizing activities.

---

27 *The Matter of Ralph A. Freundlich, Inc., and Doll and Toy Workers' Union,* 2 N. L. R. B. (old) 147 (1935).

28 For a criticism of this action, see (1935) 35 *Columbia Law Review* 1140, 1142.

29 *The Matter of Ralph A. Freundlich, Inc., etc.,* 2 N. L. R. B. 807 (1937).

30 *Ibid.,* 2 N. L. R. B. 812-815.

The board held that the evidence did not support the employer's contentions. The company had never found fault with the quality or quantity of their work. With one exception, all seven were experienced workers—as proved by the fact that the company had seen fit to give them frequent raises. The board, therefore, ordered the company to cease and desist from in any way interfering with its employees in the exercise of their rights to self-organization. It also ordered the reinstatement with back pay of those who had been discharged.[31]

The campaign to establish a union went on during 1936, and some progress was made. It was not until the following year, however, that the union won a firm foothold in the plant. By this time the group had affiliated with the Playthings and Novelty Workers' Union (C. I. O.), and organizers from the national office helped in the membership campaign. Finally, in 1937, the union secured a closed shop agreement which is still in effect. At the present time, moreover, the union reports that almost all of the workers of the company are dues-paying members.[32]

The story of this case shows the difficulties which must be overcome if contractual relations are to be maintained in certain types of firms. It suggests, also, that the Wagner Act is no guarantee that collective bargaining will continue, even in companies where it is once established. Thus the question arises whether the safeguards to unionism contained in the National Labor Relations Act should not be strengthened. Apparently the employer in this case was not at all deterred by that legislation in blocking the organizing efforts of the union. It was only because a new group came in to carry on the struggle that an agreement was finally signed. At least it seems clear that if unions hope to win and maintain bargaining privileges in situations of this sort, they must still rely chiefly on their own strategies and resources.

The Remington Rand case was posed against a similar background. Here, again, the employer was determined to break up the union and be rid of it. Here, again, the tactics to achieve this end went beyond mere appeals to the workers or even threats of discharge; the company issued warning that entire plants might be permanently closed and production shifted elsewhere, and that whole groups of workers were to be displaced. These facts attracted considerable attention while the case was being tried before the National Labor Relations Board, and do not warrant detailed review, but there

---

31 *Ibid.*, 2 N. L. R. B. 817-818.

32 Data for the period after the board hearings in 1936 were secured in an interview (December 16, 1939) with Alexander Ravitch, then organizer for the Playthings and Novelty Workers' Union. Efforts to secure an interview with the company's management were unsuccessful.

are two features which give the matter particular interest. The company, which manufactures office equipment of all kinds, is one of the country's giant business organizations; consolidated assets, as of March 31, 1938, were almost $45,000,000, and its employees at this date numbered about 16,000. The other special point is that an agreement with the Remington Rand Joint Protective Board of the Office Equipment Workers (A. F. of L.) had been in effect for over a year before there were any definite indications that a show-down fight was imminent. Relations under the agreement were for the most part harmonious after it was first signed in June 1934; not until the fall of the following year were there signs of trouble.[33]

These facts throw light on the methods which the company finally used in its attack upon the union. A large firm can resort to devices which are at once more varied and more potent than those available to a smaller enterprise; but by the same token its tactics are likely to be more easily discovered and more quickly censored, too. Furthermore, the interim period of "peace and harmony" suggests that when the company finally moved to the attack, it did so after long deliberation and after mapping the details of the campaign with considerable care. The first step in the attack was shrouded in mystery and suspense. A rumor reached union headquarters in the fall of 1935 that the company had acquired a plant at Elmira, New York, and that some of the factories, particularly the one at Ilion, New York, would probably be closed down. The union tried again and again during the latter part of 1935 and early 1936 to find out from the company whether the rumor was true; each time it was met with an evasive reply. On April 23, 1936, the company moved twenty-eight tons of dies from Ilion to Elmira. Thereupon the union tried to sharpen the issue by arguing that if the Elmira plant was being operated by Remington Rand, it should be subject to the agreement, and that if the plant was not Remington Rand's, it was a violation of Section 15 of the agreement to send work there.[34] Both then and a few months later when it became evident that the Elmira plant (known as the Elmira Precision Tool Company) belonged to the company, officials of Remington Rand refused to explain.[35]

During all the negotiations attempted at this period union officials were unable to deal directly with James H. Rand, Jr., the president of the company. The lesser officials whom they did see appeared to be singularly ill-informed on the matter. Time and again confer-

[33] *The Matter of Remington Rand, Inc., etc.*, 2 N. L. R. B. 634 (1937). It is not clear why the company suddenly took steps to break off relations with the union. Company spokesmen refused to discuss the issue.

[34] This provision prohibited sending work outside of the company's plants if it could be done by the regular employees.

[35] *The Matter of Remington Rand, Inc., etc.*, 2 N. L. R. B. 635-640 (1937).

ences were called and adjourned with no clearer picture of what was happening than before. A discussion late in the spring of 1936 between Mr. Crofoot, president of the union, and H. T. Anderson, manager of the Norwood, Ohio, plant, is indicative of the manner in which the situation was handled. The latter was asked whether there was a connection between Remington Rand and the Elmira firm. The following conversation ensued:

Mr. Anderson: I doubt that I will be able to give you a satisfactory answer. In the first place, it is evident that everyone believes the operation is a Rem-Rand operation. I am not familiar with the set-up in Elmira but I know the Elmira Precision Tool Company is not a Remington-Rand organization now. As to who may be in back of it, I do not know.

Mr. Crofoot: Is there any good reason why the officials of Remington Rand cannot give us a definite answer regarding moving the plant from Ilion?

Mr. Anderson: I do not know . . . . As far as I know, it is an entirely different company.

Mr. Crofoot: If Mr. Rand or Mr. Benner [vice-president of the company] is interested in the relations between the employees of these six plants, he could at least come down here to see us . . . . This is the second time that a direct answer has been avoided by putting a plant manager on the spot. Three times and out is enough. If we cannot meet him, it is time we found out.

Mr. Anderson: I do not think they will be here.[36]

The record indicates that no ranking company officer appeared. This deliberate refusal on the part of the management to meet with the union cannot be reconciled with its commitments under the agreement of June 1934, which provided that grievances, if not settled satisfactorily, might be taken up directly with the works manager or a higher executive of the company. Here was a legitimate matter—and a very important one—which the union could carry no further than the superintendent of one of the company's less important plants. Moreover, the immediate point at issue was not what could be done about a situation, but simply what were the facts of the case. It is very doubtful whether the company would have taken this extreme position unless it had already decided to terminate all dealings with the union. During this same period the union sought wage increases for certain groups of workers. It contended that two years earlier the company had promised a raise when its earnings were improved. In April 1936, the company replied that a wage increase was out of the question. Defeated on this issue and blocked in its efforts to get definite information about the shift in plant operations, the union armed itself with a mandate from its members to call a strike. Last-minute appeals to President Rand were unsuccessful, and strikes broke out at the various plants early in the summer of 1936.

The events which followed reveal how determined was the company to break off all dealings with the union. They are summarized only briefly here. Soon after the union secured authority to strike

---

[36] *Ibid.*, 2 N. L. R. B. 639.

from its members, the company held an election among all the workers of its six main plants to ascertain whether they favored such action. The results were almost completely at variance with those based on a similar poll taken by the union. By the end of May 1936, the strike was well under way and the union had halted production in all six plants. The company lost no time in launching a counter-attack which aimed at the resumption of operations on the management's terms of employment. The methods used in this drive were diversified, and in some instances ruthless. At Ilion, chief reliance was placed on the reaction of the town's own business groups after they were given to understand that, unless the labor difficulties ended, Remington Rand might be forced to transfer its operations elsewhere. A "Citizen Committee" was formed, which along with a group of workers who allegedly opposed the strike, induced the sheriff to swear in some three hundred special deputies. Assured of protection, a meeting was then called of all employees "who wanted to work," and on June 10, 1936, some five hundred re-entered the plant. In this way, the morale of the strikers was weakened and it required only the use of some strikebreakers, a wide publicity campaign among the townspeople, and a program of personal appeals to the workers to bring the strike to a halt.[37]

With varying emphasis the same methods were employed at the other five plants. In Tonawanda, New York, and Middletown, Connecticut, greater use was made of imported strikebreakers who opened the plants after pitched battles with the picket lines. In Syracuse the position of the union seemed particularly strong, and the company was obliged to discharge a large number of workers who were active in the union. In every case, however, the pattern was essentially the same and the campaign to break the strike uniformly successful. James H. Rand, Jr., personally announced that "two million business men have been looking for a formula like this," and said it "would go down into history as the Mohawk Valley Formula."[38]

The National Labor Relations Board issued a complaint against the company in July 1936. Two months before this, the company had unsuccessfully tried to secure an injunction against the leaders of the union for unlawful picketing near the company's Syracuse plant.[39] Soon after the board issued the complaint, Remington Rand sought to enjoin the board from taking further action on the ground that it lacked jurisdiction and that the law was unconstitutional besides. This injunction was also denied.[40]

---

[37] *Ibid.*, 2 N. L. R. B. 650-666.

[38] *Ibid.*, 2 N. L. R. B. 659.

[39] *Remington Rand, Inc., v. Crofoot*, 248 App. Div. 357, 289 N. Y. Supp. 1025 (Sup. Ct. App. Div. 1936).

[40] *Remington Rand, Inc. v. Lind*, 16 F. Supp. 666 (W. D. N. Y. 1936).

Proceedings were finally begun before the board's trial examiner on October 14, 1936. The company did not place any of its own witnesses on the stand. It tried to show, rather, that much of the testimony of the witnesses for the union was unreliable, and that the company had continued to bargain in good faith with the union. The company, in cross-examining the union's witnesses, also tried to prove that there was widespread opposition among the workers to the union and to the strike. As to charges of violence and the importation of armed guards, counsel for the defense sought to show that the violence was all on the side of the union, and that armed guards were employed only where it was necessary to protect the plant from damage by the union.[41] In reviewing the testimony, however, the board concluded that the evidence did not support these contentions. It issued its order in March 1937, about nine months after the strike was defeated. The order prohibited the company from interfering with its workers' rights to self-organization or from dominating any labor group. One section of the order specifically directed the company to withdraw all recognition from employees' associations in Ilion and Middletown; another part of the same section, which the Court of Appeals later deleted, directed the company to disestablish completely these two associations as representatives of the workers. Moreover, the company was directed to reinstate all workers dismissed after May 26, 1936. Where there were not enough openings to make this possible, new workers hired after this date were to be released and the former employees put in their places. If there were not enough openings even after this was done, the workers were to be put on a seniority list and given the first jobs that opened up in any of the company's plants.[42] Except for the change already mentioned, the Court of Appeals affirmed the board's order.[43] In its argument before the court, the company had contended that the National Labor Relations Act was void and unconstitutional; that the employer-employee relation in this instance did not directly affect interstate commerce; that the board's procedure in handling this case was "arbitrary, unfair and capricious"; and that all of the board's findings of fact and conclusions of law were contrary to the testimony adduced. When the company appealed to the United States Supreme Court, a review was refused.[44]

Long before the intervention of the board or of the courts the strike was over and the union defeated. The completeness of the defeat is evidenced by the fact that today the union has no agreement

---

[41] *The Matter of Remington Rand, Inc., etc.*, "Official Report of Proceedings before the N. L. R. B." (hearings before the trial examiner), pp. 797-798, 1310-1311, 1371-1372, 1375-1380, etc.

[42] *The Matter of Remington Rand, Inc., etc.*, 2 N. L. R. B. 744-746.

[43] Board order enforced as modified, 94 F. (2d) 862 (C. C. A. 2nd, 1938).

[44] Certiorari denied, 304 U. S. 576 (Remington Rand), 585 (Employees Association) (1938).

with the company. More than that, the Joint Protective Board apparently no longer has a majority of the workers in its membership. Nine "independent" employees' associations sprang up after the strike was broken, and in 1939 they urged the National Labor Relations Board to conduct elections at the plants. The Joint Protective Board countered with the charge that the company had sponsored these associations in violation of the board's order and that they were under the domination of the company. Following these charges, hearings were again begun before the National Labor Relations Board in the fall of 1939. The company secured an injunction against the board, ending the hearings. Later the injunction was dissolved, and hearings were resumed in January 1940. Finally, the company signed a stipulation under which it agreed to disestablish the nine employee associations and to cease urging, persuading, and warning its employees not to become members of any labor organization. On June 29, 1940, the board issued an order to this effect.[45]

The record of this case reveals again the powerful opposition which some unions must face in their efforts to win and maintain agreements. When that happens there are good grounds for doubting the effectiveness of such agencies as the National Labor Relations Board. It is true that the company-sponsored employee associations were finally disestablished. It is also true that if it had not been for the board, many workers would probably never have been reinstated. At the same time, there were so many changes in the company's personnel requirements that one wonders how many of these workers were actually restored to their jobs.[46] For example, the plant at Middletown was shut down—at least temporarily—and operations at the Syracuse plant sharply curtailed. The chances are that this has meant no re-employment for many of the workers dismissed for union activity. Even more important from the union's view, the Joint Protective Board has no agreement with the Remington Rand Company. There is the crucial issue, and there the company has prevailed. The agreement was destroyed before the board entered the picture, and nothing that the board did later has altered this fact. For the union it was a Pyrrhic victory indeed; it won its case but lost its bargaining status.

UNION-EMPLOYER STALEMATE

The steps taken by the employer to break off all dealings with the union and overthrow the union itself were as clear-cut as they were

---

[45] *The Matter of Remington Rand, Inc., and Remington Rand Joint Protective Board of the District Council Office Equipment Workers*, Case No. C-1588, decided June 28, 1940, 24 N. L. R. B. No. 118. The writer checked the sequence of events in this case after the board's first order was issued in March 1937, with William R. Carlson, Director of Personnel, Remington Rand, Inc., New York City, January 10, 1940. See also *New York Times*, June 30, 1940, sec. 1, p. 15.

[46] Efforts to secure information on this latter point were unsuccessful.

deliberate in the two cases just described. In the Wilson Line case the measures undertaken by the employer may have been no less systematic, but they were not quite so direct.[47] At the time hearings were proceeding before the National Labor Relations Board, the company operated a small fleet out of Wilmington, Delaware; its crews numbered about one hundred and fifty men, but employment was slack during the winter months. Its personnel fell into three categories, each with its own union organization. The licensed engineers, assistant engineers, etc., belonged to the National Marine Engineers' Beneficial Association, C. I. O.; the licensed deck officers, first mates, etc., belonged to the National Organization of Masters, Mates, and Pilots, A. F. of L.; and the unlicensed personnel, common seamen, etc., belonged to the Harbor Boatmen's Union, C. I. O. In 1937 these three unions established locals in the Wilson Line, and in June of that year each union signed an agreement with the company. Ten months later the agreements expired and, despite efforts by the unions, the employer refused to renew them.

According to the trial examiner, two factors were paramount in producing this result.[48] First, the employer established rival organizations which, in turn, sought to win the workers away from the "outside" unions. Second, the employer disregarded important provisions in the signed agreements, thereby rendering them of little value to the union members. Simultaneously, certain leaders of the union were discharged and other discriminatory measures taken against workers who were active in the union. Consequently, when the agreements expired, the unions no longer represented a majority of the workers still on the payrolls and the employer had matters pretty much his own way.[49] Thus, when the National Labor Relations Board took over the case, it was confronted with a *fait accompli*. True, it could order the reinstatement of workers who had been discharged for union activity and prohibit the employer from bargaining with the "company-dominated" groups; but at least for the time being, the unions had lost their status as bargaining agencies for the workers and further changes in personnel threatened to make the loss a permanent one.

According to the trial examiner, when the company first learned of the organizing activities of the unions in 1937, it lost no time forming rival groups. In February 1937, the general manager of the line called a meeting of eight ship captains, as a result of which the Marine Employees Committee was created. This committee claimed to represent a majority of the licensed personnel and two months later

---

[47] *The Matter of Wilson Line, Inc., etc.,* 23 N. L. R. B. No. 129 (1940).

[48] In connection with this case, references are to the "Intermediate Report of Trial Examiner," since the board's decision is not sufficiently detailed.

[49] *The Matter of Wilson Line, Inc., etc.,* "Intermediate Report of Trial Examiner," dated May 5, 1939, pp. 24-28, 40.

the company signed an agreement with it, covering wages and conditions of work. Another organization, known as the Unlicensed Marine Employees Committee, was formed under similar circumstances; it, too, secured an agreement. Meanwhile, the "outside" unions had been conducting their campaigns, and by May and June 1937, they likewise put forth the claim of representing a majority of the workers in their respective groups. An election was arranged by consent and, although the vote was close, the unions came out ahead (in one case, the vote was a tie). Agreements were thereupon signed with the three unions, all covering the same period from June 1, 1937, to March 31, 1938.[50] Despite this state of affairs it appears that the agreements with the two Marine Employees Committees did not become a nullity, nor did these organizations cease to exist. In fact, they seem to have remained very vigorous, the company continuing to play an important part in their activities. The result was that two sets of agreements were in effect at the same time. It indicated that recognition of the "outside" unions was more of a formal gesture than a decision made in good faith on the part of the employer. This circumstance also made the change from union to non-union conditions much easier when the final break came.

Apparently no men were discharged for union participation during the months of organizing activity prior to the signing of the agreements. But the company did make threats and showed in others ways that it opposed the unions. For example, Andrew Anderson, a member of the Marine Engineers' Beneficial Association, made the following affidavit at the time he voted in favor of the Association as his bargaining representative on March 31, 1937: "Should my signature appear on the petition for the Marine Employees Committee of the Wilson Line, Inc., it is to be understood that it was placed there under fear of reprisal."[51] Similar statements were signed by about twenty other employees of the firm. Incidentally, Anderson resigned from the Marine Engineers' Beneficial Association about a month later and was not among those who were subsequently discharged.

This phase of the company's policy had a bearing on the close balloting at the time bargaining representatives were chosen in May and June of 1937. A substantial majority of the unlicensed personnel indicated a preference for the Harbor Boatmen's Union; but the vote among the licensed deck officers was eleven for and nine against the National Organization Masters, Mates and Pilots; and among the licensed engineers, the vote was tied at eleven for and eleven against the National Marine Engineers' Beneficial Association. Part of the ex-

---

[50] *The Matter of Wilson Line, Inc., etc.*, "Official Report of Proceedings before the N. L. R. B." (hearings before the trial examiner), Board Exhibit No. 10.

[51] *The Matter of Wilson Line, Inc., etc.*, "Intermediate Report of Trial Examiner," dated May 5, 1939, p. 32.

planation of these results may have been that the workers in the higher categories felt that they were well able to take care of their own interests without the union. But there also is evidence that some of these men voted against the unions because they knew that the management opposed them. The National Marine Engineers' Beneficial Association, for example, had sixteen dues-paying members among the company's licensed engineers on April 3, 1937. Soon thereafter the company entered into an agreement with the Marine Employees Committee. By the time the election to determine bargaining representatives was held (May 18 to May 21) five members of the Association had withdrawn from that organization and joined the Marine Employees Committee; the result was the tie vote mentioned.

During the next five or six months, after the agreements with the unions were signed, the company conducted a rather systematic policy of discharging union members. In a fair proportion of cases, according to the trial examiner, the dismissals were not related to any reduction in the amount of shipping being done. In some instances the dismissals were called lay-offs, but when the time for re-hiring came new men were given the jobs. With regard to the Harbor Boatmen's Union, for example, the trial examiner declared that "practically all" of its members were discharged in 1937.[52] He found that though many of these men were subsequently re-hired, the reinstatements occurred without the knowledge of the union, a procedure violating the agreement with the Harbor Boatmen's Union which provided that all hiring of unlicensed employees was to be performed through the union. It was also disclosed at the board hearings that these workers became members of the Unlicensed Marine Employees Committee when they were reinstated. Almost equally harsh measures were taken against members of the other two unions. An article in the agreement with the National Organization Masters, Mates and Pilots provided that the company would employ as licensed officers only members of this union who were in good standing, as long as such men were available. The company, however, discharged nine of the eleven members of the organization and hired men who belonged to the Marine Employees Committee. A like provision in the agreement with the National Marine Engineers' Beneficial Association was similarly ignored. In fact, all engineers in the company who belonged to the Beneficial Association were eliminated from employment while the agreement was still in effect. Consequently, when the firm served notice in February 1938, that the agreements would not be renewed, the unions no longer represented a majority of the workers whose names were still on the payrolls.[53]

Other steps taken by the company diluted the value of the agree-

---

[52] *Ibid.*, p. 24.
[53] *Ibid.*, pp. 24-28.

ments long before the final break came. The seniority provisions assured real protection to employees, but the company virtually disregarded those commitments when the lay-offs occurred. Under Section 13 of the agreement with the union representing the licensed personnel, the employer promised to prepare a list showing "the name and seniority dating of each employee who holds rights in each class . . . ." No satisfactory list was posted for many months which, according to the trial examiner, was the result of "a system of inattention and non-compliance with the requests of the Association to negotiate the matter."[54] An acceptable list was worked out only after the matter had been referred to an arbitration committee, but by that time the company had given notice that the agreement would not be renewed. Meanwhile, attempts by the union to confer with the management over dismissals and lay-offs were uniformly unsuccessful. Where men who had seniority were offered re-employment, they were told that they would have to make individual applications for reinstatement.[55] It was on problems of this vital nature that the union was denied an opportunity for discussion with the employer. Thus it was hardly necessary for the company, in February 1938, to announce its intention not to renew since, to all intents and purposes, the agreements were already void.

Over a year after the agreements had expired—in May 1939—the trial examiner filed his report with the National Labor Relations Board.[56] He recommended that the company be ordered to withdraw all recognition of the various "Committee" groups and reinstate with back pay the twenty-two union members who had been discharged. According to union officials, the company did take some steps to comply with this report but refused to pay back wages. The men, in turn, refused to accept employment on the company's terms. The company subsequently sent individual letters to the men offering them their old jobs, but only on condition that they give up their claim to back wages and that they recognize the various "Committee" organizations as their bargaining representatives. Moreover, work was guaranteed only until September 15, 1939. Some of the men accepted these terms, but a good many still held out. Still later, the company tried to have the National Labor Relations Board reopen the case in order to introduce additional evidence, but this effort was not successful.[57]

---

[54] *Ibid.*, pp. 33-34.

[55] *Ibid.*, p. 33.

[56] *Ibid.*

[57] Data for the period after the trial examiner filed his report in May 1939, were secured in interviews (January 8, 1940) with Warren Evans, Business Manager, Local 13, M. E. B. A. and Jesse Morris, Business Manager, H. B. U. Local, Philadelphia. Efforts to secure an interview with a representative of the Wilson Line company were unsuccessful.

Hearings were held in October 1939 before the National Labor Relations Board in Washington. Its decision and order were issued in May 1940—six months after hearings before the board had commenced and more than three years after the original charges were filed with the board's regional office in Philadelphia. The board directed the company to withdraw all recognition from the two employee committees and to cease dominating or interfering with their administration. It also ordered the company to reinstate twenty of the twenty-two union men who had been discharged and to stop discouraging membership in the three unions.[58]

At the present time the unions are still without agreements with the Wilson Line. The unions have filed additional charges against the company, alleging failure to comply with the board's decision and order. Action on these new complaints is pending. But it is difficult to believe that a board ruling at this late date will substantially alter the status of the unions in the Wilson company. The crucial factor is whether the employees are willing to support the unions in their efforts to win bargaining privileges. Apparently the workers of this company are no longer sufficiently interested in the unions to make such a victory possible, but the loss of enthusiasm is certainly not surprising. Three years was a long time for workers to wait before the National Labor Relations Board took definite action on the charges brought by the unions. Even now the unions' appeal to the men must rest primarily on promises instead of gains already achieved.

WORKER DISAFFECTION

The next two cases are in many respects similar to those already considered. As before, the employers took the offensive and more or less deliberately broke off relations with the unions. Once again, lay-offs and dismissals were ordered with a view to the elimination of the workers who were most active in the unions. In the Firth Carpet Company case the familiar strategy of sponsoring rival groups among the workers was followed. In the La Favorite Rubber case the employer undermined the agreement by disregarding some of its most important provisions.

But the particular feature in both instances was the fact that a substantial number of workers deserted the union organizations and thereby ruined the very basis of the agreements. True, there were some indications of internal dissension in the five other cases, but it was impossible to say just how genuine was the workers' opposition to the unions. Indeed, where the hostility was clear, as in the Ralph

[58] *The Matter of Wilson Line, Inc., etc.*, 23 N. L. R. B. No. 129 (1940). The company was ordered to provide back pay equal to the amount the twenty men would have received if they had not been discharged, less any earnings received from private employment.

A. Freundlich case, it was apparently the result of frequent dismissals and the employment of many new workers. In the La Favorite Rubber and the Firth Carpet Company cases no such extreme measures were adopted, yet there was a marked decline in union support among the employees. Though the employers undoubtedly had something to do with this development, they were not entirely responsible for the degree it attained. These two cases, therefore, pose the question why such a drastic change of sentiment occurred and what part the disaffection of the workers played in the dissolution of the agreements.

In both instances the majority of the workers withdrew from membership in the unions before the final break took place. In the Firth Carpet Company case one of the union's officials, who later resigned, testified that at the time of the organizing strike in May 1937, Local 156 of the Textile Workers' Organizing Committee (now the Textile Workers' Union of America), affiliated with the C. I. O., had a membership of about eight hundred out of a total of nine hundred and fifty workers in the company's plant at Firthcliffe, New York.[59] The same witness testified that the auditor's report for January 1938, eight months later, showed that the union had only sixty-two paid-up members.[60] While it is true that January was a slack month in the company's operations, it is clear that the union had lost the support of a majority of the firm's workers. It is significant that when the company, in May 1938, suggested that an election be held to determine the bargaining representatives of the employees, the union refused the offer.

Equally striking was the decline in union membership in the La Favorite Rubber Manufacturing Company case.[61] When Local 133, United Rubber Workers of America (C. I. O.), first signed an agreement with the firm in June 1937, the trial examiner found that it had about ninety per cent of the company's hundred workers in its membership. Six months later he found fifty per cent of the members were three or more months behind in their dues; by February 1938, in the union president's own words, the organization had gone "to smithe-

---

[59] The company, which manufactures carpets and rugs, operates plants in Newburgh and Auburn, New York, as well as in Firthcliffe. The annual output of the three plants is valued at approximately $500,000. The Firthcliffe plant is situated in a town of less than a thousand population, about sixty miles up the Hudson River from New York City. There was no union organization in the plant before the T. W. O. C. began its membership campaign in the spring of 1937; a strike was called which ended in an agreement in May of that year.

[60] *The Matter of The Firth Carpet Co., etc.*, 10 N. L. R. B. 944 (1939), "Official Report of Proceedings before the N. L. R. B." (hearings before the trial examiner), pp. 2218-2219.

[61] The company is a small manufacturer of mechanical rubber goods, located near Paterson, New Jersey, in the town of Hawthorne. There was no union in the plant until the U. R. W. A. began its organizing campaign in the spring of 1937; after a strike which lasted about a month, an agreement was signed in June of the same year.

reens.''[62] At this point the international union suspended the local's charter for failure to keep up with the dues and reports required by the constitution and by-laws of the United Rubber Workers of America.

The withdrawal of worker support from the unions in these two cases was not uninfluenced by measures adopted by the employers. However, the testimony in the Firth Carpet Company case is not entirely clear as to the part played by the management in the dissolution of the union, since the movement to oust the union was led, ostensibly at least, by a small group of salaried workers who were classed below the rank of foreman. Nevertheless, the campaign was too costly and too elaborate to permit the belief that the company had nothing to do with the attack. When the union first began to organize the plant in the spring of 1937, some of the salaried workers started another group, known as ''Our Own Union.'' At the beginning they won little support among the other employees. But the following spring circumstances were more favorable and the same group launched another organization, known as the Firth Workers' Protective Association. By the time hearings before the National Labor Relations Board's trial examiner commenced in November 1938, one estimate put the membership of the Association at about three hundred and seventy.[63] At this latter date the employer had an agreement covering wages, hours, and conditions of work with the Protective Association, but none with the union.

The union's prestige among the workers was hardly advanced by certain developments which occurred after it secured an agreement in May 1937. In one instance, according to the local's business agent, the union unsuccessfully sought an increase in pay for painters in the plant, but shortly thereafter one of the painters received a raise through individual bargaining with the management and without the union's knowledge. A plumber's helper later obtained a raise in a similar manner.[64] On another occasion the company asked its employees whether they would rather have a week's vacation with pay or an extra week's pay with no vacation. This was done without consulting the union, although the agreement called for a week's vacation with pay. There was considerable dispute among the workers before a decision in favor of the extra week's pay was reached.[65]

---

[62] *The Matter of La Favorite Rubber Manufacturing Co., Inc., etc.*, 17 N. L. R. B. 955 (1939), ''Intermediate Report of Trial Examiner,'' pp. 4-5.

[63] Testimony of Harold Perry, President of F. W. P. A., formerly shop chairman, Local 106, T. W. O. C. *The Matter of The Firth Carpet Co., etc.*, ''Official Report of Proceedings before the N. L. R. B.'' (hearings before the trial examiner), p. 1910.

[64] Testimony of William McDonald, Business Agent, Local 106, T. W. O. C., *ibid.*, pp. 52-53, 72. There was no craft union for painters or plumbers in the plant; presumably, both men were members of the Textile Workers' local.

[65] Testimony of William McDonald, *ibid.*, pp. 69-70.

The issue causing sharpest dissension among the workers concerned lay-offs. Here again the company took a position not calculated to allay discord. During the fall and early winter of 1937 the company's business fell off perceptibly, and the question arose (first in the woolen mill) whether the available work in each department should be distributed equally among the department's personnel or whether the recent workers should be laid off. Understandably enough, this issue caused a split between the veterans and the newcomers. The union tried to straddle the issue, agreeing to the lay-off of the recently hired workers if the company would promise to give them back their jobs when conditions permitted. To this the company would not consent. Since no compromise was reached, the issue continued to divide the ranks of the workers and the union's position became more and more precarious.

The mortal blow came in January 1938, when the shop chairman of the Textile Workers' local, Harold Perry, resigned and subsequently became president of the Protective Association. Significantly enough, he was one of the older workers (having been employed by the company for nine years as a spinner) and he opposed the union's stand on the lay-off procedure. Whether the company gave him inducements to withdraw from the union is not clear; but soon afterwards he became manager of the company's baseball team and thenceforth seemed to be on more familiar terms with officials of the firm. Meanwhile support for the union dwindled steadily as agitation for the rival group increased.[66] Advertisements began to appear in the local newspapers, and speeches were made on various occasions attacking the union. At one meeting early in April, Colonel Egan, corporation counsel for the city of Newburgh, New York, spoke to the workers on their rights under the Wagner Act.[67] A couple of weeks before this meeting was held, cards were handed out among the workers of the plant for their signatures; they bore the message: "I don't want the T. W. O. C. to represent me for purposes of collective bargaining."[68] Apparently the company knew about these cards and did nothing to stop their distribution. Harold Perry testified that about six hundred workers signed the cards at that time. In April 1938, a group of union opponents met with the president of the company; they told him that they were against the union because they did not want another strike and did not desire to be represented by a Communist-controlled organization; moreover, they declared that the union's demand for a closed shop was unreasonable. The upshot was

66 It was only later that the rival group became known as the Firth Workers' Protective Association.

67 Soon afterwards Colonel Egan drew up the constitution and by-laws of the F. W. P. A.

68 *The Matter of The Firth Carpet Co., etc.*, "Official Report of Proceedings before the N. L. R. B." (hearings before the trial examiner), pp. 1818-1819.

that when the agreement with the union expired in May 1938, it was not renewed; instead the company circulated an agreement among the workers which carried the signatures of the Firth Workers' Protective Association and the president of the company.[69]

At the conclusion of the hearings before the board's trial examiner seven months later (December 1938), a stipulation was signed by the two parties. In accordance with its terms, the board ordered the company to refrain from interfering in any manner with its employees in their rights to self-organization; it further ordered the company to withdraw all recognition from the Firth Workers' Protective Association and to inform its employees that this had been done.[70]

Subsequent events in this case, as in the others, reveal the difficulties which sometimes have to be surmounted in order to maintain contractual relations between an employer and a union. They also throw light on the part which an agency like the National Labor Relations Board can play. An election was held in January 1939, soon after the stipulation was signed, and the union failed to win a majority. Difficulties between the union and employer continued, and early in 1939 the union brought additional charges before the National Labor Relations Board. The union alleged that the company discouraged union membership by granting wage increases which had been refused when requested by the union; by imposing greater restrictions on the freedom of movement about the plant of union members than of non-union workers; and by checking on the work performance of union members more rigidly than upon non-union employees. The board decided that these charges were not sustained by the evidence. The union also charged that the company discharged three workers because of union membership and refused to reinstate ten workers in the shipping department who had struck because of alleged discriminations by the employer. The board ordered the company to reinstate seven of the strikers but dismissed the charges regarding the other workers.[71] At present, the union has no agreement in this company, and apparently lacks the support of a majority of the workers.

In the La Favorite Rubber case no rival organization emerged to compete with the union for support of the workers. Yet the union's disintegration was just as striking as in the Firth case and, if any-

---

69 This agreement from the workers' viewpoint was less satisfactory than the one with the union; it did not provide for a week's vacation with pay (except on condition that business in the United States returned to 75 per cent of normal!) and at no point in the grievance procedure was there provision for intervention by impartial "outside" parties.

70 *The Matter of The Firth Carpet Co., etc.*, 10 N. L. R. B. 944 (1939).

71 *The Matter of The Firth Carpet Co. and Textile Workers' Union of America*, decided July 9, 1941, Case No. C-1597 (decision not yet published at time of writing). Board member Edwin S. Smith dissented in part.

thing, more complete. Before six months had passed after the agreement was signed, in June 1937, support for the union had turned into opposition among a majority of the workers. Moreover, the change in sentiment seemed to be not so much a product of deliberate machinations on the part of the employer as a result of the workers' own choice. Needless to say, when the agreement expired in March 1938, none took its place.

All the same, the employer had some part in the events which led to the dissolution of this union agreement. Some of the provisions of the agreement were applied in only a half-hearted manner; others were disregarded completely. In some instances, the company itself admitted that the terms of the agreement were not carried out;[72] in others, the evidence points to the same conclusion.[73] When it became apparent that the agreement was of little value, members of the union began to wonder if it was worthwhile paying dues for such small returns.[74] Meanwhile issues arose which further alienated important groups of employees from the union. The final blow came when some of the union's own officials lost interest in the organization, and the president of the union was discharged in February 1938.

Whether by accident or design, the employer in the La Favorite Rubber case pursued a very clever policy. He did not engage in any overt acts against the union, once the organizing strike was ended. After the strike, he conducted a fair and honest election in which the union got almost all of the votes. He thereupon signed an agreement which provided for an increase in wages and a reduction in working hours. As time went on, he did nothing to incur the open hostility of the workers; no rival group mysteriously appeared to compete for the support of the employees; no slanderous attacks were made upon the union; no program of discrimination or dismissals against the union men was undertaken. On the other hand, he withheld many of the gains from the workers which were rightfully theirs under the agreement; he granted favors to certain workers and not to others; and he handled some issues, like the question of payment for overtime, in such a way that dissension among the workers was almost sure to develop. The sum total of these steps did much to weaken the workers' faith in the union.

But this was not the whole story. The leaders of the union, them-

---

[72] Testimony of Edward Matsin, General Assistant to the President, *La Favorite Rubber Manufacturing Co., etc.*, "Official Report of Proceedings before the N. L. R. B." (hearings before the trial examiner), pp. 880, *passim.*

[73] Testimony of Abram Amos, President, Local 133, U. R. W. A., *ibid.*, pp 32, *passim.* The company's answer to these charges is contained in the testimony of Charles Matsin, President of La Favorite Rubber Manufacturing Co., Inc., *ibid.*, pp. 883, *passim.*

[74] *The Matter of La Favorite Rubber Manufacturing Co., etc.*, "Intermediate Report of Trial Examiner," p. 5.

selves, were not of a character to instill great confidence. Three or four of the union leaders were obviously poor workmen. Indeed, the trial examiner concluded that the four union men who were allegedly dismissed for union activity were really dropped because of their incompetence. Moreover, when the going became difficult, several union officials deserted the cause. Early in the winter of 1937, the treasurer of the union ceased keeping books for the organization altogether and discontinued sending reports to the international office.[75] Later, when the president of the local was dismissed, he wrote a letter to the president of the company, asking for reinstatement and stating: "You can rest assured that I will never have anything more to do with any union . . . as I am completely fed up on all unions. Because they never did do anything good to help me out. Only to help me out of a job."[76] Thus the union was undermined from without and weakened from within. Small wonder that the organization fell apart and that the agreement was not renewed.

The intervention of the board in this case altered the union's position in no important respect. The trial examiner did not sustain the union's charge that the employer discriminated against the discharged men named in the complaint. The only satisfaction which the union derived from the proceedings was a stipulation signed by both parties and filed with the National Labor Relations Board more than a year after the union local had disintegrated.[77] In accordance with the stipulation, the board ordered the company to cease and desist from interfering in any manner with its employees in the exercise of their rights to self-organization; it further ordered the company to inform all of its workers to the same effect. But the stipulation was of little significance since the power of the union had already been broken when its membership fell away. There is no agreement between the union and the company today.[78]

CONCLUSIONS

Light has been thrown on some of the influences which may operate within a given situation to destroy recently established systems of collective bargaining. It has been shown, in the last five cases examined, that at least a share of the responsibility for the dissolution of the agreements fell on the employers. To defeat the unions, they

---

[75] *Ibid.*

[76] *The Matter of La Favorite Rubber Manufacturing Co., etc.*, Respondent's Exhibits, 2-A and 2-B, reproduced in "Official Proceedings before the N. L. R. B." (hearings before the trial examiner), p. 450.

[77] *The Matter of La Favorite Rubber Manufacturing Co., etc.*, 17 N. L. R. B. 955 (1939).

[78] Letter to the writer dated January 17, 1940, from Miss Cornelia Anderson, Assistant Research Director, U. R. W. A. Efforts to secure an interview with representatives of the company were unsuccessful.

sometimes adopted measures both sweeping and ruthless in character, though their strategy at other times was more subtle and indirect. But whatever the technique, the employers in these situations sought to break off relations with the unions and to escape completely from their responsibilities under the agreements. The same thing was true of many other agreements investigated during the preparation of the present study. However, it should be repeated that all the agreements referred to here were "first agreements" and only recently signed. Likewise it needs to be pointed out that the material for this chapter was drawn from National Labor Relations Board cases in which employers were accused of anti-union activities in violation of the Wagner Act. It would therefore be obviously unwarranted to consider these examples of employer policies as typical of American industry as a whole.

At the same time it is clear that the record does not entirely exonerate the unions from blame. Certainly in the Sands case, the union insisted on concessions from the employer which the latter was not in a position to give and which the terms of the agreement did not justify. In other cases the local union leaders were inept in handling controversial issues and even unfaithful to the responsibilities placed upon them. The decline in union membership which occurred in every one of these cases, therefore, was not always due to the design of the employer—and an important factor in the wrecking of these locals and the destruction of their agreements was the lack of support on the part of the workers themselves.

The material also throws some light on the controls exercised by the National Labor Relations Act in the situations that have been described. Individual union members received protection from dismissal and from other forms of discrimination which otherwise they would not have had. Certain harsh and undisguised anti-union tactics of the employers were halted. As for the more subtle, though apparently no less effective methods that were sometimes adopted, the board's intervention seemed to have little consequence. The National Labor Relations Act does not prohibit all dealings with individual employees; nor does it classify agreement violations on the part of employers as unfair labor practices. Indeed, once an agreement is signed, it is of no concern to the board how it is administered, unless some steps are subsequently taken which violate the National Labor Relations Act.[79] In practice, this sometimes means that the board does not enter the scene until the agreement has been dissolved and all collective dealings terminated. At least, this was so in the seven situations here reviewed; in each, the board's action came too late

[79] William G. Rice, Jr., "The Legal Significance of Labor Contracts under the National Labor Relations Act" (1939) 37 *Michigan Law Review* 693.

to be of much help. Once an agreement is terminated and the membership of a union has become negligible, it is naive to think that a board order to reinstate certain discharged workers and to bargain with a particular organization can make a real difference one way or the other. To be effective the remedy must be applied before the dissolution, not afterwards. Otherwise, the right to bargain collectively as guaranteed by the National Labor Relations Act loses its meaning.

The chief difficulty is the slow pace at which the board machinery moves. Hearings are usually begun on a case after the main battle is over. Then there is another considerable delay before the board issues its decision and order. For example, in unfair labor cases during the period 1938-1939, there was an average of seven months between the time a charge was filed with a regional office of the board and the time a decision was rendered by the board. During the period 1937-1938, the interval exceeded a year, though in the period 1939-1940, the lapse was something less than seven months.[80] What a delay of five or six months can mean has been shown in the cases discussed. It is clear that the board's machinery must be speeded up if the objectives of the National Labor Relations Act are to materialize.

Other improvements also seem to be called for to lend substance to the rights guaranteed by the law. As indicated, there are employers who persist in anti-union policies even after they have been found guilty of committing an infringement. Such conduct raises the question whether enforcement of the act should not be tightened. Penalties might be stiffened by making violations a crime instead of becoming subject simply to a "cease and desist" order. Discharged employees might be awarded treble damages instead of mere compensatory reimbursement for loss of work. Government contracts and government loans might be withheld from firms which violate the act. However, it should be noted that there is an opposing view which holds that even the present law is too punitive; this school argues that genuine acceptance of the principles of the act depends primarily on voluntary cooperation, and insists that much of the controversy over the board's work would have been avoided if its terms had rested on such a basis. There is still another school which believes that the act is unfair in that it applies only to management, and recommends that the law be made to restrict unions as well as employers. This latter group also recommends various procedural and administrative changes

---

[80] *National Labor Relations Board* (The Attorney General's Committee on Administrative Procedure, U. S. Department of Justice, Monograph No. 18, 1940), p. 2, footnote 3, and p. 90, Appendix A. Copies are available at the office of the Attorney General, U. S. Department of Justice, Washington, D. C.

calculated to make the board more impartial in the discharge of its duties.[81]

Though an evaluation of these proposals is beyond the scope of the present study, one comment seems appropriate. Chief responsibility for establishing and maintaining stable bargaining relations lies outside the jurisdiction of government. The only parties who can make collective bargaining systems work are the unions and employers immediately involved. The cases that have been discussed show that if employers are really determined to break off dealings with unions, they can do so by one means or another. In the same sense, if unions cannot retain the loyalty of their members during a period of strife, there is little a government agency can do. For the most part, then, the solution of these problems must wait upon the good sense and resourcefulness of the employers and union leaders most closely concerned. The chief task of the National Labor Relations Board at the present time is to expedite its handling of cases and to discharge its functions in the fairest possible way.

---

[81] These various proposals are discussed in Rosenfarb, *op. cit.*, Chapter 19.

CHAPTER VI

RESPONSIBILITY IN THE AUTOMOBILE INDUSTRY

Union-employer responsibilities under certain agreements recently signed and subsequently abrogated have already been considered. The very existence of the union was at stake in each case, and the struggle over that issue shaped the course of both sides. But wherever strategies conflicted with commitments, the latter were sacrificed. Thus responsibilities, when accepted at all, were not assumed with the full intention of abiding by them.

Special interest attaches to the problem of responsibility in the automobile industry during the period between 1935 and 1940.[1] In this field, union-employer relations are on a different level from the situations previously considered. It is true that bargaining privileges and agreements with the union were granted only recently.[2] However, the union has survived the test of the crucial first years and today is assured an important position in the industry. (The reference is to the labor organization now dominant in this industry—the United Automobile, Aircraft and Agricultural Implement Workers of America, C. I. O.) Still unsettled is the question just what the union's position is to be. Labor relations in this field are midway, as it were, between industries in which collective bargaining is new and insecure as opposed to industries in which collective bargaining has been long established. The same is true of several other fields, such as steel, rubber tires, and textiles. The automobile industry was chosen for special consideration because difficulties of a fairly serious nature have

---

[1] Attention is paid here chiefly to the large manufacturers of motor vehicles and only incidentally to the small companies and parts manufacturers. The record of union-employer relations in all automobile companies having agreements with the union, however, has been much the same. Most of the material for this part of the study was gathered in 1939 and the first half of 1940.

[2] As recently as 1934 William S. Knudsen, then Executive Vice-President, General Motors Corporation, declared that the company was willing to negotiate with specified employees and meet with their representatives for a discussion of such questions as hours of employment and wages, together with systems of payments. "We are not, however, willing to recognize said union as such," he said, "nor to enter into any contract with it on behalf of our employees." Release 3827, memorandum No. 2 (March 15, 1934), National Labor Board (old). This release was secured from the Technical Service Division, National Labor Relations Board, Washington, D. C.

been encountered in the administration of its union agreements. In addition, there has been a sharpening of public interest in this industry by reason of its intimate connection with the national defense program.

To understand the position now held by the union in the automobile industry it is necessary to know the extent of its membership and the proportion of the field covered by its agreements. Though it is almost an axiom that union membership claims are not scientifically accurate, the following figures give some idea of the present strength of the U. A. W.-C. I. O. In June 1941, President R. J. Thomas asserted that paid-up membership in the union totalled 540,000 workers.[3] A year earlier, in his report to the 1940 convention, President Thomas stated that paid-up membership was 294,428, while the total roster, including "exonerations" (due to unemployment and other reasons), at that time numbered approximately 382,000. For the year ending April 30, 1940, President Thomas reported that average paid-up membership was 188,454.[4] Between the outbreak of the war in September 1939, and June 1941, there was a nearly four-fold increase. These figures include members of the union in the aircraft as well as in the automobile industry, although until 1941 membership in the former field was negligible.

But it is more important for present purposes to ascertain the number of plants under agreement with the union. According to the report of President Thomas, 647 plants in the automobile and aircraft industries had agreements with the union in 1940. The number of workers employed in these plants totalled 411,280. In 1939 only 302 plants were under agreement, whereas in 1938 there were 501.[5] In 1939 almost all of the agreements granted recognition to the union for its own members only. In 1940, sixty-seven per cent of the agreements granted exclusive bargaining privileges to the union, thirteen per cent granted union shop conditions, and eighteen per cent granted closed shop conditions.[6] The only large automobile manufacturer to sign a closed shop agreement with the union in 1940 was Reo Motors, Inc. The only major manufacturer to sign a union shop agreement was the Hudson Motor Car Company. On June 21, 1941, however, the union won a noteworthy victory when it secured a union shop agreement with the Ford Motor Car Company. This brought the last important firm in the automobile industry under union standards.

---

[3] *New York Times,* June 21, 1941, p. 1.

[4] *Automobile Unionism,* Report of R. J. Thomas to the U. A. W.-C. I. O. 1940 convention in St. Louis, Missouri, July 29, 1940, p. 7. This report is available at the Detroit office of the union.

[5] *Ibid.,* p. 6. It is impossible to determine from available figures what proportion of the various divisions of the automobile and aircraft industries were covered by these agreements.

[6] *Ibid.*

In June 1941, there were approximately 700,000 workers in automobile and aircraft plants covered by agreements with the union.[7]

Although much less serious than a few years ago, there is still conflict between the union and the automobile manufacturers having agreements with the U. A. W.-C. I. O. The union wants to have a voice with management in all important decisions bearing directly on working conditions. It wants a part in setting wage-rates, in determining hours of work, in handling lay-offs and re-employment problems, in formulating seniority rules, in determining the speed of production, and a host of related questions. Management, on the other hand, is anxious to restrict the union's participation in all these matters as far as possible. It is resolved to keep a large portion of its traditional freedom to set wages, fix hours, order lay-offs, shift personnel, and change production standards. Management knows that some of this freedom must be given up for collective bargaining makes some sharing of power inescapable. Its strategy now is a defensive one, designed to keep the union's authority within narrow bounds. Even though agreements have been signed, therefore, conflict between the two persists.

In the preceding chapter a number of situations were examined in which the contracting parties deliberately committed violations of the agreements and broke off all dealings with one another. At the present time, conditions in the automobile industry are to some degree similar. Here, as in the situations previously discussed, agreements do not accurately reflect the relative bargaining strength of the two parties. Whenever, therefore, an opportunity for maneuver arises, both sides strive to better their positions. Controversies during the life of agreements, since they make possible a show of strength, present just such openings.

A typical issue reflecting the objectives and strategies of both groups is the speed of assembly-line operations. One agreement provides that the timing of production shall be fair and equitable, "consistent with quality of workmanship, efficiency of operations and the reasonable working capacities of normal operators."[8] This clause has little meaning as it stands. The parties to the agreement must act to give it content. If the union hopes to win concessions on this score, grievances about the speed-up must be aired and the management pressed for the most favorable interpretations possible. It may be hard to determine the most effective strategy. Perhaps moderate persuasion would be a suitable method; perhaps results could be gained through extreme demands and exaggerated claims; perhaps threats of

---

[7] *New York Times*, June 21, 1941, p. 1. The chief provisions of the Ford agreement are given in this article.

[8] Agreement between the Chrysler Corporation and the International Union, U. A. W.-C. I. O. (1939), Article I (*Rates of Production*), Section 3.

strike action or other reprisals would be successful, even if such acts violate commitments made elsewhere in the agreement. Whatever the technique, the purpose is the same: to achieve a voice in the determination of production standards. But all that management is prepared to grant is a promise to be reasonable in fixing the speed of operations. "If," as the Chrysler Corporation Agreement provides, "an employee or group of employees claim the timing of their work is too fast . . . the job will be examined again . . . ."[9] This is as far as management intends to go, and any change or interpretation which would give the union a greater part in settling such questions is stoutly opposed. Possibly full and frank discussions with the union spokesmen can accomplish this end; perhaps a blunt refusal to discuss the issue at all will prove to be most successful. Thus it can be seen that considerations of strategy are equally important for both sides, while such matters as grievance procedures, promises to negotiate, and other responsibilities are reduced to secondary importance.

This condition is not surprising in view of the heavy stakes involved. If the union can gain an effective voice in such matters as distributing jobs, determining wage classifications, setting the speed of production, and formulating the order of lay-offs, its place in the industry will be secure. Not only would there be slight cause to worry over the danger of being displaced by some rival group, but the power of the union to press other demands would be greatly heightened. Management knows that this would mean that the companies would be much less free to hire whom they please, when and under what terms they care to specify. Changes in the interests of plant efficiency, departmental production requirements, or retooling operations might become difficult to secure. In dealing with problems of such crucial import, therefore, neither party feels that it can afford to be too punctilious about the rights and welfare of the other side.

At the present time, the struggle for "control of the job" in the automobile industry centers around the union's demand for a closed (or union) shop. Until recently, automobile manufacturers who had made agreements simply recognized the U. A. W.-C. I. O. as bargaining representative for its own members. Today, however, they treat the union as bargaining representative for all workers in plants in which it has the support of a majority.[10] This is in accord with pro-

---

[9] *Ibid.*, Article II, Section 3. This article provides further that all the facts "shall be made available for the parties dealing with the grievance." If unsettled, the dispute is to be referred to the regular grievance procedure.

[10] Thus the 1937 General Motors Corporation agreement provided: "The Corporation hereby recognizes the union as the collective bargaining agency for those employees of the Corporation who are members of the union." The 1939 Chrysler Corporation agreement, on the other hand, grants the union exclusive bargaining rights in accordance with the National Labor Relations Board supplemental decision and certification of representative, dated November 18, 1939.

visions of the National Labor Relations Act and constitutes a significant forward stride. However, except in the arrangements with Ford and a few other companies, membership in the union is still not a condition of employment. Under a closed shop agreement, the employer undertakes to hire only those who belong to the union. Under a union shop agreement non-members may be hired with the requirement that they join the union within a certain period. But as long as membership is not made a condition of employment, there is always a possibility that the men will drop out of the union and disintegration set in. Most of the gains secured by unions are extended to members and non-members alike. Wage increases apply to both; so do improvements in working conditions.[11] Thus, from a worker's point of view, there is the constant question, entirely aside from his feelings about the union, whether membership is worth the cost. True, initiation fees and dues at present are not high. The constitution of the international union provides that locals shall set initiation fees between two and fifteen dollars, and they usually approach the minimum. Monthly dues are one dollar, and a special assessment not to exceed the same sum can be levied once a year.[12] But if the advantages of unionism can be secured without incurring these costs, workers may decide to stay out of the union.

Moreover, under these circumstances rival groups may gain footholds in the plants. The only way one labor organization can supplant another is to win members at its competitor's expense. Such a move can always be made if a union has nothing more than bargaining privileges. But the move becomes impossible if a closed or union shop agreement prevails—of course, assuming that it is observed. This safeguard gives the union a powerful hold on the men, for workers must then look as much to the union as to the management for their jobs. Those who refuse to join, those who decline to pay dues, those who fail to fulfill the other obligations of membership will be deprived of the eligibility to get work. Those already employed who do not join the union will be ousted. The place of the union will then be relatively secure.

Similarly, as long as membership in a particular union is not a condition of employment, the question of favoritism and discrimination on the part of management is bound to arise. Employers who seek to weaken or even to destroy the union are given many oppor-

---

[11] Thus when the union won two weeks' vacation with pay from the General Motors Corporation in 1940, the same privilege was granted to all employees of the company. This question is discussed in an article by Marvin J. Barloon, "Violence and Collective Bargaining," *Harper's Magazine*, vol. 180 (May 1940), pp. 625-634.

[12] William H. McPherson, *Labor Relations in the Automobile Industry* (Washington, D. C.: Brookings Institution, 1940), pp. 27-29. All employees are eligible for membership in the union after they have worked for thirty days.

tunities. More important, even the most innocent moves come to be viewed with suspicion. New employees who refuse to join the union are immediately classed as "company stooges." Decisions on seniority which favor non-union workers as against union members are treated as steps in a concerted program to break up the union. Under these circumstances, even employers who do everything they can to administer their agreements fairly are charged with bad faith. Serious controversies are almost sure to follow.

Company spokesmen contend that the employers are fulfilling both the letter and the spirit of the agreements. If charges of discrimination and insincerity made by the union are true, inquire these spokesmen, why have not numerous actions been instigated against these companies before the National Labor Relations Board? Actually, since the signing of the agreements, few such cases have been started. Moreover, in almost every instance, the employers have been exonerated.[13] But the important point for this discussion is not whether automobile manufacturers are discriminating against union members. Much more important is the fact that under present arrangements allegations of such treatment are inevitable. So long as a substantial number of workers remains outside the U. A. W.-C. I. O., the union has good reason to fear possible moves in this direction. Until the organization's position is secure, the union cannot afford to be anything but cautious. Under union shop conditions these suspicions would be allayed. Indeed, the union would then be in an effective position to make other demands on management. Strike threats would carry more weight. The union could concentrate all of its efforts on the particular demands sought. Dissension among competing groups would be less likely to arise.[14]

Officials of the union are not so much interested in winning formal agreements which carry union shop provisions, since written agreements are not the only means of winning union shop privileges. If these privileges were established in practice, the union leaders would be satisfied. Even if agreements merely granted preference to union members in the distribution of jobs, the effect would be much the same. Furthermore, leaders of the union realize that not even all of their own members favor the union shop. In the minds of many, it means that every worker will be "frozen" to his job and that ad-

---

[13] It was impossible to check this statement against records of the National Labor Relations Board. Union spokesmen, however, corroborated it.

[14] For a more detailed statement of the union's and management's position on this issue, see the *Detroit News*, October 1, 1939, p. 12. In explaining why the union set out to gain union shop conditions, Richard T. Frankensteen, then Detroit Regional Director, declared: "The problem we now faced was a shop with union and non-union men, which is like a house divided against itself. There is a constant attempt to organize it entirely and an incessant struggle to disintegrate it completely." *Ibid.*

vancement through individual effort will become much less likely. In its campaign for this objective, therefore, the union cannot disregard possible worker opposition.

Before the automobile manufacturers can be brought to accept the principle of the union shop, however, a substantial majority of the workers must become members of the union.[15] If this goal can be achieved, probably enough pressure can be brought to bear on management (chiefly in the form of strike threats) to win the demand for a union shop. On the other hand, if management can prevent a large number of workers from actively supporting the union, the drive for a union shop can be defeated. Thus the Ford Company refused to sign any sort of an agreement with the union until this issue was decided; but when a substantial number of its workers voted for the union in a National Labor Relations Act election, the company signed a union shop agreement. In General Motors, Chrysler, and most of the other companies, the issue is still unsettled although agreements have been in effect for some time. The conflict between management and the union for "control of the worker and his job" will continue until this question is answered.[16]

It is clear that in such a vital struggle the dictates of strategy must tend to outweigh any formal commitments and responsibilities that may have been assumed. Both sides must be alert at all times to developments which could be used to further their interests. The union cannot afford to let any opportunity pass which might bind the men more closely to its organization. Inducements and pressures of many sorts, ranging all the way from promises of improved working conditions to threats of physical injury, are brought to bear on the men to accept membership in the union. With the same end in view, vigorous efforts are made to collect dues and to secure more than merely passive acceptance of the union's leadership. Throughout this program appeals to the worker's self-interest and charges of greed and dishonesty against the management play an important part.

Similarly, management takes advantage of the vague phraseology of the agreements to limit gains secured by the union.[17] True, there

---

[15] In a few industries employers have signed closed shop agreements with unions which do not have a majority of the workers as members. Apparently the step has usually been taken to avoid dealings with some other labor organization. See, for example, *Consolidated Edison Co., et al. v. N. L. R. B., et al.*, 305 U. S. 197, 59 Sup. Ct. 206 (1938), affirming as modified, 95 F. (2d) 390 (C. C. A. 2nd, 1938), modifying, 4 N. L. R. B. 71 (1937).

[16] It would be more accurate to say that the union is endeavoring to make the employees as dependent on the United Automobile Workers as they are on the employers for job opportunities and improvements in working conditions. Clearly, the union shop would go a long way in this direction.

[17] But as the personnel director of one company remarked: "At first we interpreted the provisions of the agreements as vaguely as possible. When the union started doing the same thing, we decided it would be better to interpret the terms strictly." Interview (August 16, 1939). Persons whom the writer interviewed in connection with this chapter preferred to remain unidentified.

are few instances of clear-cut violation or discrimination. Management is no longer in a position to launch attacks upon the union. It can only conduct defensive actions. It must move quietly, with little fanfare, in its efforts to check the increasing power of the union. Its most effective strategy now is to turn to its own advantage doubtful cases which may arise under the agreements. If the union lets its rulings go unchallenged, well and good. If the union objects, perhaps management can win the ensuing argument anyway. If the issue causes dissension among the workers or wins some members away from the union, management's position may be strengthened.

It would be wrong to infer that employers in the automobile industry have complete freedom of action in their dealings with the union. In this respect, the situation stands in sharp contrast to the position of the employers described in the preceding chapter. Nevertheless, there are enough doubtful cases arising under the agreements to give automobile manufacturers considerable latitude even now. The day-to-day operations of these firms require innumerable transfers of personnel and many promotions. Every year large numbers of workers have to be laid off and then re-hired. Also there is the frequent question as to when and how new employees shall be hired. On the other hand, certain departments or plants may have to be closed indefinitely and some workers deprived of their jobs. Under any of these circumstances, it is comparatively easy for the companies, without overt attacks on the union, to favor non-union rather than union workers or to create animosity against the union's policies. It is likewise simple for the union to raise discrimination charges against management. The upshot is that each side accuses the other of violating the agreements. In the words of a company official: "The automobile union has looked on these agreements as binding just the employer, not the union. It has no intention of complying with the agreements whenever there is any chance of getting something better."[18] In rebuttal, a union spokesman said: "The company that I have been dealing with tries to cut corners under the contract all the time. It has gone way out of its way, time and time again, to interpret the contract to our disadvantage."[19] The evidence would seem to prove that neither side is free from criticism on this score.

However, it would be a mistake to infer that most issues are handled in a spirit of bitterness. Substantial progress has been made on this score since 1937. In the great majority of cases both parties are now willing to be guided by the facts of the situation and to be bound by a common-sense interpretation of the agreements. If this were otherwise, relations would be impossible, and every dispute would lead

---

[18] Interview (August 16, 1939) with an automobile company official.

[19] Interview (August 22, 1939) with a union official.

to an open break. The day-to-day operation of a gigantic business enterprise involves concessions and compromises by all groups concerned. Obduracy would simply bring production to a halt. As a result, the strategy of the automobile companies and the U. A. W.-C. I. O. is to select a relatively small group of cases for aggressive action. The remainder are handled with an eye to a quick settlement and the least possible amount of argument. But though this serves to restrict the area of conflict to a considerable extent, it does not make the struggle less fierce or the outcome less important.

BACKGROUND CIRCUMSTANCES

There are certain characteristics of the automobile industry which make it possible for the companies and the union to continue jockeying for position. Business organizations in the manufacturing branch of the industry are of large size and the relation between the top management, plant superintendents, and foremen is not always a close one. Changes in policy, even when made in good faith, are therefore not immediately translated into action. Most automobile plant officials are more accustomed to attacking the union than cooperating with it. To alter habitual attitudes takes time, and occasionally even a transfer of supervisory personnel is required. An even more important consideration is the fact that the ramifications of a big organization enable the top management to disclaim responsibility when such a move seems advantageous. For the settlement of certain disputes under the agreements the automobile companies have taken pains to vest final authority in the managers of the various plants. This is true of the 1937 General Motors Agreement regarding disputes over the speed of production.[20] The same is true of disputes under this agreement concerning change-overs from the piece-rate to day-rate basis of wage payment.[21] From the standpoint of plant efficiency there are good reasons for such decentralized authority; it allows for the requisite degree of flexibility and permits the existence of differences in policy where needed. So far as the union is concerned, however, this complicates the problem of locating authority and securing enforcement, since the plant superintendents are not the "free agents" which the wording of the agreements would imply. In connection with the matter of changing from piece-rate to day-rate, one union spokesman made the following charge:

---

[20] General Motors Corporation Agreement (1937), Article C (*Timing Operations*).

[21] Of the seventy-five General Motors plants, only twelve are still on a piece-rate basis; all the rest are on day-rate.

When we went to the plant managers with proof that seventy-five per cent of the men wanted to make the change, the plant managers would simply say, "No," or else say, "It's against company policy." When we went to the company officials, they would reply, "It's up to the plant managers."[22]

This statement is not entirely justified in view of the fact that the union has been relatively successful in pushing this particular demand. It points to a type of maneuver, however, with which the record of labor relations in this industry is replete. What was said of the relation between company officials and plant superintendents is likewise true of the superintendents' relation to their foremen. According to a union leader, a favorite device of plant managers is to refer back disputes concerning the agreement to the foremen involved; another strategem is to promise to "check into the trouble" and then do nothing further about it; a third is to admit that the grievance was justified and then proceed to repeat the offense, only to admit error again at a later date.[23]

Another important element in the conflict between union and management is the powerful position of the large automobile manufacturers. A relatively small group of firms controls opportunities for employment in the industry, and cities like Detroit, Flint, and Lansing are almost entirely "one industry" towns.[24] This means that an employee who incurs the disfavor of an employer and loses his job is in a very precarious position. Until recently, at least, union activity and even union membership have been frequent causes of discharge. Today the National Labor Relations Act prevents such extreme measures and, what is probably more important, the union now has sufficient economic strength itself to discourage flagrant discrimination against its members.[25] Despite this fact the men still fear company reprisals because of their union affiliations. Much of their apprehension is unjustified, but not all of it. Moreover, not only continued employment but promotion depends on management's approval. It is therefore natural for workers to hesitate a long time before risking an employer's displeasure.

An additional circumstance which plays into the hands of those who are directing maneuvers in this conflict is the continuously changing labor requirements of the industry. The production of new models each year is one of its outstanding achievements. Aside from the tech-

---

[22] Interview (August 10, 1939) with union official who, until 1939, was manager of relations between the U. A. W.-C. I. O. and the General Motors Corporation.

[23] Interview (August 17, 1939) with a plant committeeman.

[24] In 1929, for example, ninety per cent of the factory wage earners in Detroit were dependent on the automobile industry for employment. Leon Henderson, *Regularization of Employment and Improvement of Labor Conditions in the Automobile Industry* (N. R. A., Division of Review, Preliminary Report, 1935), p. 41.

[25] As a matter of fact, during 1938 and 1939 the large automobile companies discharged only a few men.

nical problems involved, it entails laying-off thousands of men annually, and then reassigning them a month or so later to jobs frequently quite different from positions previously held. During the course of a production season, moreover, numerous shifts in personnel occur as operations in certain departments are expanded, reduced, or altered in any one of a number of ways. These changes give ample scope to partisans of both camps to press their claims for the workers' support. Opportunities are sure to arise in which employers, if they choose, can penalize workers for supporting the union—the National Labor Relations Act to the contrary notwithstanding. Similarly, spokesmen for the union sooner or later receive cases in which discrimination, fancied or real, has occurred. The following quotation from the minutes of one of the plant committee meetings with company representatives tells of one such grievance pressed by the union:

> In the past it has been the practice of the management to contract work out to the job shops; some are considered alley [i.e., shops not under union standards] and non-union scab shops. We consider this undermining the union. We request that at this time the management allow no work to be let out until all the men working in A and B departments on the seniority list are working not less than 40 hours per week and that the chief steward be notified by letter of all work being contracted out, and to what shop or company this work goes.
>
> The corporation [replied that it] will continue to place in outside shops whatever tool room work they think is advisable and will so allocate it. Information will not be furnished chief committeemen in connection with what work is placed in outside shops.[26]

It is out of such issues that "worker loyalty" is fashioned. If the union had been able to win its point in the case cited, the workers in these two departments would have had concrete proof of the union's worth. Losing it must have made the men more dubious. How these issues are handled, therefore, assumes crucial importance.

Although these circumstances do not make for stable relations, they do not destroy the basis for a strong labor organization. Unions frequently thrive on adversity. Indeed, spokesmen for both the union and the companies agree that the U. A. W.-C. I. O. exists today chiefly because employment conditions in the industry had become so bad. Said one union organizer who had worked twelve years in the industry:

> The union grew because the men needed it. Nobody was sure of his job. Nobody knew how much money would be in his envelope on pay day. Nobody trusted the boss, except a few of his pets. What do you expect, when foremen fired anyone they didn't like and gave the jobs to men who were willing to buy them liquor or pay them "kickbacks" for a chance to work?[27]

---

[26] The meeting was held in the spring of 1939. The minutes of shop committee meetings in various plants were made available to the writer for 1938 and 1939 with the understanding that the names of the plants and of the parties concerned would not be disclosed. The minutes referred to in this chapter were written by company spokesmen; they were made available by the union.

[27] Interview (August 14, 1939).

According to the same organizer, these abuses were to be found throughout the industry during the 1920s. But there were also other sources of unrest. Company spies were frequently employed to keep employers informed about the activities of the men.[28] Charges against the speed-up were not uncommon, and even in those years men were being displaced at an age that seemed too early.[29]

However, these considerations should not be allowed to obscure the fact that employment conditions in other respects were far better than in most industries. The volume of employment during the 1920s was large and the hours of work were not unreasonable; hourly wage-rates were high and even annual earnings were good. Moreover, during this period there was a phenomenal improvement in the industry's product—although, according to one authority on labor problems, the intense competition which underlay this improvement was based in no small measure on the companies' freedom to handle their employees as they chose.[30] After 1929 mounting unemployment and lower annual earnings crystallized sentiment among the men against the employers and opened the door to "outside" union organizations. The workers turned to the union, said the personnel director of a parts-manufacturing company, because they needed its protection.[31] The results of the elections recently conducted in the industry by the National Labor Relations Board would seem to bear out this contention.[32]

Many of the difficulties between the union and the companies today are a legacy of the past. During the 1920s the industry attracted thousands of young workers from the South and Middle West, many of them from rural towns and farms. A survey of unemployment conditions in Detroit, for example, showed that less than one per cent of the heads of all relief families in 1934 were born in that city. Over forty-seven per cent had come to Detroit between 1920 and 1929; only five per cent had arrived during the years 1930-1933.[33] Their new surroundings and the poor chances of getting another job in case of "a fight with the boss" made the men relatively tractable. Employers had little trouble in handling the men as they chose. As the new

28 See *Violations of Free Speech and Rights of Labor*, Hearings before a Subcommittee of the Committee on Education and Labor, U. S. Senate, 75th Cong., 1st sess., pursuant to S. Res. 266 (1936), Part 4, pp. 1115, 1127; Part 5, pp. 1621-1622.

29 See, for example, Henderson, *op. cit.*, p. 5.

30 Interview (June 13, 1939) with Dr. David J. Saposs, then Chief, Technical Service Division, National Labor Relations Board, Washington, D. C. In this connection, the following statement in the Henderson report is significant: "The competitive conditions of the past few years [referring to the early 1930s] have reached down to the time-study men. These have been forced to show how to make inequitable reductions in working to hold their own jobs." Henderson, *op. cit.*, p. 6.

31 Interview (August 21, 1939).

32 The results of these elections are given on p. 123.

33 Henderson, *op. cit.*, p. 43.

workers became familiar with their environment, however, resentment against employment abuses began to mount. After 1929 the movement of workers from outlying areas into the automobile centers virtually stopped. Companies could no longer take on "green hands" who would accept without protest virtually any conditions. Unrest increased as the depression further demoralized employment standards. At this juncture, extremist groups began to make their influence felt. The workers were urged to join together and to adopt violent methods if other forms of protest failed. The aftermath of this period of ferment is well known. Between 1934 and 1938 an aggressive campaign of union organization was undertaken. Violent methods and radical demands were part of the campaign. But since that time extremist tactics have been used only sparingly.

According to company spokesmen, however, radical groups—either Communist party members or sympathizers—still figure prominently in the U. A. W.-C. I. O. Most members of these groups, so employers allege, have either secured employment in the industry only recently or have never worked in the plants at all. While it must be admitted that there certainly is some truth in these charges, it must likewise be clear that the appeal of these groups has been based on abusive employment policies and depressed industrial conditions. If conditions are improved, the influence of radical elements will probably diminish.

Nevertheless, the struggles of the last few years have left their mark on the administration of the agreements. The story of this conflict is too familiar to warrant detailed repetition here. Between 1933 and 1940 a battle was fought on two fronts. First, the union carried on a vigorous organizing campaign for the purpose of wresting bargaining privileges from the employers. In the course of this struggle all of the common techniques of industrial warfare were employed, together with some less familiar. Of the latter the most spectacular was the union's use of the "sit-down" or "stay-in" strike. Under this strategy, used most extensively during the first half of 1937, the men stayed in the plants for the duration of the strike. Coupled with mass-picketing and large-scale demonstrations of "worker solidarity," it had every appearance of outright insurrection. More important, from management's view, it was very effective in shutting down the plants and in preventing strike-breakers or non-union workers from being brought into the factories. The "sit-down" disappeared after 1937, but it has not yet been forgotten by either side. The bitterness and mutual distrust which it engendered has to some extent been carried over into everyday negotiations between the two parties. In the same way, the militant tactics of the employers—the use of armed guards, tear-gas, and the policeman's "billy"—have left their mark on present-day relations.

Jurisdictional differences among various labor organizations formed the second front on which conflict occurred after 1933. In that year the American Federation of Labor set up union locals, based on the industrial form of organization, which were affiliated directly with the Federation.[34] But other groups soon sprang up. For example, in the Dodge factory in Detroit, many of the employees became dissatisfied with the Federation local and formed the Automotive Industrial Workers' Association; employees in other plants, notably in the Hudson factory, also withdrew and, in 1934, formed the Associated Automobile Workers of America. Still another organization known as the Mechanics Educational Society of America had been organized in 1933. In contrast to the other organizations its membership consisted almost entirely of tool and die workers. Some of the manufacturers also established company unions at this time. However, the great majority of workers remained unaffiliated with any bargaining group in 1934.

In the spring of that year the Federation unions threatened to call widespread strikes in an attempt to win recognition and to halt discriminatory practices against their members. Under an agreement secured by President Roosevelt the Automobile Labor Board was appointed to settle these issues. The terms of the President's agreement provided for the election of bargaining committees in the various plants on a proportional representation basis. Since this procedure prevented the Federation unions from achieving positions of primacy in the plants, they soon withdrew from the agreement. The board was disbanded in June 1935 when the Supreme Court invalidated the National Industrial Recovery Act.[35]

The American Federation of Labor, in August 1935, combined its federal labor unions into a single organization, the International Union, United Automobile Workers of America. For a time the Federation continued to appoint and pay its officers. But strong opposition to the Federation's supervision and cautious policies soon developed. Although the Federation granted the union full autonomy, in July 1936 it proceeded to change its affiliation to the Committee for Industrial Organization (now the Congress of Industrial Organizations). At the same time, a number of rival groups, notably in the Dodge and Hudson plants, joined the international, numerous strikes were called,

---

[34] Unions of this type are referred to as federal labor unions. At the outset, the automobile unions had no immediate association with one another, but they were supervised by a single A. F. of L. representative. In 1934 the automobile unions elected eleven of their members to a national council to advise the A. F. of L. representative.

[35] For the terms of the President's settlement and a review of the board's work, see *Final Report of the Automobile Labor Board*, Dr. Leo Wolman, Chairman, August 6, 1935. A mimeographed copy is available in the Business School Library, Columbia University, New York City.

and the organizing campaign was pushed more aggressively than ever. By July 1937, according to one observer, the union had approximately 370,000 members (with 400,000 claimed) and some five hundred agreements.[36]

No sooner had the different groups been brought together, however, than factional disputes broke out again. A struggle developed between two groups within the union for control of the organization, centering around President Homer Martin. Efforts at conciliation, in which C. I. O. representatives figured prominently, were unsuccessful. In 1939 President Martin called a special convention and sought to suspend fifteen of the twenty-four members of the executive board. The board countered by suspending Martin and electing R. J. Thomas in his place. The Martin group then called a separate national convention at which a rival organization was set up. In June 1939 the Martin organization reaffiliated with the American Federation of Labor. Both groups conducted vigorous organizing drives during 1939, and in some cases employers were caught between the two warring factions. In most of the plants, however, it soon became apparent that the C. I. O. group was much the stronger. Elections were held to determine the issue during 1939 and the first half of 1940. Counting all elections held in the automobile and aircraft industries, the National Labor Relations Board conducted polls in one hundred and sixty plants between January 1, 1939, and July 1, 1940. These plants employed 259,540 workers. The United Automobile Workers of America, C. I. O., won majorities and was certified as sole bargaining agency in one hundred and ten of these elections. The United Automobile Workers of America, A. F. of L., won fourteen, while other craft unions affiliated with the A. F. of L. won thirteen. Independent labor organizations won the remaining twenty-three contests. There were 260,000 workers eligible to vote in all of these elections; approximately 235,000, or ninety per cent, cast their ballots. The votes were distributed according to the following table.

N. L. R. B. ELECTIONS IN THE AUTOMOBILE INDUSTRY
JANUARY 1, 1939—JULY 1, 1940[37]

Bargaining Representative	*Total Votes*
U. A. W.-C. I. O.	165,725
U. A. W.-A. F. of L.	36,944
Independent	5,930
Others	20,760
None	2,544
Void, etc.	2,807

[36] McPherson, *op. cit.*, p. 18. One year earlier the union had only about 27,000 members (though claiming 40,000) and twenty-one agreements. Much of the data for this period is taken from McPherson's study.

[37] *Automobile Unionism*, Report of R. J. Thomas to the U. A. W.-C. I. O. 1940 convention in St. Louis, Missouri, July 29, 1940, pp. 5-6 and Appendix A.

At the various Chrysler plants the C. I. O. group received 41,553 votes or nearly ninety per cent of all votes cast. At the General Motors plants the C. I. O. group received 91,852 or about two-thirds of the votes cast.[38] The election at the two main plants of the Ford Motor Company on May 21, 1941, is not included in the above figures. There the C. I. O. union received 51,866 votes, or seventy per cent of the total; the A. F. of L. union received 20,364 votes, or twenty-seven per cent.[39] It is clear from these figures that the U. A. W.-C. I. O. is now the dominant labor organization in the automobile industry.

DISPUTED ISSUES

These background circumstances provide the setting against which both sides are maneuvering for "control of the worker and his job"—the employer seeking to retain control, the union seeking to share it. The period of open conflict, for the time being at least, seems past, but the struggle will continue in modified form until this basic issue is settled. During the life of the agreements, strikes or stoppages will probably be less frequent than in the past. The companies report that in 1939 and 1940 disruptions were negligible. According to an official of the union[40] not a single strike has occurred under any of its agreements since Homer Martin was suspended from office in January 1939.[41] Nevertheless, despite the absence of strikes, other tactics that are hardly less effective are still practiced. The companies charge that in some plants slow-downs take place, which violate the agreement.[42] In this type of action, certain men on the assembly line reduce the speed at which they perform their particular task. Usually they accomplish this by working at the regular pace but letting every every third or fourth job-operation go undone or partially so. At other times, protest assumes an even more overt form. The expansion in employment and the rise in living costs connected with the current defense program have already occasioned an increase in the number of such protests.

At first glance these events would seem to be nothing more than

[38] *Ibid.*, Appendix A.

[39] *New York Times*, May 23, 1941, p. 1.

[40] Interview (August 1940).

[41] The 1939 Chrysler agreement, in Article 4, provides that: "The union will not cause or permit its members to cause, nor will any member of the union take part in, any strike or stoppage of any of the corporation's operations or picket any of the corporation's plants or premises until all the bargaining procedure as outlined in this agreement has been exhausted, and in no case until after the negotiations have continued for at least five days and not even then unless sanctioned by the International Union, United Automobile Workers of America."

[42] *Ibid.* Article 4 further provides that: "The union will not cause or permit its members to cause, nor will any member of the union take part in, any sit-down, stayin or slowdown in any plant of the corporation, or any curtailment of work or restriction of production or interference with production of the corporation."

expressions of sporadic, local protest. In one plant, for example, a small group of workers initiated a slow-down because of excessive heat in their department; the management reported that they were able to reduce production of the entire plant by nearly one-third for a short period of time. Later in the same plant another group of men did the same thing because they wanted two more employees to help them on their job.[43] Similarly, a stoppage occurred in another plant because the company laid off a union committeeman for insubordination; in still another, a stoppage occurred because a union member was discharged for alleged incompetence.[44] Other protest actions were staged because the men wanted to "get rid of their foreman"; because they were being worked more than thirty-two hours a week at the same time that other workers were unemployed; and, in one case, because they demanded an increase of ten cents an hour.[45]

The minutes of plant meetings between union and company spokesmen show how grievances of this sort crystallize into overt action, and how the companies deal with them. The following excerpt from one of these records is typical:

> At the start of this model a number of temporary employees were hired in order to take care of certain non-standard conditions and other production difficulties. These conditions are now cleared up, the men are not needed any more, and it has been proposed the men be laid off.
>
> The union committeemen were protesting this proposed lay-off complaining that they had been offered no actual proof of the time study figures through the plants. They charged that no work had been taken out of the department to make up for the suggested lay-off of manpower and stated, in case the lay-off was put into effect, they could not be responsible for production.[46]

The dispute was not settled at the meeting at which these minutes were taken, and the next day there was a slow-down of production in the division involved. A special shop committee meeting was called the day following, at which the plant manager pointed out that the division was running greatly over standard cost and that manpower exceeded production requirements. He went on to say that unless this condition was rectified, production would be forced to "outside plants or other plants of the corporation where a product of the same quality can be made fairly at a cheaper price."[47] This and additional meetings failed to settle the dispute, the union charging that the company was attempting to introduce a "speed-up." Finally, a representative of the international union entered the negotiations. Together with two company representatives he inspected the operations in question, later stating that "it was his opinion, if the management wanted

---

43 Interview (August 15, 1939) with company spokesman.

44 Stoppages occurred on April 19, 1938, and April 26, 1938.

45 Stoppages occurred on April 14, 1938, October 7, 1938, and November 30, 1938.

46 These minutes refer to a plant meeting held on January 3, 1939.

47 Minutes of January 5, 1939.

to get production out of this location, they would have to put back to work the men laid off." When the management refused to do this, the union did not push the issue further.[48]

Even though such incidents were scattered and localized, they also constituted a phase of the broader union strategy previously outlined. These disruptions placed management under immediate pressure to accept the union interpretations of the agreements. To the union there seems to be no choice other than action along such lines, for the position of the union, vis-à-vis management and the men, is still insecure. Moreover, the terms of the agreements are so vaguely phrased that they can easily be rendered worthless by an alert and determined management. There is the further consideration—and a not unimportant one—that the union finds the chance in these situations to dramatize itself, demonstrating to the men that it is a vital and militant organization. Though it is true that the agreements provide a definite procedure for the settlement of disputes and that the companies have repeatedly insisted that the union abide by the prescribed methods,[49] the fact remains that the U. A. W.-C. I. O. is still engaged in a campaign to consolidate its position among the workers of the industry and to achieve a share of control over labor policies. It still believes that management is ready to take every opportunity to rob it of gains already won and to weaken it in the eyes of the men. The union, therefore, feels entirely justified in disregarding established procedure in order to press home every advantage.

Perhaps at no point is the conflict between strategy and responsibility more sharp than in regard to campaigns for new members and for the collection of dues. The agreements with the manufacturers specify that the union will not intimidate or coerce employees in any way nor solicit membership on corporation time.[50] Prohibitions against solicitation of members on company properties, however, have been dropped from most of the agreements. Union spokesmen admit that these provisions have been violated, but insist that this is the only way to deal with "hitch-hikers," employees who receive the benefits of union agreements but refuse to join or pay dues.[51] During the fall of 1938, for example, the union staged a concerted drive for new members and for the payment of back dues. Appeals were made to the men en route to work, while at the plant, and on returning home.

---

[48] Minutes of January 7, 1939.

[49] The personnel director of one of the large manufacturers stated that the grievance procedure clause was violated more frequently than any other. Often cases were brought directly to the personnel office rather than to the foremen and stewards as provided by the agreement. Interview (August 20, 1939).

[50] For example, the Packard Motor Car Company Agreement provides that the union or its members will not intimidate or coerce employees in any manner or at any time, nor solicit or sign up members on company time. Article I, Section 2 (b); agreement signed September 26, 1939.

[51] Interview (August 17, 1939) with plant committeeman.

Where verbal appeals were unsuccessful, threats of coercion and physical violence were sometimes made. The employers allege that the men were harassed at their places of employment "in every conceivable fashion, including threats, assaults, destruction of lunches, and clothing, and concealment and larceny of tools."[52] In some cases men were "escorted" from the plants and given to understand that they would not keep their jobs unless they accepted the union's demands. In other instances the union staged "dues picketing" drives. Employees on coming to work were obliged to pass through a "gauntlet" of union men before entering the plant. Those who could not present proper credentials were sometimes subjected to physical assault and to other forms of abuse.

Though spokesmen for the companies emphasize the seriousness of these agreement violations, it is likely that they are exaggerating the importance of the problem. Indeed, an examination of the minutes of meetings between officers of local unions and various plant managers during 1938 and 1939 revealed only a few instances in which this matter came up. In one case the following colloquy took place:

> The writer [Labor Relations Supervisor of the plant] questioned the committee as to their attitude on what took place last week with respect to collection of dues and escorting employees out of the plant, particularly in Department X where Committeeman Smith was a leader in the eviction. Committeeman Jones stated that according to his information Mr. Smith had not been the leader in this matter, but might have been one of the group . . . . The writer also called Committeeman Brown's attention to the part he played in the coercion of employees to join the union in Department Y, it being the writer's opinion that members of our shop committee who know that this is a direct violation of our agreement should use their influence to prevent rather than encourage such actions.[53]

The same issue has come up on a few recent occasions during shop committee meetings with company representatives. However, spokesmen for the companies are unanimous in saying that since the fall of 1938 union actions of this nature have become infrequent. Indeed, if such tactics were pushed too far they would produce results precisely opposite to those desired. Nonetheless, so long as the union's campaign for union shop conditions continues, some instances of extremist action are almost sure to occur, for on this issue militant measures represent the only hope of gain for the union.

The seniority system and problems relating to the order in which men are laid off and rehired present another situation which both sides hope to turn to their advantage. Contrary to general belief, in the automobile industry at least, the administration of a seniority system under which men are released from or added to the employment rolls

---

[52] *Sitdown* (Automobile Manufacturers Association, 1939), p. 6.
[53] Minutes of shop committee meeting in plant A, dated October 11, 1938.

in order of length of service need not present complex problems.[54] This is true even of such large firms as General Motors and the Chrysler Corporation in which thousands of men are employed and in which virtually all the workers are laid off at least once each year. Nevertheless, seniority rules can be interpreted in such a way as to cause confusion and dissension. That is the path that has been chosen by both the union and the manufacturers, both having tried to turn the issue to their advantage. The employers have used the seniority question as a device to set old against young, experienced against inexperienced, with a view to weakening the position of the union. Clauses granting exceptions of one sort and another have permitted the employers to show preference to some workers and neglect others, to cause dissension among the men, and to bind favored groups more firmly to the companies. For its part, the union has also made good use of the vaguely worded seniority rules. Cases have been taken up which are groundless but which demonstrate to the men that the union is an aggressive fighter. Interpretations have been demanded which have brought certain groups closer to the union, even though in doing so other groups have been alienated.[55] Here, then, is an issue that goes to the heart of the union's campaign for union shop agreements and for a share in the control of the worker and his job. While this campaign is in progress, therefore, the conflict over seniority may be expected to continue.

The 1937 General Motors agreement is typical of the other agreements in regard to seniority. It provides that all employees who have worked six months are to be placed on a seniority list for their respective departments or occupational groups, in order of the date of hiring. The agreement then states:

> In a reduction of the working force in any department or occupational group affecting employees with seniority, employees with less service shall be laid off before employees with longer service according to the seniority list . . . In increasing the working force in any department or occupational group, employees will be called back in the reverse order in which they were laid off.[56]

This would seem straightforward enough. The difficulty comes in connection with the various exceptions and qualifications that have

---

[54] The *Final Report of the Automobile Labor Board*, 1935, p. 4, states: "The making and administering of seniority rules is likewise a straightforward and relatively simple undertaking." But, continues the *Report*: "While seniority rules are still new and, perhaps, not so fully appreciated as they later may come to be, the representatives of both employers or employees may be tempted to throw the weight of their influence in favor of seniority claims which cannot be supported by the record and of general interpretations of seniority which cannot be sustained under the prevailing rules."

[55] In fact, the personnel director of one of the companies remarked in an interview (August 20, 1939), "Some day seniority is going to wreck the union and it will be its own fault."

[56] General Motors Agreement (1937), Article B (*Lay-off, Transfer and Rehiring Procedure*).

been introduced. Thus, those who have worked for less than six months (temporary employees) do not have seniority privileges. Similarly, men who have been unemployed for twelve months or more lose their seniority. The same holds true of men who quit voluntarily or who are discharged.[57] The agreement also distinguishes between reductions in plant operations which are "temporary" and those which last "for extended periods." In the former circumstance, "the work week may be reduced before any employees are laid off"; in the latter, "temporary employees will be laid off first and thereafter the work week will be reduced before employees with seniority are laid off."[58] The General Motors Agreement also makes provision for a special group of employees whom the company desires to retain regardless of seniority rank. This clause reads as follows:

> The management in each plant will prepare a separate list of employees, who in the judgment of the management should be retained or recalled to work, regardless of any other provisions, in order to facilitate tooling or rearrangement of the plant, the taking of inventory and the starting of production and similar situations. In the selection of this list, length of service shall be secondary to other qualifications, but should be given reasonable consideration . . . The members of shop committees shall be included in this list.[59]

These exceptions seem reasonable. To distinguish between temporary lay-offs and more extensive shut-downs, for example, is to make a distinction as advantageous to the union as to the employer. Similarly, the "special list" provision, if administered in good faith, simply gives the company an opportunity to keep men whose work is indispensable. But such exceptions and distinctions present exactly the opportunities that both sides are waiting to exploit.

Many of the plant shop committee meetings with company representatives at which grievances are discussed and settled are devoted almost exclusively to this and related issues. In one of the plant committee meetings, for example, there was a lengthy discussion over a complaint that the company had re-employed certain workers who possessed less seniority than other men qualified for the jobs. The company spokesman answered that the latter were already employed in other departments and that they would be given back their old

---

[57] An employee who is notified of work and does not report within three days, or does not give a satisfactory explanation for not reporting, is considered a voluntary quit.

[58] General Motors Agreement (1937), Article B (*Lay-off, Transfer and Rehiring Procedure*). As regards the rule that employees are to be laid off according to seniority, the agreement contains this further qualification: "If in the judgment of the management, production in the plant must be materially reduced for an extensive period, thus creating a social problem in the community, this rule will be modified in a manner satisfactory to the employees to give preference in the available employment to employees with dependents as against employees without dependents."

[59] *Ibid.*

positions "when production opens up in our various departments."[60] In a later meeting with company representatives the same shop committee raised questions about employees in two departments that had been closed down. The union demanded that employees be given the choice of remaining on the seniority list or accepting employment in the truck plant. The company officials made the following reply:

> At the present time there are no openings in our truck plant inasmuch as there are still men with seniority who have not been recalled to work. However, where it is necessary to increase the man power in any department above their present seniority list an opportunity will be given those employees to accept such employment.[61]

At all of these meetings the union brought up many seniority complaints on behalf of individual employees, but only in a few instances did the companies accept the union's version of the facts or accede to its demands.

The provision in the automobile agreements which allows certain employees to be retained regardless of their seniority rating has caused innumerable disputes. In the spring of 1939, for example, a walk-out occurred in the district of a plant where a group of workers of "exceptional ability" were not included in a general lay-off in the car assembly division. The company replied that the agreement allowed this distinction to be made and requested that the employees return immediately. Spokesmen of the international union declared at later meetings that "the intent of the agreement had been to keep exceptional employees only at the beginning and not at the end of a model," an interpretation which would have made the "exceptional ability" clause quite meaningless. They argued further that the regular men could handle production in this division satisfactorily. The union spokesmen admitted that the men were wrong in walking off their jobs but added "it would now be the policy of the union to not cooperate with the corporation and to snipe at them at every opportunity."[62] But, even though disorders occurred in various departments during the next week and production schedules were generally disrupted, the company refused to modify its original decision. Instead it ordered the men back to work and penalized the ring-leaders with two week lay-offs. Further protests by the union were fruitless.[63]

The question of transfers, promotions, and job classifications is another contentious issue which both sides are trying to turn to their advantage. The agreements give employers almost complete authority over these matters, but they prohibit employer discrimination for union membership or union activity. Naturally, a worker who feels

---

[60] Minutes of shop committee meeting in plant B, dated August 9, 1938.
[61] Minutes, dated November 8, 1938.
[62] Minutes, dated May 2, 1939.
[63] Minutes, dated May 8, May 9, and May 10, 1939.

that he is not receiving his due job classification quickly raises the charge of "discrimination." This gives the union an opportunity to limit the employer's authority and to prove the union's worth to the men. Employers, on the other hand, can use the issue to sow seeds of dissension among the men and to bind "loyal" employees more closely to the companies. In view of the campaign now being conducted in the automobile industry, it is not surprising that this kind of dispute should arise more frequently than almost any other.[64]

Plant committee meetings are often transformed into prolonged discussions of the requirements of particular jobs and the qualifications of particular workers. In one instance, an employee on the transmission assembly line demanded a "utility" classification because of his special ability. After an investigation of the case, the company refused the request.[65] The following is another grievance over discrimination which came up in a plant committee meeting:

> Conveyor loaders in Department 83 engaged in transferring freshly painted stock from spray lines to oven lines have a very tedious and painstaking job, as all stock, some of it very heavy, must not be permitted to come in contact with their person or any other object. This necessitates holding each and every part at arm's length . . . . This job should be reclassified and paid a higher rate to bring it in line with other classifications.[66]

The company put another man on the operation and no further complaints were heard. In some discrimination cases the union endeavored to get wage increases for certain men. In others it tried to have them transferred from one department or plant to another.

CONCLUSIONS

Disputes over union membership drives, dues payments, seniority rules, job transfers, and promotions may arise under any system of collective bargaining, but they have a special significance at the present time in the automobile industry. In the conflict over seniority rules, for example, if the union is able to win numerous concessions from the companies and prove its effectiveness to the men, the goal of the union shop can be brought much nearer. The same is true of other issues which arise during the life of agreements—the duties of certain workers, charges of speed-up, shortage of personnel, distribution of work, unsatisfactory work conditions, and the like. At another time these issues would be far less likely to lead to serious disruptions. Now, however, they are part of a broader struggle. Neither side,

---

64 In a classification of grievances in one plant of the General Motors Corporation during 1938, the question of job transfers was the one most frequently raised.

65 Plant Committee Grievance Report, Local Y, U. A. W.-C. I. O., dated February 14, 1939.

66 Minutes of shop committee meeting in plant C, dated April 27, 1939.

therefore, can allow these issues to be adversely decided without making firm protest and even a show of strength.

Until the conflict over the union's share in the control of labor policies is settled, the industry will probably be subjected to intermittent disturbances. In large measure the issue will turn on whether the union can win union shop privileges. The disputes will not necessarily take the form of strikes or overt acts of sabotage. The national defense program now under way will place both sides under great constraint to avoid any extensive interruption of production. If special machinery is established in the shape of an arbitration board, the likelihood of important disruptions during the life of agreements will be further reduced. Both sides have shown a willingness to keep disturbances at a minimum. Nevertheless, below the surface of everyday events the struggle will continue. Even if powerful pressure is exerted to maintain peaceful relations, the possibility of a serious breach still remains.

Conditions under new agreements such as those in the automobile industry are quite different from conditions under long-established systems of collective bargaining. Both sides are still prone to settle issues by trial of combat. Basic questions concerning recognition and bargaining privileges remain open. Though formal relations may be in effect, the substance of true collective dealings may be lacking. Under older systems the struggle over status is much less likely to develop. Both sides are more ready to accept a policy of "live and let live." There is greater willingness to agree. Under these circumstances, the difficulties that persist are not to be attributed to "power politics" or to shifts in relative bargaining strength. Such difficulties are due to broad economic factors—a phase now to be considered.

CHAPTER VII

ENFORCEMENT IN THE COAT AND SUIT INDUSTRY

To the investigator's dismay an analysis of enforcement problems under union agreements in the clothing industry raises such broad questions that the topic of main interest may be overshadowed. Thus, while many of the departures from contractual standards in this industry seem traceable to the small contractor who works up material on orders from some jobber, closer inspection reveals the former as part employer and part employee, and the latter turns out to be as much of an absentee landlord as he is a jobber. Considerations of this sort quickly carry the inquiry far afield. Similarly, an analysis of the arbitral machinery in the clothing industry makes little sense apart from the interests of various groups within the industry and the circumstances which give rise to them. As a consequence, it is impossible to confine the subject to such narrow questions as what provisions in the agreements are frequently disregarded or how impartial chairmen handle charges of agreement violations. Instead the inquiry involves the much broader effort of analyzing the economic characteristics of the industry and showing how they impinge on the problem of this study.

The field here has been restricted to the women's garment industry of New York City, with particular reference to the branch concerned with the manufacture of coats and suits. Output of women's garments for the entire country runs to something over a billion dollars a year although there are wide fluctuations in the sum from year to year.[1] The manufacture of coats and suits accounts for about twenty-five per cent of the total value of goods produced, while the manufacture of dresses comprises about forty per cent.[2] Approxi-

[1] *Census of Manufactures, 1937* (U. S. Department of Commerce, Bureau of the Census), Part I, p. 419. For earlier years, see: *Census of Manufactures, 1935*, p. 396; *Census of Manufactures, 1933*, p. 192; *Census of Manufactures, 1931*, p. 324; Mabel A. Magee, *Trends in the Location of the Women's Clothing Industry* (Chicago: University of Chicago Press, 1930), pp. 126-132. The term "women's garment industry" as used here is classified in the *Census of Manufactures* as "Women's, Misses' and Children's Apparel Not Elsewhere Classified."

[2] *Census of Manufactures, 1937*, Part I, pp. 419-420; *Census of Manufactures, 1935*, pp. 396-397. The figure for the coat and suit industry includes "separate skirts."

mately three-fourths of the industry's total output is centered in and around New York City where, of course, the stronghold of the International Ladies' Garment Workers' Union is also to be found. According to the union, about ninety-four per cent of the country's coat and suit workers are members of the union, as opposed to about eighty-one per cent of the dress workers and about fifty-five per cent of the workers in other branches of the industry. On January 1, 1940, the union reported paid-up membership of 241,000, about 150,000 of this number being in New York City. Though these figures may overstate the union's strength, it is impossible to say by how much.[3]

Unlike its counterpart in automobiles and steel, the bargaining system in this industry has been in effect for many years. Twice since it was first established in 1911, the bargaining machinery has broken down—once during the first World War and later in the mid-twenties. Today, however, the union is solidly entrenched in the coat and suit and dress sections of the industry. Closed shop conditions are now in effect. Agreements in New York City provide for a thirty-five hour week and minimum wage rates ranging from $0.46 to $1.81 an hour. Twenty-five years ago the same agreements provided for a fifty hour week and wage rates ranging from $0.12 to $0.50 an hour.[4]

Consequently, the emphasis of union policy in these two branches of the industry has shifted. At one time the union's chief concern was the winning of higher standards. Today its principal objective is to enforce the provisions of agreements as well as to bring non-union employers under similar standards. This circumstance brings the union face to face with the economic difficulties of the industry, since they lie at the root of the problem of enforcement. It also gives the union's program a character quite different from that of its counterpart in more recently organized fields. The explanation for such a shift in policy is to be found largely in the nature of the industry. Competition is intense; the mortality or turnover of firms is high; production and employment fluctuate widely during the year, as well

[3] Value of output, classified by states, is given in *Census of Manufactures, 1937*, Part I, pp. 421-424. The proportion of workers in the various branches of the industry who belonged to the union, as of January 1, 1940, is given in a release of the Educational Department, I. L. G. W. U., *Trends and Prospects in the Women's Garment Industry* (1940), p. 8. The figures on the extent of unionization in the dress industry include both cotton and silk dresses. There are twelve other branches of the women's garment industry, as classified by the union, of which the most important are embroidery, rainwear, and neckwear.

[4] *Ibid.*, p. 11. The comparison between present day standards and standards existing twenty-five years ago pertains to all union agreements in the coat and suit and dress industry considered as a group. Agreements signed with particular employers might show much less of an improvement in standards. This is true, for example, of agreements with the Association of Manufacturers in the coat and suit industry. The lowest minimum wage rate provided by the 1916 agreement with this group was 24 cents an hour; today it is 66 cents an hour.

as from one year to the next. Under these conditions violations of commitments are bound to be widespread. It is not surprising, therefore, that in the coat and suit and dress industries the union has come to concentrate its efforts on enforcing the standards incorporated in its agreements.

ENFORCEMENT DIFFICULTIES

The greatest obstacle in the path of policing union agreements in this field is the industry's peculiar jobber-contractor system of manufacturing and distributing its product. True, some of the firms in the industry (the so-called "inside" shops) are manufacturers in the usual sense of the term, purchasing their own materials, working them up on their own premises, and arranging for their sale. But since the first World War garments have for the most part been produced by contractors or sub-manufacturers, who work according to the specifications of some jobber on materials owned by him. Having purchased materials and employed designers to create new styles, the jobber then contracts for the manufacture of the desired garments according to specifications which he sets. Under this system of production the immediate employers are the contractors; but the ultimate employers are the jobbers, for they keep title to the materials sent to the "outside" shops. Today, even some of the manufacturers employ this system of production, making only a part of their garments in their own shops and sending out the rest to contractors or sub-manufacturers.[5] This setting is a favorable one for employers who seek to escape standards provided by union agreements. Jobbers, charged with responsibility for violations of the agreements, reply that they have no direct dealings with workers in the industry. Contractors, faced with a similar charge, argue that employment standards are beyond their control, dependent as they are on the amount of work jobbers send to them and on the price jobbers are willing to pay. Under this system of divided authority it is easier to evade contractual standards than if responsibility were centered in a single group.

There are other characteristics of this system of production and distribution which help to explain the difficulties that are faced in enforcing union agreements. The number of contractors mounted so rapidly after the first World War that by 1924, according to a commission appointed by Governor Alfred E. Smith, there were at least 1,200 contracting shops in the coat and suit industry alone, doing work for only about 200 jobbers. This system of production accounted for approximately three-fourths of the industry's total output in 1924,

---

[5] At one time it was customary to distinguish between contractors and sub-manufacturers on the grounds that the former only made up garments which had already been cut. Today the two terms are used interchangeably in all branches of the industry. The present study follows current practice.

whereas before the war most garments had been made in the shops of "inside" manufacturers.[6] As the number of contractors increased during the decade, competition for the jobbers' business grew keener. Fixed costs like rental payments and charges for equipment made competition more active since sales at any price above current expenses were better than none at all. From the jobber's viewpoint the result was that he could farm out his materials to a shifting group of contractors, playing off one against the other, and giving his orders to those able to make the lowest bids. During a single season of production most of his business went to a relatively few contractors, the little that remained being fought for by all the others. Thus, in 1925 it was estimated that, on the average, 86.3 per cent of the work for each jobber in the coat and suit industry was turned out by 18.5 per cent of all the contractors working for him during the year.[7] Many contractors therefore found themselves under strong pressure to reduce their costs, and one way of doing so was to cut corners under their agreements with the union. To a lesser extent manufacturers felt the same compulsion as their position in the industry became more difficult.

The rapid growth of the contracting system during this period was the employers' answer to the union's campaign for higher standards of employment. In essence, it represented an effort to escape those standards. True, other causal forces were active. Thus under this system firms which contracted out work were able to increase or decrease production more easily than when they worked up their own materials. Moreover, the jobber-contractor system made it possible to put marketing operations on a large-scale basis.[8] But the chief cause lay in the threat of the union's campaign for higher wages and shorter hours. Largely because of the growth of the jobber-contractor system employers were able to check this campaign during the post-war decade. In fact, the development of this system undermined the entire structure of the union's organization.

Though not quite to the same degree as before, the jobber-contractor system persists today as the dominant form of production in the coat and suit industry. A 1935 survey of all establishments showed that 395 were jobbers, 934 were manufacturers, and 1,025 were contractors. The same survey revealed that in metropolitan New York the "inside" shops handled 39.3 per cent of all garments produced,

---

[6] *Final Recommendations* (Governor's Advisory Commission, Cloak, Suit and Skirt Industry, New York City, 1926), p. 8. The number of members in the manufacturers' association of the coat and suit industry dropped from 440 in 1916 to 188 in 1924; the decline reflected the growing importance of the jobber-contractor system.

[7] *Ibid.*, p. 7.

[8] Lewis L. Lorwin, *The Women's Garment Workers* (New York: B. W. Huebsch, Inc., 1924), pp. 409-417.

while the "outside" shops accounted for 60.7 per cent.[9] Moreover, competition among contractors remains intense. Data on the volume of business available to contractors in the coat and suit industry are not available for late years. A recent survey in the dress industry, however, revealed that 78 per cent of total production was in the hands of 37 per cent of the contractors in the industry.[10] Despite efforts by the union to reduce the number of contractors, the competition for a limited volume of business continues. Consequently the pressure to cut costs and evade union standards is hardly less compelling than it was fifteen years ago.

But these are not the only disturbing factors. The importance of style in the coat and suit industry increases the unpredictable element in carrying on operations. Variations in demand may sharply reduce sales in the course of only one or two seasons. Firms agreeing to pay certain wage-rates one year may not be able to do so the next. The agreements, however, rest on the assumption that broad variations will not occur. They fix standards which do not change from year to year, much less from month to month. Thus the likelihood of violations is great, for one way in which an employer may try to adjust operations to a bad season is to undercut the going rate. Pressures of this sort subject the structure of union standards to serious strain.

In this light, seasonal changes in demand are seen to be an important factor. Many firms experience wide fluctuations in their operations during a single year, depending on the "interaction of calendar, weather, and style."[11] One survey, covering an extensive variety of industries, revealed that producers' sales of women's clothing undergo wider seasonal fluctuations than those of any other industry except ice cream manufacture, shipments of fruit and vegetables, and production of refined cottonseed oil.[12] Some firms can operate more months of the year than others because they know their way "around the agreements." The seasonal factor presents particularly serious problems in connection with employee dismissals. A firm

---

[9] *Summary of Statistical Report, 1934-1935* (Coat and Suit Code Authority, National Recovery Administration), p. 1. The *Summary* is available at the National Coat and Suit Industry Recovery Board, New York City.

[10] The survey was made by the New York Dress Joint Board, cited in Lazare Teper, *The Women's Garment Industry* (New York: I. L. G. W. U. Educational Department, 1937), p. 13.

[11] Harry A. Millis and others, *Collective Bargaining in the U. S.* (Twentieth Century Fund), chapter by Patrick M. Malin on the women's garment industry. At the time of writing, this study was not yet published. References, therefore, are to Mr. Malin's original manuscript.

[12] Simon S. Kuznets, *Seasonal Variations in Industry and Trade* (National Bureau of Economic Research, New York, 1933), pp. 209-211.

closes down at the end of one season and may open at the beginning of the next with a different set of styles. It may contend that some of its former workers are not equipped to do the new type of work and that others must be secured to take their place. The agreements allow firms to effect bona fide reorganizations, necessitated by a permanent curtailment or a fundamental change in business, and to dismiss workers for incompetency or misconduct.[13] But the proper interpretation of these provisions in specific situations is not clear. It should be pointed out, parenthetically, that these observations apply primarily to the contractors and only incidentally, if at all, to the "old line" manufacturers.

Changes in manufacturing methods are another source of agreement violations. Alterations in methods of manufacture are being made continuously, with direct effects upon the job requirements and earnings of various groups of workers. This circumstance is not one calculated to simplify the union's task of enforcing employment standards. When questions concerning job classifications arise, disputes over wages are sure to follow—particularly in the contractor shops. These issues are discussed at a later point in the present chapter.[14]

Employers also face the threat of competition from firms making garments at lower cost under non-union conditions of employment. This problem, closely associated with the rise of the jobber-contractor system of production, became so serious during the post-war decade in the New York coat and suit industry that union standards were completely demoralized. At the same time firms began to spring up in towns around the New York metropolitan area where the union had not penetrated. This movement has continued. In the dress industry, for example, between 1927 and 1935 nearly three hundred and fifty factories, employing about 30,000 people, were established in nearby towns in Connecticut, New Jersey, and eastern Pennsylvania.[15] In the coat and suit industry, between the years 1933 and 1939, the number of manufacturing and jobbing firms in New York City declined, while the number in out-of-town districts remained about the same; the volume of sales in the two areas, however, showed little change. The table below makes the comparison.[16]

---

[13] Agreement of Industrial Council of Cloak, Suit and Skirt Manufacturers, Inc., with I. L. G. W. U., etc. (1937), Articles 21, 25. Agreements cited in this chapter are available in the office of the international union, New York City.

[14] See pp. 158-161, *infra*.

[15] Letter dated December 19, 1935, from David Dubinsky, President, I. L. G. W. U., to Frank J. Taylor, Comptroller, City of New York, reprinted in *Justice*, January 1, 1936, p. 1.

[16] Data on contract firms were not available; the figures therefore understate the movement to out-of-town centers.

ESTIMATED NUMBER OF MANUFACTURING AND JOBBING FIRMS AND VOLUME OF SALES, COAT AND SUIT INDUSTRY, 1933-1939

	New York City			*Out-of-Town*		
Year	*Number*	*Sales**	*Firms Not Reporting Sales*	*Number*	*Sales**	*Firms Not Reporting Sales*
1933	837	$199,064	78	271	$41,536	17
1934	783	182,291	74	288	44,173	26
1935	714	184,294	65	258	43,009	11
1936	702	207,610	58	266	48,268	15
1937	709	214,240	60	278	52,359	16
1938	724	163,984	129	263	44,924	24
1939	624	197,624	92	264	52,164	27

*In terms of thousands of dollars.
Source: National Credit Office, New York City.

Though the union has made substantial headway in organizing production centers nearby New York City, it must now cope with a trend away from New York to Pennsylvania, Maryland, and even more distant states. At the present time this constitutes the most serious threat to agreement standards that confronts the union.

Finally, there is the difficulty of fulfilling commitments under union agreements in any industry where earnings are scanty and financial resources are limited. In 1938, for example, the National Credit Office reports that 80 out of 724 manufacturing and jobbing firms in the New York City coat and suit industry failed to meet current obligations. Failures in the industry as a whole for this year numbered 97 out of 1,011 firms; their liabilities amounted to $1,721,-000.[17] A survey made by Dun and Bradstreet in 1937 ranked thirty-five manufacturing lines in the order of their relative profitability. The ratio of net profits to net sales in a sample of 114 coat and suit jobbers and manufacturers averaged only twenty-two per cent and ranked eighth from the bottom of the list. Figures showing the ratio of net profits to tangible net worth ranked the industry almost equally low.[18] There is every reason to believe that the financial position of the contractors is, generally speaking, even more perilous. This fact goes a long way toward explaining the many attempts to elude standards provided in agreements with the union; it is particularly true

[17] The number and the liabilities of jobbing and manufacturing firms in the coat and suit industry which failed during the years 1932 through 1939 are reported by the National Credit Office, New York City, as follows:

	1932	1933	1934	1935	1936	1937	1938	1939
Number of Failures	181	75	85	101	73	70	97	61
Liabilities*	$4,919	$1,154	$1,550	$1,694	$920	$1,377	$1,721	$1,093

*In thousands of dollars.

[18] The figures from Dun and Bradstreet were secured by Patrick M. Malin.

of contractors, in whose shops wages take up anywhere from seventy to seventy-five per cent of total receipts.[19]

The foregoing analysis illuminates the difficulty encountered by the union in preventing individual workers in contracting shops from accepting employment at terms below the union's standards. If competition for the available business is intense among contractors, competition among workers for the jobs offered by contractors is much greater. Changes in employment opportunities, elimination of lines of work, seasonal fluctuations in output all make for active bidding among the workers of the industry for whatever employment in contracting shops is available. Generally speaking, job opportunities are limited to the beginning of each season; a worker must find employment in his line at that time or run the risk of idleness for the entire year. After the peak season, when employment starts to slacken, the pressure to accept work below standards set by the union becomes still greater. On this score the Governor's Advisory Commission reported as follows:

> When work is scarce, as it usually is except for a few weeks in each season, the workers are told that in order to meet the exigencies of price competition and to bring some work into the shop, they must enter into secret arrangements contrary to the minimum labor standards which have been agreed upon, and which are pretty successfully enforced in the larger shops of the ("inside") manufacturers.[20]

Since 1926, the time of the Commission's report, collusive dealings between employers and workers have become less widespread. But, according to the executive director of the Industrial Council of Cloak, Suit and Skirt Manufacturers, there are a good many firms in which such surreptitious arrangements exist even today.[21] This is particularly true of contractor firms, not only in outlying districts (outside New York City) but in the metropolitan area itself.

As these circumstances help explain the many attempts to escape union standards, so closely related factors show how hard it is to detect the violator once an evasion occurs. Reference has already been made to the difficulty of determining who is responsible for agreement violations under the jobber-contractor system of production. There is the additional difficulty that most of the contractors, who are small employers, find it relatively easy to set up their machines in remote lofts during the season of active business. According to the 1937 Census, the average contractor in the coat and suit industry only

---

19 *Census of Manufactures, 1937*, Part I, p. 422. The census figures do not show the proportion of jobbers' and manufacturers' income going to labor. Dr. Lazare Teper, Director of Research, I. L. G. W. U., in an interview with the writer, estimated the proportion to be about twenty-five per cent. This could be misinterpreted since jobbers pay "wages" indirectly as payments to contractors.

20 *Final Recommendations* (Governor's Advisory Commission), p. 5.

21 Letter to the writer, dated November 22, 1940, from Samuel F. Klein.

employed twenty-five workers.[22] Figures for the manufacturers showed that they generally had a work force not much larger than the contractors. Indeed, women's clothing is an industry of small establishments in all of its branches; a 1933 survey of eighty-four different manufacturing fields ranked it at the very bottom of the list in degree of business concentration.[23]

Detection of agreement violations is further complicated by the high degree of unit mobility, particularly among contracting firms. Caught in a violation, contractors can pull out their machines, choose another name, and start operations elsewhere. This aspect of the industry has recently received considerable attention in connection with the so-called "run-away" shop. It is important here in showing how easy it is to escape union standards. Even if the union is quick to catch the fugitive employer, it may be too late since many of the orders received by contractors are small and can be completed before the union "controllers" are able to get to the shop.[24] Figures on mortality in the industry are indicative of the "fly-by-night" character of many of these firms; they fail to distinguish, however, between employers who are permanently eliminated and those who reappear elsewhere in the industry. The Governor's Advisory Commission found that during 1924 thirty-eight per cent of the contractors and thirty-four per cent of the manufacturers in the coat and suit industry closed their doors.[25] A study by the Coat and Suit Code Authority of the National Recovery Administration showed that during 1934 about sixteen per cent of all manufacturing firms in the New York market area went out of business.[26]

This review of some of the characteristics of the coat and suit industry would seem to lead to the conclusion that the barriers to effective enforcement are formidable indeed. Yet for every influence that tends to undermine contractual standards there is a counter influence working toward the opposite result. Some employees, it is true, feel compelled to accept work on any terms they can find; but most of them, thanks largely to innumerable exhortations from their union leaders, are aware of the menace to their own working standards which such collusive arrangements always contain. This ten-

---

22 *Census of Manufactures, 1937*, Part I, p. 422.

23 Rufus S. Tucker and others, *Big Business—Its Growth and Its Place* (Twentieth Century Fund, Inc., New York, 1937), pp. 42-43.

24 See "Among the Cutters of New York," *Justice*, August 1, 1935, p. 15. According to the union, "controllers" are able to perform their policing functions without resort to violence or coercion. On some occasions, however, it is probably true that they fall back on "strong-arm" methods.

25 These figures are cited in Teper, *op. cit.*, p. 17.

26 *Summary of Statistical Report, 1934-1935* (Coat and Suit Code Authority, National Recovery Administration), p. 1.

dency is further encouraged by rules of union membership prohibiting work below union rates. Union regulations also prevent employees from moving from one job to another in the course of a single season. Similarly, unauthorized stoppages and "outlaw" strikes are prohibited. Violations of these rules carry the threat of money fines, lay-offs, and even expulsion from union membership. So far as stoppages are concerned, however, penalties imposed by the union are of little importance, since the union hardly ever declares a stoppage to be unauthorized.

Nor should the influences working for compliance on the side of employers be overlooked. Their importance is attested by the experience in the coat and suit industry where the enforcement program has given these favorable elements every opportunity to make themselves felt. This has contributed in no small measure to whatever success the enforcement program has achieved. Most employers, of course, are not particularly eager to fulfill their commitments under union agreements, but they frequently find the cost of not doing so greater than the gain. Once they come to this conclusion, therefore, employers readily agree to policies adopted by the union and their employers' association to bring competitors into line. Many of the manufacturers (as opposed to the contractors) in the coat and suit industry discover themselves in this situation. Most of them have considerable capital invested in their enterprises, usually varying between twenty-five and fifty thousand dollars. For employers on such a level, the price of disregarding the provisions of their agreements with the union is frequently prohibitive since escape is difficult and penalties are severe (referred to in the agreements as "liquidated damages"). More important, they realize that their position in the industry has been seriously weakened by the spread of the contracting system; they see in the union's program, if it can be strictly enforced, a means of bringing this dangerous movement under control. As a result, the association representing the manufacturers in the coat and suit industry (known today as the Industrial Council of Cloak, Suit and Skirt Manufacturers, Inc.) has shown greater willingness to cooperate with the union's enforcement program than have the associations representing the other employer groups. The Governor's Advisory Commission commented on this fact when it observed that the manufacturers were less prone than the other employers to violate their agreements with the union.[27] It is not surprising, therefore, that as long ago as 1926 this group was willing to accept the union's demand for limiting each jobber and manufacturer to a certain number of contractors; the same group has actively supported other phases

---

[27] *Final Recommendations* (Governor's Advisory Commission), p. 7.

of the program as well, in the hope that the program will "stabilize and standardize the industry."[28]

The same influences operate among the jobbers and contractors, though to a lesser degree. While jobbers have few workers in their immediate employ, their firms are small in number and relatively well financed. Once jobbers assume obligations under the agreements, violation is not easy. The difficulty has been to induce them to accept responsibility for employment standards in their contracting shops, since they do not directly hire or supervise these workers. Today jobber responsibility is provided for under the agreements. But in some instances the change seems to be more nominal than real. The contract shops, as is well known, continue to present many serious enforcement problems. In their case all the troublesome features still prevail—small size, rapid turnover, low earnings, intense competition, and high labor costs relative to total costs. A few of the contractors have made substantial investments or have established a reputation for exceptional work in one or two lines. These employers are more ready to support efforts by the union to maintain standards and extend their coverage. But the investment of the great majority of contractors varies anywhere between one thousand and five thousand dollars.

Out of these circumstances, interests, and points of view has emerged the elaborate machinery for policing union agreements in the women's garment industry described in Chapter III. Like the factors that conditioned its development, this machinery reflects both unifying and conflicting elements within the industry. On the whole, the main thrust in launching the program and carrying it forward has come from the union. As already noted, active support has also come from the manufacturers.[29] The other two employer groups have simply tried to temper some of the program's harsher features and, in certain instances, tried to derive from it some positive benefits for themselves. All three employer groups have supported that part of the program designed to eliminate stoppages and other disruptions. But major

---

[28] Letter to the writer, dated November 22, 1940, from Samuel F. Klein, Executive Director, Industrial Council of Cloak, Suit and Skirt Manufacturers, Inc. The late Raymond V. Ingersoll, first impartial chairman of the New York coat and suit industry under rules established by the Governor's Advisory Commission, stated in an interview (October 23, 1939) that the two groups which gave most aid in the enforcement program during the 1920s were the union and the manufacturers.

[29] Provision for a permanent impartial chairman, for example, was made in 1924 under rules established by the Governor's Advisory Commission. While all groups in the industry cooperated in this undertaking, main credit for getting it under way belongs to the union and to the manufacturers' group. In fact, immediately prior to 1924, these two groups had maintained a system of choosing impartial chairmen from a previously selected panel. Interview (October 23, 1939) with Raymond V. Ingersoll.

responsibility for the introduction and development of the program rests with the union.

The next step in the analysis deals with the problems which the enforcement program faces and the way they are handled. This subject is approached by comparing the program at two stages in its development: the first, between 1924 and 1926 when many features of the present program were introduced and the second, between 1935 and 1939. The role played by the impartial chairman in the handling of enforcement problems possesses special importance.

THE 1924-1926 PERIOD

During the period of the first World War and even more during the business recession of the years 1920-1922, the strength of the International Ladies' Garment Workers' Union in the New York coat and suit industry ebbed perceptibly. The agreements won in 1916 were weaker than some of the earlier agreements, while in the case of the 1919 agreements, though substantial gains were made, violations of contractual standards soon became widespread.[30] With the revival in business which began in 1922 the union was able to increase its membership substantially. At the same time a program was formulated which the union hoped would end once and for all violations of contractual standards by employers.

The main objective was to win provisions in the 1924 agreements which would make possible the effective policing of contractual standards. By that time the jobber-contractor system had become the dominant form of production, and the union leaders were convinced that enforcement would never be secured unless this system were brought under effective union control. The 1919 agreement with the "inside" manufacturers provided for a preferential union shop and was fairly detailed in its provisions.[31] But the only clause in the 1919 agreement with the jobbers' association (the Merchants' Ladies' Garment Association, Inc.) which bore on this issue guaranteed that all the work of jobbers would be sent to union shops.[32] There was nothing else in the agreement which limited the number of contractors a jobber could have or which insured that the available work would be distributed equally among his contractors. Nor did the agreement provide satisfactory means whereby the union could discover whether work was going to non-union contractors. Article 1 directed the job-

---

[30] Lorwin, *op. cit.*, pp. 309-311, 342-351.

[31] Agreement between the Cloak, Suit and Skirt Manufacturers' Protective Association and the I. L. G. W. U. and the Joint Board of Cloak Makers' Union of the City of New York (1919).

[32] According to one union official this was the only provision in the agreement that "amounted to anything." Statement by Harry Wander, Vice President, I. L. G. W. U., *Justice*, March 14, 1924, p. 5. The 1919 agreement, renewed with slight modifications in 1922, expired in 1924.

bers to send the union, by way of the Merchants' Association, the names of any of their contractors which were not on the union's list of approved shops; but the absence of teeth in the clause robbed it of much meaning.[33] Moreover, this system of production allowed the jobbers to enjoy the advantages of active bidding among the contractors for their business. Thus, despite the fact that jobbers, indirectly at least, exerted an important influence on employment standards in the contracting shops, the 1919 agreement placed no corresponding responsibilities on their shoulders. Finally, the impartial machinery for settling disputes under the agreement was inadequate and almost entirely without effect,[34] and the question of damages in the event of a violation of the agreement was mentioned only incidentally in Article 4.[35]

Determined to remove these deficiencies the union in 1924 placed the following demands, among others, before the jobbers' association of the coat and suit industry as well as the association representing the manufacturers and contractors:

1. The members of the association shall be limited to a particular group of "steady" contractors, their total number to be equal to the number of members in the association multiplied by five.
2. These "steady" contractors shall be apportioned ratably among the members of the association on the basis of their average volume of business for the last three years. No member shall give work to any other contractor if his "steady" contractors are not working at full capacity; under the latter circumstances, the work is to be divided equally among the "steady" contractors alone.
3. The jobbers shall be responsible for one week's wages to members of the union working in the jobbers' "outside" shops.
4. The union shall have the absolute right to examine all records which, in the opinion of the union, are necessary to ascertain whether work is being done in accordance with the agreement.
5. All disputes shall be investigated jointly by the manager of the association and the union, or by their deputies. In case of their failure to agree, the disputes are to be submitted to a trial board or to the impartial chairman who is to be designated.

The union also made a sixth demand. In asking that jobbers deal only with union shops it sought a redefinition of the term "union shop" so that the very small contractors would be eliminated from the industry; the device hit upon was simply to require that all union

---

[33] Agreement between the Merchants' Ladies' Garment Association, Inc., and the I. L. G. W. U. and the Joint Board of Cloak Makers' Union of the City of New York (1919). A plan agreed upon after this agreement was signed provided that jobbers would give the names of all their contractors to the union and would deal only with contractors whom the union approved. Apparently it was not generally observed. Statement by Harry Wander, *Justice*, March 14, 1924, p. 5.

[34] The impartial machinery in the coat and suit industry, established under the Protocol of Peace in 1911, had been virtually abolished in 1916 by action of the employers. For an account of this earlier period, see Lorwin, *op. cit.*, Chapters XII-XXVIII.

[35] Agreement between the Merchants' Ladies' Garment Association and the I. L. G. W. U. and the Joint Board of Cloak Makers' Union (1919).

shops must have at least fourteen machine operators.[36] The employers in the coat and suit industry, particularly the jobbers, vigorously resisted these demands. Anticipating a deadlock in the negotiations, Governor Smith appointed a fact-finding advisory commission. Its report, which recommended a compromise favorable to the union, was accepted by the manufacturers' and contractors' associations. The jobbers did not give in until a general strike seemed imminent. On July 16, 1924, uniform agreements were signed with the three associations.

The union won its demand on the fourteen machine operator requirement.[37] It also won the right to examine, on its own request, the books of any jobber belonging to the Merchants' Association, but only in company with a representative of the jobbers' association and only for the purpose of "determining whether such a member is giving work to non-union shops."[38] The union was likewise successful in regard to the imposition of penalties upon jobbers found dealing with non-union shops. The employers' association agreed to impose a fine for the first offense which "shall be sufficiently high to offset the advantage gained by the member through such transaction, together with an appropriate penalty. A second offense shall mean expulsion."[39] The association also agreed to keep an up-to-date list with the union of all contractors with which its members had dealings; no member was to employ a contractor not included in the latest corrected list of union shops furnished by the union.[40] In addition to these obligations, jobbers were henceforth to be responsible for the wages of workers in their "outside" shops.[41] Finally, the agreement set up the arbitration machinery described in Chapter III.

The union, however, did not gain its demand to limit the number of contractors with which the jobbers' association, or rather each individual jobber, could deal. Nor was it successful in winning adoption of its scheme to share work equally among the "steady" contractors when times were slack. These matters, the Governor's Advisory Commission believed, called for further study and they were not included in the recommendations made by that body in 1924.[42] In-

---

[36] For the other demands made by the union at this time, see Lorwin, *op. cit.*, pp. 422-424.

[37] Agreement between the Merchants' Ladies' Garment Association and the I. L. G. W. U. and the Joint Board of the Cloak, Skirt, Dress and Reefer Makers' Union of the I. L. G. W. U. (1924), Article 2.

[38] *Ibid.*, Article 6.

[39] *Ibid.*, Article 5.

[40] *Ibid.*, Article 3.

[41] *Ibid.*, Article 7. If a contractor failed to turn over money to the workers which the jobber had provided, the jobber was still responsible for seven days' wages.

[42] These principles, however, were included in the Commission's *Final Recommendations* in 1926.

deed, these two principles were not to be incorporated in agreements with employers until 1933.

Having achieved an agreement that at least gave indications of being enforceable, the union proceeded to try to make this hope a reality. At first its efforts were fairly successful. The union had already called walk-outs against shops in the coat and suit industry during the period of negotiation over the new agreement. These walk-outs were continued against any firms which did not live up to the standards of the new agreements; the last walk-out was not ended until August 19, 1924, over a month after the agreement was officially in effect. The union was particularly determined not to allow any shop to re-open that had failed to comply with the fourteen machine operator clause. One group that was active in this phase of the work was the cutters' local, then under the leadership of David Dubinsky.[43] If this clause could be enforced, the cutters saw an opportunity to have at least one of their number employed in every shop. Therefore no shop was approved unless it complied with this rule. Two weeks after the signing of the agreement about fifteen per cent of the 2,114 registered cutters had still not been returned to their work or were employed in shops not yet sanctioned by the union.[44] Among the thousand or more shops that the cutters' local allowed to re-open by this date twenty-two were suspected of violating the fourteen machine operator clause. Dubinsky dispatched controllers to these shops and adjustments were made where violations were uncovered.[45]

Once the shops were "settled," the union took steps to insure continued compliance with the agreement. Here, again, the work of the cutters' local illustrates the kind of action that was taken. Manager Dubinsky first thought his local would need special controllers to police the shops for only a few weeks following the general walk-out. He later came to the conclusion that a continuing system of supervision was necessary. Enforcement measures were formulated to check violations of union rules by union members and to curb offending employers. For example, in a little over one week during September 1924, the cutters' local collected fines under the agreements totalling $2,000.[46]

Soon the program of this local was broadened to include the policing of many clauses in the new agreement. Since they wished to provide their own members with as much work as possible, the cutters were particularly active in checking on employers suspected of sending materials to non-union shops. The case of a firm on Madison

---

[43] However, it should not be inferred that this local was or is more active than other locals in enforcing the agreements.

[44] "The Week in Local 10," *Justice*, August 15, 1924, p. 12.

[45] *Ibid.*

[46] *Ibid.*, September 12, 1924, p. 12.

Avenue where the cutters were not getting a full week's work during the early summer was an instance in point. As the firm was usually busy at that time of the year, the union began to investigate. The partnership papers of the company were examined to see if there were any direct connections with non-union employers. The contractors working for the firm appearing on the company's list were inspected to ascertain whether the work was being done by union cutters. But nothing irregular was uncovered. Surmising that the company's list of contractors was incomplete, one cutter finally followed a case of piece-goods to its destination. Consulting its own records, the union found that the shop receiving the material was non-union. Thereupon the firm which had given out the work was fined and told either to withdraw its orders or to see to it that the non-union shop was organized. A strike was then called against the latter firm, and when it refused to sign an agreement the union instructed the other to withdraw its work. At that juncture, the non-union shop readily gave in.[47]

The cutters were also active in checking on their own members. On Labor Day, 1924, Manager Dubinsky made an intensive drive against shops which were staying open on the holiday. At seven o'clock in the morning he assigned fifty men to subway stations between Chatham Square and Third Avenue and 34th Street and Seventh Avenue. These patrols turned back any cutters coming to work as soon as they stepped off the trains. During the day the union "policemen" also visited some two hundred shops suspected of planning to work on Labor Day.[48] Members of the local who were subsequently caught working on holidays or after-hours were fined, after the first offense, anywhere from ten to one hundred dollars by the executive board of the local.[49]

It was amid these circumstances that the apparatus of the impartial chairman, under the guidance of Raymond V. Ingersoll, began to function in 1924. The manner in which this agency settled disputes under the agreements and interpreted their various provisions is a story by itself. But its work was also an important part of the program to secure compliance with the agreements in the coat and suit industry, since in cases coming before the impartial chairman, the charge was almost always made that one party or the other had violated the agreement. Whenever this charge was sustained, the decision was, in effect, an order to comply with the agreement. Indeed, there is reason to believe that the advantage of having some impartial enforcement agency was an important factor in establishing the three-man trial board and impartial chairman in 1919. For after the arbitration machinery was discarded in 1916, infractions became so

---

47 *Ibid.*, June 6, 1924, p. 12.
48 *Ibid.*, September 5, 1924, p. 12.
49 *Ibid.*, September 26, October 17, and November 7, 1924.

frequent and disputes so bitter that by 1919 both sides were ready to go back to the former system.[50] Sometimes the dominant role of the impartial chairman was that of judicial arbitrator and interpreter; at other times, his role as enforcement officer was the more important. In almost all of his decisions, however, both functions were present to a greater or less degree.

As an illustration of the way in which the role of the impartial chairman as enforcement officer became interwoven with his other functions, the series of cases against the firm of R. Sadowsky, Inc., is worth reviewing. This was a company which had work done in both an "inside" and certain "outside" shops. It did not belong to the association of manufacturers but, instead, had an independent agreement with the union. The firm had just been reorganized and the union had agreed to the reorganization only on the basis of the agreement. In the first case the union made two complaints before the impartial chairman. The union charged that the firm was giving all of the work in its "inside" shop to four out of the sixteen cutters, contrary to Articles 3 and 17 of the agreement, and that these four cutters who had been performing special or supervisory tasks before the reorganization were doing the work of regular cutters. The firm answered that while the working time of the twelve cutters was reduced, their pay checks were not; moreover, the so-called supervisory employees had all joined the union as regular cutters. On the basis of the evidence submitted, the impartial chairman ruled that the twelve cutters were not entitled to money damages. He did find, however, that a foreman not a member of the union had done some work belonging to the cutters; the employer, therefore, was fined forty-four dollars for breaching the agreement.[51]

In the second complaint of this case, the union charged that the workers in the firm's "outside" (or contracting) shops were getting no work while workers in the "inside" shop were busy, contrary to Article 3 of the agreement.[52] The employer answered that this provision calling for equal distribution of work was to apply only to situations specified in Article 4, and that none of the provisions in

---

[50] Lorwin, *op. cit.*, pp. 333-334.

[51] Raymond V. Ingersoll, Impartial Chairman, New York Cloak and Suit Industry, *Decisions*, Section 1, Case 26, pp. 20-23. These decisions, along with those of Impartial Chairmen Alger and Rosenblatt, are available in bound form at the National Coat and Suit Industry Recovery Board, New York City.

[52] Article 3 of the agreement with this company declared "that all former workers of the employer, whether retained in its inside shop or placed in any of the said contractors' shops, shall . . . receive the same wages, opportunity to work and treatment as if they had continued in the inside employ of the employer."

Article 4 required an equal division of work between employees in the "inside" and "outside" shops. On this complaint the impartial chairman ruled in favor of the union, deciding that the provisions of Article 3 were explicit and were not limited to the provisions of Article 4.[53]

A short time later an application by the firm for a rehearing of the case was denied by the impartial chairman.[54] Still later the union brought another complaint against the firm, this time alleging that the decision of the impartial chairman ordering equal distribution of work between the "inside" and "outside" shops was being violated. To this charge the employer answered that the character of his business had changed in such a way that most of his work was now done on individual samples, duplicates, special orders, and alterations, and that this kind of labor could be done best in the "inside" shop. The union rebutted that the "outside" workers, if they had remained "inside," could have done much of this work; that a clause in the agreement specifically provided that workers going into the "special and exclusive" shops of the manufacturer were to have the same work opportunities as though they had continued in the one shop; that work was still being sent out to firms entirely unconnected with the concern and that substantial orders were being given to one non-union shop which had not been unionized until after the complaint had been filed. The decision of Chairman Ingersoll ruled that the union had correctly interpreted the agreement, but that the evidence did not indicate deliberate bad faith on the part of the employer. He, therefore, ordered that the employer pay the aggrieved workers for three-fourths of the time they had lost on the basis of calculations submitted by the union.[55] He declared, further, that it was expected the employer would be able to manage his business so as to bring about an equalization of work in accordance with the agreement; also that he

[53] Ingersoll, *Decisions*, Section 1, Case 26, pp. 23-25.

[54] *Ibid.*, Section 2, Case 26 (b), pp. 1-2.

[55] A fair adjustment of money damages under these circumstances is no easy matter. In case of a violation by the employer, Article 24 of this agreement merely provided that: ". . . the employer shall pay to the union a sum of money sufficient to compensate the union for such violation." In computing the money damages, the union first presented figures taken from the books of the employer showing in detail the apparent discrepancies in the *number of days* worked from the time the contract was signed until November 22, 1924. The union then presented figures showing the *number of hours* that *each* employee actually worked in each trade or line of work. The average number of hours of employment for *all* the employees in each line of work was then computed. If it was found that any worker in one of the "special outside" shops worked less than the average number of hours for his line, the union claimed for him an amount of damages sufficient to bring him up to that average. *Ibid.*, Section 2, Case 26 (c), pp. 4-5.

would take precautions not to send any more work to a non-union shop.[56]

This series of cases suggests some of the difficult enforcement problems encountered in the women's garment industry. It is particularly helpful in indicating the part that the impartial chairman plays in handling these problems.[57] Many observers have emphasized the fact that even where an impartial chairman is present, most disputes are settled by direct negotiations between the parties themselves. This was, in fact, true of the period 1924-1926 in the New York coat and suit industry.[58] However, the influence of the impartial chairman's decisions was considerably greater than the relative number of cases coming before him would indicate. Employers who pondered the decision just discussed, for example, would think twice before they engaged in similar practices themselves. Moreover, as the number of decisions multiplied, covering a wider and wider variety of case situations, the enforcement work of the impartial chairman became more generally felt. To suggest the range of problems he confronted, the following table lists the complaints filed with the impartial chairman in the order of their frequency during the period between September 1924 and June 1926. The complaints listed here, which total ninety-six in number, refer only to disputes between the union and employers and not to controversies among employers alone. In a few instances more than one complaint was charged in a single case.

ARBITRATION CASES, 1924-1926

Nature of Complaint	*Frequency*
Reinstatement of workers	19
Discharge of workers	16
Eligibility for membership in employers' association	15
Stoppage by workers	10
Reorganization of firms	9
Refusal to pay wages; underpayments	7
Unequal distribution of work (mostly concerning workers in a given shop)	5
Dealings with non-union firms or non-union workers	4
Miscellaneous	11
Total	96

Source: Raymond V. Ingersoll, Impartial Chairman, New York Cloak and Suit Industry, *Decisions*, Sections 1-5 (September 15, 1924-May 3, 1926).

[56] *Ibid.*, Section 2, Case 26 (c), pp. 2-6. In April of the following year the union again filed a similar group of complaints against this firm. Impartial Chairman Ingersoll this time ordered the firm to pay additional damages to cover violations between November 22, 1924 and April 4, 1925 (amounting to about $4,900). He also ordered the firm to reopen certain "outside" shops which it had tried to dispense with and to cease making purchases from non-union jobbers. *Ibid.*, Section 3, Case 26 (concluded), pp. 34-44. This was one of the few instances where three complaints—at least in such a short period of time—were brought against a single firm.

[57] In the New York coat and suit industry the impartial chairman also arbitrates disputes among the various employer groups; this part of his work is not treated in the present study.

[58] Out of the thousands of complaints brought by the union and employers during this period, less than ten per cent reached the impartial chairman. Estimate of Raymond V. Ingersoll in an interview (October 23, 1939).

Of the ninety-six complaints filed during this period only ten were made by employers against the union. All of them charged illegal stoppages of work. Where it was found that the stoppages had occurred before hearings were held by the impartial chairman, he invariably ordered the men to return to work at once, in accordance with the terms of the agreement. Where the workers were still on strike twenty-four hours after the union had ordered them to return to their jobs, the impartial chairman ruled that the employer was justified in regarding their jobs as abandoned; under these circumstances Ingersoll ordered the union to cooperate with the aggrieved employer in securing new workers.[59] In the preparation of the present study no instances were discovered in which the union failed to abide by the decision of the impartial chairman in cases of this type.[60]

In connection with managerial policies, the most vexing problems coming before the impartial chairman concerned changes in production schedules, alterations in lines of work, reductions in volume of output, etc. Frequently, for example, employers wished to reorganize their firms on a reduced scale of operations because of a falling-off in business. The union, on the other hand, often suspected that the real motive was to escape union standards of employment. Under agreements with the employers' associations, employers were allowed to reorganize their firms only if "necessitated by a permanent curtailment" in their business.[61] In applying this provision to specific situations, the impartial chairman looked for evidence to indicate that the business of the employer was really little changed in volume; thus, in one case, he ruled against a manufacturer who wanted to reduce the number of employees in his "inside" shop when he found that the employer was continuing to send most of his work to "outside" shops.[62] He also refused to allow reorganizations where the reduction in the volume of business was only temporary in character. In one case he permitted the reorganization on the ground that the change in type of work was a genuine one; but he refused to allow the employer to change his entire staff of workers since the shift in his business was not of the sort that required it.[63]

Less sweeping changes introduced by employers in their shops

---

59 *Ibid.*, Section 3, Case 66, p. 6.

60 In an interview (October 23, 1939) Mr. Ingersoll corroborated this statement.

61 See Agreement between the Industrial Council of the Cloak, Suit and Skirt Manufacturers' Protective Association and the Joint Board of the Cloak, Skirt, Dress and Reefer Makers' Union of the I. L. G. W. U. (1924). This article appeared in the agreement with the manufacturers' association as long before as 1919.

62 Ingersoll, *Decisions*, Section 2, Case 43, p. 12.

63 *Ibid.*, Section 4, Cases 168, 168 (a), pp. 13-19. In these cases the firm was allowed to replace not more than one-third of its "present force." *Ibid.*, Section 4, Case 168, p. 17.

proved to be just as difficult of satisfactory settlement. Sometimes employers claimed they were producing more "special" or "sample" work than before and that this work could be done only by highly skilled workers or by the foremen themselves.[64] In this connection the impartial chairman was guided by the article in the agreements providing that work should be divided as equally as possible among all the workers in the shop competent to do the work.

A superficial examination would lead one to believe that the impartial chairman's work during these years met with great success. Actually, the program sponsored by the union and employers was encountering serious obstacles. As already noted, the chief one was due to the practice of sending out work to contractors. In dealing with this problem the impartial chairman was unable to take effective action, since the agreements at this time did not limit jobbers to a certain number of contractors. Nor did they require jobbers to distribute work equitably among their contractors. All that the agreements contained on this point was a general statement prohibiting dealings with non-union contractors. The omission had not a little to do with the violations of agreements which by 1926 had become widespread. There is little doubt that by that time the elaborate enforcement program had become seriously impaired. Cases began to arrive before the impartial chairman in which it appeared that sending work to non-union shops had been a regular and long-standing practice among certain employers; in one case the firm declared that: "This [practice] had been going on so openly and for such a long period that it assumed there was no serious objection by the union."[65]

Even statements of union officers during the period point to this conclusion. David Dubinsky, then manager of the cutters' local, had become sufficiently alarmed over the situation to declare: "The conditions in the shop . . . [during the latter part of 1925] have reached such a stage that the union must exert all its energies towards keeping a close watch over the shops."[66] The General Manager of the New York Cloak and Dress Joint Board, Louis Hyman, stated before the Governor's Advisory Commission that over fifty per cent of the members of the Industrial Council (the manufacturers' association) were not living up to the fourteen machine operator rule.[67] Even though this statement is misleading in that no employer could remain a member of the Industrial Council or of any of the other employer associations without the approval of the union, it nevertheless indicates the extent of the difficulties which the program was encountering. More-

[64] See the case where a jobber tried to classify sample tailor finishers as sample workers; the impartial chairman agreed with the union that their work was an integral part of garment production. *Ibid.*, Section 2, Case 41, pp. 10-11.

[65] *Ibid.*, Section 5, Case 247, p. 23.

[66] "The Week in Local 10," *Justice*, January 15, 1926, p. 12.

[67] "The Union's Position Outlined and Restated," *Justice*, March 12, 1926.

over, as time went on, agreement violations became more, rather than less, widespread. Indeed, what had previously been frequent evasion was to become, after 1926, a virtual breakdown in contractual relations. In the period between 1925 and 1929 the International Ladies' Garment Workers' Union was seriously weakened by internal strife and its officers no longer had as much time for policing the agreements as before. During the depression years of 1929 through 1932 the union's strength and enforcement activities were further reduced; at its low point in 1932 membership fell to about forty thousand.[68]

The question of why this elaborate enforcement program was unsuccessful is an important one. In regard to the period after 1926 the answer seems more obvious than for the earlier period. In the later period the sweep of events was simply too great for enforcement measures to remain effective; a union that is first split wide open by factional strife and, in addition, is subsequently obliged to cope with all the rigors of a major depression cannot be expected to maintain contractual standards in an industry where enforcement problems are difficult enough at best. These reasons, however, cannot be applied to the period between 1924 and 1926. The explanation advanced at the time by union officials was simple enough. They held that violations became widespread because the 1924 agreements did not provide for limitation of contractors and for equal distribution of the available work among them; nor did they place sufficient responsibility on the jobber for employment conditions in the shops of their contractors. The argument is a sound one. These omissions did seriously weaken the efforts to enforce the agreements, making it much more difficult for the union to check the spread of agreement violations, once they got under way.

On the other hand, even if the agreements had contained these provisions, serious enforcement difficulties would undoubtedly have occurred. In view of the economic characteristics of the industry and the barriers to enforcement described before, in view of the union's standards of employment and its failure to bring all competing producers under its system of agreements, a breakdown was hardly to be avoided. The handicaps under which union firms labored because of their agreements exerted a continual pressure on these firms to escape from the union's control. Economic difficulties besetting the entire industry intensified these pressures manifold. Thus, in 1925, when employment declined from the previous year and the average annual earnings of workers were lower,[69] violations of agreements be-

---

[68] Leo Wolman, *Ebb and Flow in Trade Unionism* (National Bureau of Economic Research, New York, 1936), Appendix, Table I, p. 183.

[69] Morris Kolchin, *Employment and Earnings of Workers, 1925* (submitted to the Governor's Advisory Commission, Cloak, Suit and Skirt Industry, New York City, 1926), p. 37.

came more widespread. During the same year factional disputes within the union increased in number and severity. These were the factors which undermined the union's agreements; and a mere tightening of enforcement procedures, as advocated by the union, would hardly have been enough to preserve the system of collective bargaining.

THE 1935-1940 PERIOD

The record of recent years may serve as a test of the hypothesis that enforcement difficulties in the field under examination are rooted in its economic characteristics and that, barring a fundamental reorganization of the industry, the union will always confront serious handicaps in enforcing its standards. Since 1932 the union has added large numbers to its membership; today it claims a membership of nearly 250,000.[70] The weaknesses due to factional strife have largely been eliminated. When the National Recovery Administration's program was launched in 1933 the union and employers under government sponsorship established a code of business practices and labor standards which included many of the principles long sought by the union. The code provided for the limitation of contractors, equitable distribution of work among contractors, and jobber responsibility for employment standards in contracting shops.[71] These provisions were also included in the agreements signed in 1933 and, despite the termination of the National Recovery program in 1935, they have appeared in all the other agreements since that time. In the current agreements the first two of these provisions follow the lines of the union demands of 1924, as described above. The third appears in different parts of the agreements; one provision obligates the jobber to pay his contractors enough so that they can comply with the agreement's wage-scale and still cover their overhead; another provision requires that piece-rates paid in the contracting shops are to be settled by direct dealings between the union and the jobber.[72]

Like their predecessors, the present agreements provide that there shall be no general strike, individual shop strike, or shop stoppage "pending the determination of any complaint or grievance."[73] In the event of a stoppage or shop strike, the union upon being notified obligates itself to return the strikers to their work within twenty-four hours. If there is a substantial violation of this provision, in the judgment of the impartial chairman, the employer's association has

---

[70] See p. 134, *supra*.

[71] *Code of Fair Competition for the Women's Coat and Suit Industry* (National Recovery Administration, 1933), Part I, Article 9.

[72] See, for example, Agreement between the Merchants' Ladies' Garment Association, Inc., and the I. L. G. W. U., etc. (1937), Articles 6 (g) and 14.

[73] *Ibid.*, Article 22.

the option of terminating the agreement. Similar prohibitions are placed on lock-outs called by employers.[74]

Despite these restrictions upon direct action and the elaborate machinery which has been established primarily with a view to avoiding such action, strikes still occur during the life of agreements. In New York City during 1938, for example, the International Ladies' Garment Workers' Union called approximately seventy-six strikes during the life of agreements, involving about 2,775 workers. Forty-one of these strikes were in the coat and suit branch of the industry and twenty-seven in the dress branch.[75] These estimates, which are based on strike reports sent to the United States Bureau of Labor Statistics, considerably understate the actual situation, since the bureau's strike reports exclude strikes lasting less than a day and strikes involving less than six workers. Many strikes occurring during the life of agreements in the women's garment industry are of this sort. The Industrial Council of Cloak, Suit and Skirt Manufacturers, for example, reports that during 1938 ninety-four stoppages, involving 1,577 workers, were called against its members alone.[76] Membership in the Industrial Council at this time totalled about three hundred firms. Even the Bureau of Labor Statistics figures suggest there is extensive unrest in the industry. The bureau figures already noted refer simply to New York City. This is the area in which the arbitration system has reached its fullest development. Yet strikes during the life of agreements in that region form a large proportion of all strikes occurring in the industry. During 1938, according to strike reports sent to the bureau, the International Ladies' Garment Workers' Union conducted a total of 320 strikes, in which 24,458 workers were engaged. These included not only strikes occurring during the life of agreements but also strikes to organize non-union shops in various parts of the country and to renew agreements. Of all strikes, then, in which the union participated during 1938, nearly twenty-four per cent were called under agreements in New York City; and of the total number of workers who engaged in strike actions during the year, over ten per cent were New York City workers who participated in strikes while agreements were still in effect.

---

[74] *Ibid.*

[75] The writer secured these figures from strike reports sent to the U. S. Bureau of Labor Statistics. The figures, however, have not been checked by any member of the bureau's staff. Beginning in 1938, the bureau received full cooperation from the union in the collection of the figures, so within the limits indicated, they may be taken as reasonably reliable. The figures do not correspond exactly to classifications used by the union since the bureau sometimes classifies a strike action against a group of firms as a single strike; the I. L. G. W. U., on the other hand, always classifies actions against each firm as a separate strike.

[76] Letter to the writer, dated November 22, 1940, from Samuel F. Klein, Executive Director of the Industrial Council of Cloak, Suit and Skirt Manufacturers. Figures from the union were not obtainable.

Regarding the issues and causes underlying these strikes in New York City, in every instance the union alleged that the employers were violating the terms of agreements. The data do not permit any clear-cut classification of the alleged violations. When the material available for the preceding year of 1937 is also utilized, however, this phase of the picture becomes somewhat clearer. Most of the complaints charged wage-underpayments of one sort or another and violations of piece-rate standards. A good many alleged that non-union workers were employed or that standards were lowered through a shift in the place of operations. Some declared that employees were working on holidays and after hours or that rules about the distribution of available work were being violated. In a few instances the charges were without much foundation, serving simply as an excuse for the union to extend its influence and control. In the great majority of cases, however, the charges of violation were apparently well founded.

As a typical instance, the union local charged an employer with operating a "dummy" subsidiary elsewhere in New York City under non-union conditions. Ninety-four workers walked out and after eleven days a settlement was reached. Under its terms the employer admitted that the subsidiary belonged to him and promised that union standards would be met.[77] In the case of one coat and suit firm the employer resigned from the employers' association and his firm's operations were closed down. Soon afterwards, the union cryptically reports, this case was "settled."[78] In still another case the union took similar action against a coat manufacturer who had transferred his main operations from New York to Lindenhurst, New Jersey, after having previously moved to Westbury, Long Island; in this instance also the union secured a satisfactory adjustment.[79] In the case of another strike in the coat and suit industry called during the life of an agreement, the employer had refused to abide by a decision of the impartial chairman.[80] In another, the union called a strike against an employer who had allegedly violated the agreement's wage-scale many times. The employer retorted that the union had acted in an unreasonable and arbitrary manner during negotiations over these issues. After a seven day strike involving 150 workers a compromise solution was reached.[81] In another case the union called a strike on the ground that the employer had disregarded overtime provisions of the agreement. At the same time the union was engaged in a juris-

[77] Strike called by I. L. G. W. U. local, New York City, May 17, 1937. Because of the confidential nature of this information no further identification of these strikes is possible.

[78] Strike called by I. L. G. W. U. local, New York City, January 3, 1938.

[79] Strike called by I. L. G. W. U. local, New York City, February 10, 1938.

[80] Strike called by I. L. G. W. U. local, New York City, July 28, 1938.

[81] Strike called by I. L. G. W. U. local, New York City, March 3, 1937.

dictional dispute with another labor organization, and this apparently was the real cause of the dispute. It is not clear just how this particular controversy terminated; but whatever the outcome, the employer was obliged to bear the brunt of the cost.[82]

After a careful study of hundreds of these disturbances it must be confessed that exclusive blame for their occurrence cannot be ascribed to one side or the other. In some cases the local union acted in an arbitrary and irresponsible manner; in others, the employer was primarily at fault. To an impartial investigator, however, this aspect of the problem seems somewhat irrelevant. The important point is that in the face of vigorous efforts on the side of both employers and union to eliminate these disruptions, they still occur. Despite the elaborate procedure that has been constructed to handle disputes without resort to strikes, they are far from being a thing of the past. Whether the impartial arbitration machinery can go much further in this direction is extremely doubtful. In an industry in which employers have countless ways to escape standards established by the union and in which the pressure to commit such acts is so great, local union groups sometimes feel it is absolutely imperative for them to assume all the duties of sheriff, prosecutor, jury, and judge. If they always waited for the wheels of the impartial arbitration machinery to begin to turn, they would frequently find that the worst of the damage had already been done. Many employers in this field are prepared to close down their shops after four to six months of operations and start up next season in quite a different locality. If they can escape the notice of the union's agents for two or three months and a similar length of time passes before the impartial chairman's office takes action, their main objective is achieved. It is little wonder that on occasion the union feels that it must act with the greatest possible vigor and dispatch.

Today enforcement problems in the New York coat and suit industry have been greatly complicated by the spread of piece-rate methods of wage payment. Approximately sixty-five per cent of the city's output is now under this system of wage payment.[83] The 1933 agreements were the first since the end of the previous war to permit the piece-rate as well as the week-work system.[84] The reasons for the change throw considerable light on the difficulties besetting this industry.

During the 1920s more and more firms operated under piece-rate conditions, although the agreements supposedly prohibited the prac-

---

[82] Strike called by I. L. G. W. U. local, New York City, May 28, 1937.

[83] Letter to the writer, dated December 17, 1940, from Samuel F. Klein.

[84] Agreement between the Merchants' Ladies' Garment Association and the I. L. G. W. U., etc. (1937), Article 10. Piece-rate payment has long been the prevailing practice in the dress branch of the industry.

tice. This development occurred in conjunction with the spread of the jobber-contractor system of production already discussed. At this time the principle of jobber responsibility for employment conditions in contract shops was not yet incorporated in the agreements. One means that was used to get around union standards was to introduce piece-rate systems in contract firms. This put the "inside" manufacturers at a serious competitive disadvantage, explaining in large measure the high mortality rate of these firms and the movement of manufacturers into the rank of the jobbers. By 1933 the situation was so serious that permission was granted manufacturers and other firms to introduce piece-rate methods of wage payment. The union hoped that this change would remove the competitive handicaps under which union firms were operating.

Under the present agreements the procedure involves fixing piece-rates in such a way that a reasonably competent worker will earn the amount agreed upon for his type of work. Thus, one agreement specifies that machine pressers "of average skill" are to be paid at rates which will yield them $1.81½ an hour. The same agreement provides that no machine presser is to receive less than $1.43 an hour. Similar average and minimum standards are provided for other operations such as those performed by skirt operators, piece tailors, and jacket under-pressers.[85]

Next, the union and employers must classify every job operation in all of the shops in accordance with the general piece-rate classifications of the agreement. These individual job classifications depend not only on the type of job involved but on the price category of the particular garment under consideration. As regards the manufacturing shops, these matters are ironed out in dealings between the employers and the union. As for the contracting shops, the individual shop classifications are worked out in direct dealings between the union and the jobbers who send the contractors their work. Detailed classification sheets are made up for each shop. If at this point a dispute over the classifications cannot be settled, it is referred for decision to a branch of the arbitration machinery known as the Labor Bureau.

This bureau, although financed by the National Recovery Board of the coat and suit industry, works in conjunction with the office of the impartial chairman.[86] The bureau employs a staff of "deputies" whose chief duty is to settle disputes over the classification of job operations in the various shops. Just how much authority is vested

---

85 *Ibid.*, Article 10.

86 The Recovery Board was set up by joint action of the union and of the employers in 1935 for the purpose of preserving the fair trade and employment standards established under the N. R. A. code for the coat and suit industry. See F. Nathan Wolf, "The Only Voluntary Code," *Justice*, March 1, 1938, p. 15.

in the bureau the agreements do not make clear.[87] If a manufacturer refuses to comply with its findings, he is subject to a fine or even to expulsion from his association. Similar penalties apply to contractors and jobbers. In practice, however, the penalty provisions are rarely invoked in disputes over piece-rates. Compliance rests almost entirely on voluntary acceptance of the decisions of the Labor Bureau.[88] Indeed, one of the main criticisms raised by certain employer spokesmen is that the Labor Bureau really has no power to settle disputes over piece-rate classifications.[89]

Disputes over the classification of various manufacturing operations for the purpose of setting piece-rates are numerous. Certain operations, such as making button-holes, are fairly uniform and present no great problems. But there are others like the making of pockets and sleeves, where the matter of styling is important. Here, classification becomes difficult because of the considerable variety of operations involved. Moreover, before specific piece-rates can be determined, account must be taken of the price of the particular garment being manufactured. Such complexities make disputes almost unavoidable.

But the problem of enforcement does not end even at this point. After a firm begins production of a certain line of garments, the employer may decide to make various alterations. He may want to have a different neck cut or another type of sleeve. He may also decide to put the garment in a different wholesale price classification than before. Changes of this sort affect the earnings of workers and require corresponding changes in the schedule of piece-rates. Frequently employers make these changes without prior notice to the union. If they result in lower wages than the workers had expected, protests soon come to the union agent. He tries to secure an adjustment with the employer, but if he is unsuccessful, the disputes are referred to the Labor Bureau for settlement. The office of the impartial chairman is also on the alert for firms trying to evade piece-rate standards. A staff of accountants is attached to this office and part of their duty is to detect violations of this type.[90] The staff numbers between five and thirty accountants, depending on the time of year and on the amount of work to be done. Since these men have the further task of checking on violations of other provisions of the agreement, in ad-

---

[87] See, for example, Agreement between the Industrial Council of Cloak, Suit and Skirt Manufacturers, Inc., and the I. L. G. W. U., etc. (1937), Articles 13 and 14.

[88] Interview with Louis Heit, Director of the Labor Bureau, Coat and Suit Industry, New York City, June 16, 1940.

[89] Letter to the writer, December 17, 1940, from Samuel F. Klein.

[90] This differs from the procedure in the dress branch of the industry where the union's own accountants do such work.

dition to piece-rate standards, their work is described at a later point in the discussion.

In handling disputes over the settlement of piece-rates, the union has dealt directly with the jobbers. The determination of piece-rates for the contracting shops, in the first instance, is fixed in this way. Once the rates are fixed, moreover, the jobbers guarantee that they will be enforced. If a contractor refuses to abide by these standards, the jobber agrees not to send him any more work. But if he persists in doing so, he is subject to a fine or expulsion from his association.

Piece-rate disputes, however, are not primarily an indication of procedural difficulties in setting or enforcing rates. Rather they reflect the competitive burden under which union firms labor. It was pointed out earlier that the union allowed firms to change from week-work to piece-work in 1933, because under the old system the union firms were operating under a serious handicap. The same problem persists today in an only slightly different form. There are enough firms outside the union's system of agreements to put firms within the system at a marked disadvantage. The latter are therefore under continuous pressure to violate the union's piece-rate standards. This compulsion is the chief cause of most of the disputes over piece-rates in the New York coat and suit industry.

In this phase of the enforcement program the union's part has been chiefly one of ferreting out violators and reporting them to the accounting staff of the impartial chairman. The union has been equally active in policing other provisions of the agreement. In fact, the enforcement program, while essentially similar to its counterpart of the earlier period, is being pushed more aggressively than ever before. The various locals, for example, have appointed Building Committees whose duty it is to patrol the shops, particularly for the purpose of checking on hour standards and holiday regulations. The system of "controllers" has been broadened to include out-of-town employers who have agreements with the union; thus, in August 1935, the cutters' local reported that their "controllers" had just checked on employers in several small towns near New York, and found that wages being paid to cutters were generally well below the minimum specified in the agreement.[91] Vigorous measures have also been taken against union members who accept employment at standards below those established in the agreement. The cutters, for example, passed a resolution imposing a fine of fifty dollars on any member who violated the rule against working more than thirty-five hours a week; if repeated, the cutter could be expelled from the union.[92]

In recent years the Cloak Joint Board has attempted to strengthen its enforcement program by bringing all the "inside" and contracting

---

91 "Among the Cutters of New York," *Justice*, September 1, 1935, p. 15.
92 *Ibid.*

shops of a particular jobber or manufacturer under the supervision of a single business agent. Previously agents had been assigned to districts, not to firms. The union's enforcement program in the New York coat and suit market is now centered in the Control Department, established by the Cloak Joint Board in February 1938. This department has evolved an interesting enforcement technique. Under the present agreement jobbers must deliver and receive goods in trucks driven by members of Local 102, affiliated with the Cloak Joint Board. A bottleneck is thus created, making it easier for the union to keep a continuous check on jobbers suspected of dealing with non-union or non-designated contractors. The truckers are required to make reports to the Control Department, showing the destination, assortment, and quantities of each delivery made from the jobber's office to the various contractors; before any delivery can be made, the truckers' reports must be verified by one of the inspectors from the Control Department.[93] These reports are examined in the Control Department to see if any of the jobbers are dealing with non-union or non-designated contractors. If so, word is sent to the department or district office of the union in whose jurisdiction they fall, and the business agents, in turn, take whatever steps seem advisable.

Another part of the strategy brings into action the shop chairmen of the contracting shops to which the goods are delivered. They send daily reports to the business agents of their department or district office, showing the quantity of goods received and the amount produced each day. Since the business agents have already been supplied with copies of the corresponding reports made by the truckers, they can quickly detect any discrepancies and act accordingly. If full cooperation can be secured from the truckers and shop chairmen, this new enforcement instrument promises to be an effective one.[94] At all events, the new weapon gives the union greater power to prevent violations of standards.

Moreover, the impartial chairman seems to be in a better position to help in the enforcement program than in the earlier period. In the 1926 agreements he was given the power to investigate on his own motion any firms suspected of violating the agreement. So far as the present study is concerned, this marks the most significant development in his work since the 1924-1926 period. Today, a staff of accountants is attached to his office which carries on investigations along this line. They have access under the agreements to all books and

---

93 There were nine such inspectors on duty in the garment district during the day and two during the night at the time the program first got under way in 1938.

94 The foregoing was taken from an article by Isidore Nagler, "Cloak Control in New York Market Analyzed," *Justice*, June 1, 1938, p. 7.

records of employers, and failure to meet such a request is considered a violation of the agreements. The accountants are especially watchful for any dealings with non-union or non-designated contractors and for attempts to distribute work inequitably among them. They also are on guard against attempts to pay wages below the prescribed scale and to classify job operations in a manner different from that agreed upon. These additional powers have made the impartial chairman's office even more of an enforcement agency than before. Technically, he still cannot move to eliminate agreement violations until a complaint reaches his office; but since investigations on his own initiative frequently provide the evidence on which such complaints are made, this distinction should not be overemphasized. On the whole, the augmented authority suggests that the impartial chairman wields more influence than in the earlier period and that his effectiveness as an enforcement officer is substantially greater.

For the most part, his policing work follows the lines of the earlier period although the specific issues most frequently encountered have undergone a change. In this respect, it is illuminating to compare the charges most often brought before Sol A. Rosenblatt with those brought before Mr. Ingersoll. (Mr. Rosenblatt preceded James J. Walker, the present impartial chairman.) The table below presents this comparison for two periods: the first covers the twenty months between September 1924 and June 1926; the second deals with the twenty-one months between August 1935 and June 1937. During the first period, ninety-six complaints involving union-employer relations were filed; during the second period there were 101 complaints, including eight concerning inequitable distribution of work among contractors.

COMPARISON OF ARBITRATION CASES
(*1924-1926*)
Chairman Ingersoll

Nature of Complaint	*Frequency*
Reinstatement of workers	19
Discharge of workers	16
Eligibility for membership in employers' association	15
Stoppage by workers	10
Reorganization of firms	9
Refusal to pay wages; underpayments	7
Unequal distribution of work (mostly concerning workers in a given shop)	5
Dealings with non-union firms or non-union workers	4
Miscellaneous	11
Total	96

(*1935-1937*)
Chairman Rosenblatt

Nature of Complaint	*Frequency*
Refusal or concealment of records	17
Non-union or non-designated dealings	17
Non-compliance with agreement or impartial chairman's decision	10
Stoppage by workers	9
Inequitable distribution of work (among contractors)	8
Eligibility for membership in employers' association	7
Price settlements; refusal to submit lines	6
Refusal to pay wages; underpayments	6
Miscellaneous	21
Total	101

Source: Ingersoll, *Decisions*, Sections 1-5 (September 15, 1924-May 31, 1926) and Sol A. Rosenblatt, *Decisions*, Sections 1-2 (August 16, 1935-June 12, 1937).

The chief differences appearing in the two series can be attributed to clauses in the agreements that have been added since the earlier period. Almost all of the cases classified under the first three headings in the 1935-1937 period, as well as those concerning inequitable distribution of work among contractors and price settlements, relate to new provisions in the agreements which limit jobbers to a certain number of contractors and which establish a procedure for settling piece-rate disputes.[95] The complaint that occurred most frequently grew out of attempts by employers to defeat enforcement of these recently established principles. In the earlier period, on the other hand, the impartial chairman was most often faced with questions about the rights and duties of individual workers and employers under the agreements; by 1935 these principles were pretty well clarified and cases of this sort could generally be settled by direct dealings between the employers and the union. Complaints charging stoppages of work were about as frequent in the later period as before.

While the policing agencies that have been described seem more adequately equipped to do their work than ever before, enforcement problems, as already indicated, still present serious difficulties in the New York coat and suit industry. It is probably true that evasions of contractual standards are considerably more rare today than in the period 1924-1926. The improvements in the enforcement program have gone a long way toward eliminating these difficulties. Regarding the problem of non-union dealings on the part of jobbers, for example, a comprehensive investigation by the union in 1938 disclosed that only four per cent of all garments in the New York coat and suit industry were being made in non-union contracting shops.[96] But a spokesman

---

95 Thus, cases involving non-unions or non-designated dealings were much more frequent in the second period than in the first, since in the first period jobbers were not restricted to a certain number of contractors.

96 Nagler, "Cloak Control in New York Market Analyzed," *Justice*, June 1, 1938, p. 7.

for the "inside" manufacturers reports that on August 16, 1937, there were 135 non-union firms in the New York coat and suit industry. On February 13, 1939, there were 181 non-union firms. In 1938 the latter firms had a turnover only slightly in excess of $22,000,000, a relatively small percentage of the total sales in the New York area. However, in February 1939, according to the same spokesman, non-union operations accounted for twelve per cent of total output in the New York City area.[97]

What is more significant, many New York coat and suit firms are apparently union firms in name only. Violations of piece-rate standards established by the agreements are particularly widespread. The following statement by a vice-president of the union may be an exaggeration, but it is also a straw in the wind:

> Everybody knows, and it is an open secret that the garments which the jobber displays in his showroom when prices [piece-rates] are to be settled, and the garments which are later sent out to the contracting shops, are as different as day is from night.[98]

This statement is corroborated by a spokesman for the coat and suit manufacturers. The executive director of the Industrial Council of Cloak, Suit and Skirt Manufacturers characterizes the piece-rate structure in the New York coat and suit industry as an "anarchy of rates." As matters now stand, he asserts, piece-rates are not being paid as settled; instead garments are being "settled in one grade and produced in another."[99] Consequently, as already emphasized, employers who try to live up to the agreements are operating at a competitive disadvantage. This inequitable situation has come about in various ways:

> In some piece-work shops, the 1937 [ten per cent wage] increase has been eliminated by union officials, either by arriving at the final price, with the ten per cent included, or by reducing the individual items, principally differentials, to the extent of ten per cent.
>
> Collusive deals between workers and their employers have added to the competitive disadvantages of contract-abiding firms.
>
> The rates of pay in the section work shops, operating on either a piece-work or week-work basis, are not based upon any standards that enable them to be interpreted in terms of the agreement. Different rates of pay prevail in week-work and section work shops in different sections of the city.
>
> Where no special consideration is given in the settlement of piece-rates, either through price committees, business agents or deals with workers, firms are

---

97 *Report on the Labor Situation in the Coat and Suit Industry* by Samuel F. Klein, Executive Director of the Industrial Council of Cloak, Suit and Skirt Manufacturers, given at the annual meeting of the organization on February 28, 1939. This report is available at the office of the Industrial Council, New York City, in mimeographed form.

98 Statement by Joseph Breslaw, Vice-president, I. L. G. W. U., *Justice*, May 1, 1935, p. 10.

99 Statement by Samuel F. Klein at a conference between the I. L. G. W. U. and the coat and suit trade associations, May 3, 1939, p. 5. This statement is available at the office of the Industrial Council of Cloak, Suit and Skirt Manufacturers, Inc., New York City.

making more desperate efforts than ever to escape contractual obligations. Reports of firms joining the "special privilege" contingent in the trade are often heard.[100]

The same spokesman contends that employment standards other than piece-rate provisions of the agreements are also being disregarded. He charges that secret wage concessions in week-work shops have been made, sometimes in return for a guaranteed period of employment; that the provision in the agreements requiring every shop under agreement with the union to employ at least fourteen operators is in many instances not being observed; that some firms in the popular-priced field, nominally under agreements, continue to operate in general disregard of union standards. According to him:

> Small a few years ago, the production volume of these firms has increased to a point where it has the earmarks of a monopoly on certain types of goods and menaces the survival of their legitimate contemporaries. The latter have seen much of their mail order and chain store patronage preempted by these nominally union firms. Twelve houses in this aristocracy of the cloak trade did a volume of $11,000,000 last year [1938], according to a conservative interpretation of authentic records.[101]

Instead of a uniform system of labor standards, there is really a wide variety of systems. In this connection, the executive director of the Industrial Council makes the following assertion:

> There are among others, the Brooklyn system, the New Jersey system, the "special dispensation" system, the section work system and the system in which week-work finishing converts Grade One operating into Grade Three garments. There is the system of week-work firms that pay below the scale and those that pay well above it. There is a dual system in piece-work that contains as many as, or more than, the inequalities existing between piece-work and week-work. There are numerous other systems, all of which conspire to jeopardize the future of those who adhere to the letter of the piece-work provisions of the current agreements.[102]

It is not surprising to find that the spokesman for the "inside" manufacturers views the present situation with alarm; membership in the association of manufacturers—the Industrial Council—has been falling rapidly. In 1933 membership totalled 442; in May 1939, the total was only 259.[103] He recommends that the Labor Bureau be

---

100 *Ibid.*, p. 6.

101 *Report on the Labor Situation in the Coat and Suit Industry* by Samuel F. Klein given at the annual meeting of the Industrial Council of the Cloak, Suit, and Skirt Manufacturers, Inc., February 28, 1939, pp. 14-15.

102 *Ibid.*, p. 13.

103 Statement by Samuel F. Klein at a conference between the I. L. G. W. U. and the coat and suit trade associations, May 3, 1939, p. 2. Changes in the membership of the manufacturers' and jobbers' associations in the New York coat and suit industry between August 16, 1937, and February 13, 1939, are as follows:

	—*Number of Members*—	
	Aug. 16, 1937	Feb. 13, 1939
Industrial Council	342	266
Merchants' Ladies' Garment Association	170	159
Infants' and Children's Coat Association	77	87
American Coat and Suit Association (manufacturing members only)	3	3

given authority to establish and enforce piece-rates; that the Labor Bureau in its efforts to establish uniform labor costs be given authority to investigate inequalities in rates between piece-work and week-work firms; that the advantages now enjoyed by nominally unionized firms be eliminated; that the union and employer associations make joint efforts to organize non-union firms. To this end the executive director of the Industrial Council believes that authority in the union over piece-rate negotiations should be centralized. At the present time, he asserts, local and regional union leaders are still able to grant special favors to employers or to withhold them pretty much as they please.[104]

In the negotiations for new agreements in 1940, spokesmen for the "inside" manufacturers urged that a commission be set up to investigate and act on these issues. As a result, a Board of Stability and Control was established. It is made up of "one representative of the union and one representative of each employer association under collective agreement with the union."[105] This board is empowered to ascertain whether the agreements are being enforced; to verify the weekly reports on garments sent to contracting shops and the reports on piece-rates and earnings of employees which employers are required to file with the impartial chairman; to investigate the extent of non-union production in New York, Pennsylvania, Connecticut, New Jersey, and Massachusetts and to adopt a program to eliminate competition from this source; to ascertain who produces garments below employment standards set by the agreements; to adopt a program which will achieve the following purposes:

> . . . curb the practices of purchasers who (1) create unfair competition between manufacturers, jobbers, contractors and sub-manufacturers who are in contractual relations with the union and manufacturers, jobbers, contractors and sub-manufacturers who manufacture garments under sub-standard and non-union conditions, and/or who (2) induce the breach of existing collective agreements which manufacturers, jobbers, contractors and sub-manufacturers have entered into with the union, and/or (3) whose practices undermine or cause deterioration of the labor standards and conditions of work prevailing throughout the industry.[106]

The decisions of the Board of Stability and Control, if unanimous, are binding upon the parties signing the agreements. If the board cannot reach a unanimous decision, the issue is to be decided by the impartial chairman.

CONCLUSIONS

It is not yet possible to say what steps this board will take. It may be, as the union contends, that the charges of the "inside" manu-

---

[104] *Ibid.*, pp. 7-8. Mr. Klein makes other recommendations bearing on related problems.

[105] Agreement between the Industrial Council of Cloak, Suit and Skirt Manufacturers, Inc., and the I. L. G. W. U., etc., Article 44, as amended July 19, 1940. The 1940 agreements took the form of a series of amendments to the previous agreements, signed July 12, 1937.

[106] *Ibid.*, Amendment 5 to the agreement signed July 12, 1937.

facturers are exaggerated. But if true only in part they contain for the union an ominous warning. If the International Ladies' Garment Workers' Union hopes to maintain labor standards in the coat and suit industry, it must address itself to the economic difficulties confronting union firms.[107] At the present time employers who try to comply with the agreements appear to be operating at a serious competitive disadvantage. This handicap must be removed. As suggested by the executive director of the Industrial Council, the problem will have to be approached in various ways. First, non-union firms that are in competition with union firms will have to be organized and brought under the standards of the agreements. Second, enforcement of the agreements will have to be tightened. This means taking action against firms that are at present union in name only. It also means taking disciplinary action against union members who work below standard rates.

These measures, however, would simply carry forward a program already in effect. It seems clear that these steps would not be enough to place collective bargaining in this industry on a secure footing. Positive measures more immediately effective in removing the disadvantages under which union firms now operate must be devised. These measures need not lower or imperil existing employment standards in union shops to any serious degree. Union shops might be granted greater preference in the market for finished garments.[108] Doubtless, production costs in many union firms could be reduced. Up-to-date machine equipment might be installed. Materials might be furnished to union firms at lower costs than at present. Other efficiencies might be worked out in the distribution and sale of the finished product. Still other improvements might be obtained through changes in internal shop management—rearrangement of existing facilities, re-routing of materials, changes in the distribution of work, shifts in the duties and responsibilities of certain types of workers, and careful classification of individual workers according to their daily output. A system of production which contains many possibilities is the section work method. Under the present plan all tasks before a garment goes to a machine are performed by a single worker. Thus, the same operator makes the outer shell of the garment, joins the parts of the lining together, and with the help of a machine attaches the lining to the body. This procedure, in which full-fledged mechanics are employed, is known as the over-all system. In the section work system, these operations are performed by several workers, the number depending on the development attained in the shop. In the men's clothing industry, where the section work system was first introduced about

[107] Presumably this applies to the dress branch of the women's garment industry as well.

[108] Some steps, of course, have already been taken toward this end in connection with the union label system.

thirty years ago, machine work on a man's suit jacket is divided into approximately one hundred and fifty separate operations.[109]

Of course, serious difficulties would have to be overcome before such a system of production could be established in the coat and suit industry. In the first place, women's garments are less standardized than men's clothing because the style factor is more important. This makes it harder to subdivide operations and put production on a large-scale basis.[110] On the other hand, large-size firms were the dominant type of organization before the previous World War. Apparently a system of subdivided operations is therefore possible. More formidable is the question of labor displacement. If such a system were introduced, the older and more skilled workers would be displaced by younger workers. The bulk of the union's strength is among the former group. Consequently, the union is opposed to the section work system. Perhaps a compromise of some sort can be reached. The scheme might be introduced gradually. Efforts might be made to transfer workers faced with displacement. Funds might be advanced by both the union and employers to workers deprived of their jobs.

The union should not hesitate to spend time, effort, and money in seeking improvements along all or several of these lines. What is at stake is the survival of the New York coat and suit industry—on which the union's own life depends. This is not to say that the union has blocked efforts to improve economic conditions within the industry. Indeed the union has probably contributed more to the development of the industry than any other element in the field. Today all sections of the trade look to the union for leadership. But this makes it all the more important for the union to meet its economic responsibilities in a statesmanlike manner. These are obligations which must be faced sooner or later under every long-established system of collective bargaining. In the New York coat and suit industry the union has apparently achieved the highest employment standards that conditions within the industry, as it is now organized, will allow. Unless the union grants relief to union firms and takes steps to help reorganize the industry, its system of collective agreements will be destroyed. During the mid-twenties, as already shown, the destruction was complete. The next chapter deals with another system of collective bargaining where the same result occurred.

---

109 In the dress branch of the New York women's garment industry at the present time, the union is making an effort to improve production methods. Under the 1941 agreement an "efficiency department" has been set up in the office of the impartial chairman to assist employers in bettering the efficiency of their shops. Provision has also been made to raise funds in an effort to increase New York City's importance as a style center. *New York Times*, February 19, 1941, p. 37. Efficiency rules for shops making low-priced dresses were announced by Impartial Chairman Harry Uviller in July 1941. *New York Times*, July 29, 1941, p. 29.

110 Carter L. Goodrich and others, *Migration and Economic Opportunity* (Philadelphia: University of Pennsylvania Press, 1936), pp. 346-348.

CHAPTER VIII

BREAKDOWN IN THE COAL INDUSTRY

A union cannot feel that its position in an industry is secure even when it has agreements covering most employers in a particular market. It must also reckon with the economic characteristics and problems of the industry. A union which disregards economic conditions may well contribute to the industry's difficulties and even undermine its own position. The story of labor relations in the New York coat and suit industry, as shown in the previous chapter, illustrates this point. An even more striking example is afforded by the bituminous coal industry between the years 1920 and 1928.

At the beginning of this eight-year period there was a comprehensive system of union agreements in the bituminous coal industry. Chief in importance were the agreements covering the Central Competitive Field. This field included the soft coal sections of Illinois, Indiana, Ohio, and western Pennsylvania, which in 1920 accounted for about one-third of the nation's bituminous coal output. Basic terms of the agreements were formulated at joint interstate conferences of union and employer spokesmen. These terms also guided negotiations in the Southwest and other important coal fields. By 1920 the United Mine Workers had even been able to extend its system of agreements to many areas hitherto non-union. By the end of 1927, however, the greater part of this structure lay in ruins.

The path leading to this climax was marked, of course, by many serious disputes. Spokesmen for both sides, for the most part, viewed these controversies in narrow and vindictive terms; only a few treated them simply as symptoms of the industry's difficulties. Soon after 1920 a mounting number of firms, first in the South, then in the West, and finally in the North, terminated contractual dealings with the union. These steps, the union declared, repudiated the agreements and in many cases directly violated their terms. Convincing evidence on the latter issue is lacking. The one area in which many employers probably violated their agreements with the union was the southern coal fields. In any event, many firms went non-union. In terminating relations, employers contended that the United Mine Workers were trying to hold union employers to a scale of wages which, in effect, gave more and more of their business to non-union operators. It was the union's obstinate refusal to accept a lower rate, they argued, which caused all the difficulty.

This spirit of personal animosity characterized almost all discussion of the problem. Testifying before a Senate committee in 1928, John L. Lewis, President of the United Mine Workers of America, in language both picturesque and exaggerated, hurled many charges against the employers. At one point he quoted President Wilson as saying that "faithful compliance with agreements" was now an accepted principle in American life. Mr. Lewis continued as follows:

> I repeat that statement: "A principle now accepted in American life." Gentlemen of the committee, accepted by whom? Not by the Pittsburgh Coal Company. Not by the Consolidation Coal Company. Not by the Bethlehem Mines Corporation. Not by the Buffalo, Rochester and Pittsburgh Railroad Company. Not by any employer who has struck down, violated, and trampled upon his agreement with the United Mine Workers of America, all of whom have dishonored the very principle of collective bargaining in America . . . . Surely somewhere in this broad land of ours, surely somewhere in the various branches of our Government, there is some balm of Gilead, there is some relief for our members. Surely there is somewhere that public opinion can be crystallized in America, to the end that its moral force may be felt, a forum where our people will receive a modicum of justice.[1]

In explaining how these agreements were undermined, spokesmen for the union placed considerable emphasis on efforts made by various railroads to break the strength of their organization. It was their contention that railroads like the Pennsylvania, New York Central, and Baltimore and Ohio, as the most important buyers of coal in the country, were taking advantage of their position to discriminate against union employers in favor of non-union operators. According to spokesmen for the United Mine Workers, this policy was pursued until almost all of the operators were faced with the choice of going non-union or going out of business. In summing up its case, the union made this declaration:

> We charge that full responsibility for the present deplorable conditions in the above-named coal mining fields rests upon the shoulders of those coal companies that so brazenly and immorally repudiated their agreements with the United Mine Workers of America, and those great interstate railroad companies that forced these companies to take such action. We charge that the present chaotic condition in the bituminous coal industry is due solely to this railroad-coal company conspiracy.[2]

The employers countered with arguments couched in language that was equally personal and vindictive. In reply to a letter of inquiry from John D. Rockefeller, Jr., principal owner of the Consoli-

---

[1] *Conditions in the Coal Fields of Pennsylvania, West Virginia, and Ohio*, Hearings before the Committee on Interstate Commerce, U. S. Senate, 70th Cong., 1st sess., pursuant to S. Res. 105 (1928), pp. 422-423.

[2] *Ibid.*, Statement by the United Mine Workers of America addressed to members of the Committee on Interstate Commerce, dated January 17, 1928, p. 9. For railroads which allegedly discriminated against union producers, see *ibid.*, pp. 5-8.

dation Coal Company, C. W. Watson, President of the company, stated:

When the Consolidation Coal Company found that its cost of producing coal was far in excess of the best price obtainable, it notified Mr. Lewis and his representatives that its mines would have to be closed indefinitely. This action was taken only after months of effort on the part of the management to avoid it. A state of widespread suffering, due to idle mines and idle men, did not disturb the officers of the United Mine Workers, nor was any criticism forthcoming on that score. On the contrary, they have insisted that the Consolidation Coal Company should continue to enforce, by the duress of unemployment, conditions of work and wages which this union itself has been unable to maintain over its own members. In other words, it has seemed to be Mr. Lewis's contention that either our men should work under conditions of his choice or they must not be allowed to work at all.[3]

As for the alleged conspiracy on the part of railroads against the union, the employers explained that it was merely a matter of buying coal where it was cheapest. Since the non-union mines during the period 1920-1927 were operating under lower wage-scales and since the cost of labor formed about two-thirds of the total cost of mining coal, the non-union operators could sell coal to the railroads at lower prices. Therefore they got the business.[4] The employers who were under agreement with the union claimed that this factor deprived them not only of the railroad business but of most of their other patronage as well. Despite repeated efforts by employers, the United Mine Workers refused to make any concessions during the years 1920-1927, and the union employers were faced with a steady loss of tonnage as a result. This was the argument, for example, that was advanced by Charles O'Neill, at that time Secretary of the Central Pennsylvania Coal Producers Association, in explaining the difficulties faced by union employers:

The poverty in Central Pennsylvania mining communities did not begin with July 1, 1927, when the union miners and operators [of this field] severed a relationship of 30 years' standing. It began seven years ago when the wage rates, contained in the Jacksonville agreement, first went into effect in the face of low wage rates in the non-union fields and continued to grow steadily worse until the climax was reached and bankruptcy faced the entire industry. The operators, who had continued joint relations with the United Mine Workers of America until July 1, 1927, decided that they must open their mines on a competitive wage scale after they had exhausted every effort to negotiate a competitive wage scale with the union.[5]

More sweeping in its condemnation of the union's policy was this statement by a non-union operator in West Virginia.

That the union, as exemplified by the United Mine Workers of America, has failed, would seem to be obvious. It only seems to have brought disaster

---

[3] *Ibid.*, letter to John D. Rockefeller, Jr., dated July 1, 1925, p. 1124.

[4] *Ibid.*, testimony of J. D. A. Morrow, President, Pittsburgh Coal Company, Pittsburgh, Pennsylvania, pp. 163-164; testimony of Langdon Bell, Director, The Red Jacket Consolidated Coal and Coke Company, Inc., Columbus, Ohio, pp. 1854-1855.

[5] *Ibid.*, p. 342.

to those who have entered into contracts with it on the side of the operators; but, what is still sadder is that it has brought misery and poverty to the rank and file of is members . . . . Unwillingness to deal with the United Mine Workers of America implies no condemnation of the principle of collective bargaining, because that organization by its stupid policies and indelible record has put itself outside of the circle of those who can claim the protection collective bargaining affords.[6]

Another illustration of the spirit in which disruptions and violations during the life of agreements are usually handled is found during the first World War. At that time conditions in the coal industry were in sharp contrast to those prevailing in the 1920s; prices, profits, employment—all were mounting. Moreover, in the earlier period the cost of living was rising rapidly, and the union made vigorous efforts to secure corresponding increases in the wages of its members. The shoe was then on the other foot. Some gains were secured in the agreements signed for the two-year period between April 1, 1916, and March 31, 1918; for example, the agreement in the Central Competitive Field increased wage-rates of tonnage workers three cents per ton, about five and one-half per cent above the 1915 rate. The wage-rates of day men were increased about five per cent.[7] But within six months the union was seeking further increases. Strike protests soon broke out in central Pennsylvania, Illinois, and northern West Virginia; similar difficulties, it is worth noting, also occurred in the non-union areas of Alabama, eastern Kentucky, Tennessee, and Virginia. In this instance it was the employers' turn to charge the union with deliberately disregarding its solemn obligations; and it was the union's turn to reply that the employers' obstinate refusal to grant reasonable increases was the source of all the difficulty. Despite an agreement reached in April 1917, providing for further increases, labor disturbances in Illinois and other parts of the Central Field multiplied during the summer of 1917.[8] Thus, at a time when the country was involved in a great war effort, a coal shortage threatened. Disturbances in other industries also threatened to impair the national program. Congress therefore enacted a measure known as the Lever Act which penalized any conspiracy to limit or restrict the production of food and fuel products.[9] This gave the Federal government additional authority with which to deal with labor disturbances in the coal

[6] *Ibid.*, testimony of J. D. Bradley, President, Elk River Coal and Lumber Company, Dundon, West Virginia, pp. 1768-1769.

[7] Under this agreement payment for tonnage was henceforth to be based on weight of the coal as it came from the mine rather than on the amount of coal that would pass over screens of a certain mesh and area (i. e., the run of mine method was substituted for the screened method of wage-payment). All agreements signed by the United Mine Workers of America are available at the office of the international union, Washington, D. C.

[8] The agreement signed in April 1917, increased rates for pick and machine mining ten cents, and rates for day men sixty cents a day. No increase for yardage and dead work was allowed.

[9] 40 Stat. 276 (1917). The law was later amended, 41 Stat. 297 (1919).

fields and in certain other industries. Fuel Administrator Harry Garfield called a conference in Washington and soon afterwards, on October 6, 1917, another agreement was signed. It granted further wage increases and provided for penalties against any workers who went on strike without first bringing their grievances to the Fuel Administration. Similarly, penalties were placed against any employer who ordered a lock-out during the period of emergency.[10] The two increases in 1917 raised wage-rates of union tonnage men about thirty-six per cent above their 1916 level; the rise in wage-rates of day men was about seventy-four per cent.[11] In the fall of 1917 President Wilson, also acting under powers granted to him by the Lever Act, ordered the existing scale of coal prices to be increased by forty-five cents in order to cover the increase in labor costs.

Appeals for higher wages were only temporarily silenced; in 1918 the union sought still further advances, but during that year no wage increases were secured. Verbal protests in 1919 subsequently took the form of direct action and despite an injunction secured by the government,[12] a bitter strike occurred in the winter of that year.[13] Needless to say, both sides accused the other of irresponsibility, ruthlessness, and greed.[14]

On hindsight, these personal recriminations appear to have had little justification. Neither the alleged violations committed by the union during the war years, nor the alleged violations committed by employers between 1920 and 1927, were the responsibility of any particular individuals. Rather, they were the product of the whole

---

[10] Under this agreement, known as the Washington Agreement, day rates were increased $1.40 per day as against an increase of 10 cents per ton for pick and machine mining.

[11] Waldo E. Fisher and Anne Bezanson, *Wage Rates and Working Time in the Bituminous Coal Industry, 1912-1922* (Philadelphia: University of Pennsylvania Press, 1932), table 7, p. 51, table 19, pp. 88-89.

[12] Injunction granted in the case of *U. S. v. Hayes*, District Court of Indiana (1919), unreported. Text is given in Francis Sayre, *Cases on Labor Law* (Cambridge, Massachusetts: Harvard University Press, 1923), p. 757. The injunction was followed by contempt proceedings and criminal prosecutions against some of the strike leaders.

[13] The U. S. Bureau of Mines estimated that the 1919 strike tied up 71 per cent of the coal producing capacity of the country and that 418,279 men, or 67.2 per cent of all employees in the industry engaged in the struggle. For data on strikes in subsequent years, see Fred E. Berquist and associates, *Economic Survey of the Bituminous Coal Industry Under Free Competition and Code Regulation* (National Recovery Administration, Division of Review, Work Materials No. 69, 1936), vol. II, Appendix III, tables 42-45, pp. 626-629.

[14] This strike was terminated December 12, 1919, by the Garfield Award. The Award granted still further wage increases. Rates of union tonnage men, for example, were raised fourteen per cent above their 1918 level. Additional gains were also secured in 1920 under the award of the U. S. Bituminous Coal Commission. Wage-rates of union tonnage men, for example, were increased about sixteen per cent above their 1919 level. The two increases raised tonnage rates about thirty per cent above their 1918 level. Fisher and Bezanson, *op. cit.*, table 7, p. 51.

situation in which the viewpoints and actions of particular persons or groups of persons played but a minor part. The same can be said for the acts which finally abrogated or terminated the agreements. In both periods broad and powerful influences were at work which involved far-reaching changes and undermined established relations within the industry. The system of collective bargaining, as an integral part of the industry's structure, was unable to withstand the impact of these changes. Whether this débâcle could have been avoided is a question discussed at a later point. But to say that someone was "to blame" or that "there ought to have been a law" to prevent its occurrence is to take too simple a view of the problem. The same point was made in connection with the coat and suit industry. Its applicability to post-war developments in the bituminous coal industry is even more striking.

CHARACTERISTICS OF THE INDUSTRY

Part of the explanation of the breakdown of union-employer relations in bituminous coal mining lies in certain characteristics of the industry itself. Coal producers, in a geographical sense, operate in an extremely broad, competitive market. Coal falls into classifications that are relatively well standardized. It is produced in widely scattered areas of the country. Buyers go long distances to get "the cheapest and the best." A coal company well established one year in a market some five hundred miles from its mines may find itself without this outlet a few years later. Changes in any one of a number of factors may bring this about—shifts in the type of coal demanded, differences in the quality of coal produced, changes in production costs, and, probably most important, changes in selling prices. Indeed, there are few industries in the country in which competition among producing units is as active over as wide an area as in bituminous coal. In 1929, for example, only about one-fourth of total shipments were intra-state. Not a single coal-producing state entirely supplied its own coal requirements.[15] Indianapolis, Indiana (a fairly representative city) obtained fifty-three per cent of its all-rail coal deliveries that year from Indiana mines and its other shipments from mines in twenty-five districts in eight other states.[16] A little over 6,000 mines were in operation that year, scattered over thirty states. Output amounted to approximately 535 million tons.[17] In 1937 there

[15] Berquist and associates, *op. cit.*, vol. I, p. 140. A complete file of N. R. A. Work Materials is available in the N. R. A. Records Section, U. S. Commerce Building, Washington, D. C.

[16] *Report of the Committee on Prices in the Bituminous Coal Industry*, Waldo E. Fisher, Chairman (National Bureau of Economic Research, 1938), p. 9.

[17] *Mineral Resources of the United States, 1930* (U. S. Department of Commerce, Bureau of Mines), Part II—"Non-metals," table 22, p. 640.

were 6,548 mines in operation, which produced nearly 446 million tons of coal.[18]

These circumstances compel the union to have dealings with a large number of firms in widely separated parts of the country. If a group of employers in one area is allowed to disregard the union's standards, competitive pressure would soon force employers in contiguous areas to do likewise. This, in turn, would lead to similar pressures on more distant firms, with similar results. The movement might easily spread in wider and wider circles until the whole system of collective bargaining would be destroyed. Although closely bound economically, bituminous coal properties are geographically widely scattered. Important producing centers are located in areas as far apart as Alabama, Illinois, Washington, and Wyoming. Even more inaccessible to union representatives are coal mines in the mountain fastnesses of eastern Kentucky and Tennessee or in the sparsely settled sections of Arkansas. The eastern coal market includes producers as far west as the Mississippi River and as far south as Alabama, although producers in the latter state do not figure importantly. In order to maintain its position in that market the union must hold employers in line, as well as retain at least the tacit support of their workers, in all parts of this wide domain.

Nor does the nature of the miner's job and the attitude towards working rules which it fosters simplify the task of maintaining union standards.[19] The miner's place of occupation is not in an urban factory building where he is in close daily contact with hundreds of his fellows. He works underground, in some remote passageway or room. Save for one or two companions he is generally isolated from the other men. Aside from occasional contacts with the "mine boss," he is also pretty much on his own. As a loader he works largely at his own speed. As a cutter or a driller "at the face" he enjoys a measure of the skilled workman's independence. Companies have not been too much concerned about this attitude, since most miners are paid on a piece-work or tonnage basis and if they choose to work at a leisurely pace or leave early—or not come to work at all—their earnings are correspondingly less. Moreover, even men working on a day basis, such as engineers and maintenance employees, have a surprising amount of the same spirit. In recent years the introduction of power-driven machinery and other efficiencies have involved some increase

---

[18] *Minerals Yearbook* (U. S. Department of Interior, Bureau of Mines), table 2, p. 771. For neither year were mines producing less than 1,000 tons annually included.

[19] This is discussed at somewhat greater length in Chapter III *supra*.

in management supervision, but the essential outline of the picture remains unaltered.[20]

The wide diversity of working conditions also complicates the union's job of maintaining uniform standards. As noted in Chapter III, this becomes most evident in regard to the determination of piece-rates. At least some of the miner's earnings depends on what he can secure by himself, through direct, individual negotiations with his employer. Additional compensation for timbering, for excessive amounts of impurities in the coal, or for work in seams that are unusually narrow is determined in this way. Considerable progress has been made toward standardizing pay-rates for this so-called yardage and dead work. Indeed, the district agreements even specify in a general way what those standards are. But the task of deciding specific rates still falls in part on the individual miner (acting with or without his pit committee) and the mine executive immediately in charge.[21]

These characteristics of the job make for independence, a circumstance not calculated to simplify the problem of discipline either for the management or for the union. Not that there is any lack of solidarity among the men; all observers agree that precisely the contrary is true.[22] But it is just as likely to be a solidarity of small groups as of large. Given provocation, either by a management that is too belligerent or by a union leadership that is not belligerent enough, the men are prone to take matters into their own hands. The phenomenon of the local or outlaw strike testifies to this fact. The numerous struggles within the union, which became particularly serious during the 1920s, are not unrelated to the same spirit.

Factors bearing upon the situation of the mine operators also complicate the problem of maintaining stable union-employer relations. Many bituminous coal companies are small, poorly financed concerns. Operations from the outset are frequently on a "shoestring" basis. True, a few large corporations hold a substantial proportion of the total assets of the industry. In 1929 the seventeen largest companies (those producing three million tons and over annually) accounted for about twenty per cent of the total output. But there were 2,277 companies which produced less than ten thousand tons each. Although the latter represented about forty-nine per cent of the total number of producers in the country, they accounted for

---

[20] Goodrich, *The Miner's Freedom,* Chapters 3-5.

[21] Joseph H. Willits and associates, *Labor Relations in Bituminous Coal Mining* (Report of the U. S. Coal Commission, Part III, 1925), p. 1313.

[22] See Goodrich, *The Miner's Freedom,* pp. 56-59.

only a little more than one per cent of total production in 1929.[23] The presence of these many small firms involves serious problems in the administration of the union agreements.

Another characteristic of the industry which constitutes a continual threat to union standards is the type of capital outlay and cost structure that is involved. Entry into the industry is relatively easy, for soft coal in its natural state is both abundant and accessible. When prospects for the industry improve, new firms quickly spring up. But once the necessary capital outlays have been made, withdrawal is not easy. The equipment is too specialized to be of much value in other lines of activity and fixed costs like charges for maintenance of equipment and for interest on investments are likely to make shut-downs prohibitive. Moreover, changes in the geological conditions of a particular operation or in general market conditions may seriously affect the cost position of operators. Relatively slight changes in freight rates, for example, may cause drastic changes in sales outlets. All these are cost changes over which the individual operator has little control. Frequently, his only hope is to reduce labor costs, particularly since they form at least two-thirds of total production costs.[24] The most obvious way to achieve this end, of course, is to reduce wage-rates.

BASIC CHANGES

The problems posed by these circumstances were made much more serious by the sweeping changes of the war and post-war years. During the first part of this period the lure of expanding war de-

---

[23] *Mineral Resources of the United States, 1930,* Part II—"Non-metals," table 24, p. 644. These figures overstate the degree of concentration in the industry since wagon mines producing less than 1,000 tons a year are excluded. Data for more recent years are not comparable with the figures for 1929 because more adequate coverage has been secured and the figures relate only to size of mines, as opposed to size of companies. Even so, as the following figures show, data for later years present much the same picture. *Minerals Yearbook, 1939,* table 10, p. 784.

COMMERCIAL BITUMINOUS COAL MINES IN 1937

(*Exclusive of Truck and Wagon Mines Producing Less Than 1,000 Tons*)

Firms Producing 500,000 Net Tons and Over				
Year	*Number*	*Percentage of Total*	*Output in Net Tons*	*Percentage of Total*
1937	212	3	167,660,000	38
Firms Producing Less Than 10,000 Net Tons				
Year	*Number*	*Percentage of Total*	*Output in Net Tons*	*Percentage of Total*
1937	3,853	59	11,610,000	3

[24] *Report of the Committee on Prices in the Bituminous Coal Industry* (National Bureau of Economic Research), pp. 21-22. Total production costs referred to here do not, however, include ". . . selling costs, administrative expenses [other than supervisory and clerical work immediately involved in mine operations], interest on investments, and most taxes." Figured on this basis, labor costs amount to about sixty-five per cent of total costs, supplies about sixteen per cent, depreciation and royalties about nine per cent.

mands and mounting profits increased the number of commercial mines in operation by well over one-third and raised production from about 478 million tons in 1913 to 564 million tons in 1920. Capacity of bituminous coal mines calculated on a 308-day basis rose correspondingly—from about 635 million tons in 1913 to 796 million tons in 1920.[25] When demand fell off from its war-time peak, capacity was not, of course, immediately reduced. Indeed, it was raised still further since plans to expand output were in many cases not undertaken until the end of the war. Between 1920 and 1922 capacity was increased from 796 million tons to 916 million tons; by 1923 it had reached 970 million tons.[26] The perverse course of investment made the industry's post-war condition even more difficult. It served to focus almost the entire pressure of adjustment on the price and cost structure, and particularly on the wage structure of the industry. The system of collective bargaining was an integral part of this same structure, so that it, too, was subjected to unusually heavy strains.

Still, these pressures might not have been enough to undermine established union-employer relations if certain influences bearing on the demand for coal had not also been at work. Bituminous coal enjoys a diversified demand ranging all the way from industrial to domestic use. Well over three-fourths of annual output, however, goes to industry. Since coal is a relatively minor cost element in most industrial operations, a drop in its price may occasion little increase in the amount sold. The price decline in the post-war period, therefore, gave no relief to the industry on this score. If demand had been more elastic, the pressures on other elements in the industry, including the structure of wage rates, would have been less severe. These pressures became especially powerful during the post-war period through a long-term decline in the demand for bituminous coal, a decline which the war period had only postponed. For many years prior to 1919 there had been a steady expansion in sales of bituminous coal, but after that year the curve tilted downward. In almost every year since the war, output has been below the 1920-1923 average.[27] The reasons

[25] *Mineral Resources of the U. S., 1930*, Part II—"Non-metals," table 22, p. 640, and table 5, p. 620. In 1913 there were 5,776 commercial bituminous coal mines in operation; in 1920 there were 8,900. The figures on production and number of mines seriously under-estimate the increase, since wagon mines producing less than 1,000 tons annually are not included. The figures on capacity, however, take these mines into account.

[26] *Ibid.*, table 22, p. 640. Figures on the number of mines are as follows:

Year	*Number of Mines*
1920	8,921
1921	8,038
1922	9,299
1923	9,331

[27] *Report of the Committee on Prices in the Bituminous Coal Industry* (National Bureau of Economic Research), p. 16. In 1920, production was 564 million tons; in 1927, it was 518 million tons; and in 1932, it was 310 million tons.

for this reversal of a long-term trend have been fully considered by other investigators. The most important seem to be economies in the use of coal by various industries; competition from other sources of energy, notably, oil, gas, and hydro-electric power; reductions in the use of coke; and declines in the rate of growth of important coal-consuming industries.[28] The significant point for present purposes is that this persistant contraction in the market for coal intensified the problem of restoring some degree of balance between supply and demand in the post-war years. Along with the pressures already at work, the addition of this factor contributed greatly to the demoralization of the industry.

As if to make disaster doubly sure, the full weight of all these difficulties fell upon the industry within a four- or five-year period. Many companies that had enjoyed good earnings in 1920 were in serious financial difficulties by 1925. Such changes necessitated rapid and far-reaching adjustments, but the adaptations were confined to only four elements in the industry's structure—prices, profits, employment, and hourly earnings. These elements stood in integral relation to one another and to the system of union-employer relations which had gradually emerged during the preceding thirty years. Thus the same pressures which upset the relationships among these strategic elements in the industry undermined the system of contractual relations as well. Here lies the principal explanation for the breakdown of the union agreements.

Between 1922 and 1927 (the year in which collective dealings in the Central Competitive Field terminated) the average value per net ton of coal at the mines fell almost without interruption from $3.02 to $1.99; between 1927 and 1932 the average value figure dropped steadily lower, in the latter year reaching $1.31. In the first five-year period average value declined about one-third and in the ten-year period, as a whole, well over one-half.[29] The contraction in the demand for bituminous coal and the steady fall in prices at the mine took a heavy toll of company earnings. Indeed, the evidence indicates that throughout the eleven-year period from 1922 through 1932, the industry was, in general, operating at a deficit. Figures are available for only a few of these years. The peak apparently was reached in 1920 when the industry had a net income (before income and excess profits taxes) of over 249 million dollars. In 1925 net income had turned into a net loss of over 22 million dollars. Every year between 1928 and 1932 the industry operated at a deficit; the largest

---

[28] For discussions of the long-term decline in the demand for coal, see F. G. Tryon and H. O. Rogers, "Statistical Studies of Progress in Fuel Efficiency," in *Transactions* (Second World Power Conference, 1930), vol. 6, Section 12, pp. 343-365; and Berquist and associates, *op. cit.*, vol. I, pp. 22, *passim.*

[29] *Mineral Resources of the U. S., 1930*, Part II—"Non-Metals," table 28, p. 647, and *Minerals Yearbook, 1939*, table 11, p. 786.

net loss, over 51 million dollars, occurred in 1932.[30] During the period 1925-1929 only four other industries, as classified by the United States Bureau of Internal Revenue, showed deficits.[31] The decline in company earnings was enough to force many firms into bankruptcy and to eliminate a number of mines from operation. In 1920 there were 6,277 commercial coal companies operating 8,921 mines; in 1929, there were only 4,612 companies operating 6,057 mines.[32] This represented a drop of over twenty-five per cent in the number of companies functioning in the industry.

Similar declines occurred in employment during the post-war years. In 1920 bituminous coal mines gave employment to nearly 640,000 men; in 1927 the number stood at approximately 594,000, and in 1932, at approximately 406,000.[33] Furthermore, the men retained on the payrolls received less work than before. In 1920 bituminous coal mines worked an average of 220 days; in 1927 the average was 191 days; and in 1932 it had become only 146 days. If account were taken of the decline in the number of hours which the men actually spent each day underground, the contrast would be even sharper.[34]

The rapidly mounting difficulties of the period which are reflected in these figures placed corresponding burdens on the cost structure of the industry. Many firms faced the alternative of reducing expenses or going out of business. Their only immediate salvation was to reduce labor costs. Other items like taxes, interest on invested capital, administration expenses, transportation costs, and selling expenses were either fixed or beyond their immediate control. Aside from these costs, outlays for labor, as already noted, formed at least two-thirds of their costs of production.[35] This circumstance placed greater and greater weight on the wage structure of the industry. The available evidence (which is examined in detail below) reveals that hourly earnings of day men declined anywhere from 25 to 33$^1/_3$ per cent during the twelve years from 1920 to 1932. Data on hourly earnings of

---

30 These figures compiled by F. G. Tryon from various sources, were taken from Berquist and associates, *op. cit.*, vol. I, p. 63.

31 Berquist and associates, *op. cit.*, vol. I, p. 60.

32 *Mineral Resources of the U. S., 1929*, Part II—"Non-metals," table 24, p. 715. The figures do not include the so-called "country banks" and "wagon mines" so that the decline from the 1920 level is somewhat under-estimated. In calculating the number of companies in operation, no account is taken of interlocking ownership or interests. The number of commercial mines in operation in 1937, not strictly comparable with the figures for 1920 and 1929, was 6,548 (*Minerals Yearbook, 1939*, table 10, p. 784).

33 *Mineral Resources of the U. S., 1929*, Part II—"Non-metals," table 36, p. 742, and *Minerals Yearbook, 1932-1933*, "Statistical Appendix," table 2, pp. 376-377.

34 *Mineral Resources of the U. S., 1929*, Part II—"Non-metals," table 38, p. 744, and *Minerals Yearbook, 1932-1933*, "Statistical Appendix," table 2, pp. 376-377.

35 *Report of the Committee on Prices in the Bituminous Coal Industry* (National Bureau of Economic Research), pp. 21-22, referred to on p. 178, *supra*.

piece workers, although scanty, point to the same conclusions. Earnings calculated on a weekly or annual basis show declines running from $33^1/_3$ to 50 per cent. Probably few industries in the country have experienced a more rapid or a more extreme wage deflation in a comparable period of time.

IMMEDIATE CIRCUMSTANCES

Whether these powerful influences would alone have been enough to destroy the industry's long-established system of union-employer relations is perhaps debatable. In any event two circumstances were present which made disaster virtually inevitable. First, the union attempted to maintain wage-rates at the level reached in 1920. Second, huge supplies of coal were available in the South, an area which lay outside the union's system of agreements. Employers in the latter region were therefore able to effect wage reductions which union operators in the North could not secure. In this way they gained an enlarged share of the market. During the war northern operators could disregard the rising tide of southern coal since mining facilities everywhere were taxed to the limit. After the war, however, the industry faced a contracting market and the distribution of the available business became of crucial importance. Thanks in large measure to their wage advantage, the southern firms were able to shift the burden of these difficulties onto the shoulders of the northern operators. Given this circumstance and the decision by the union not to permit any wage concessions, northern employers were faced with one of two alternatives: either to terminate dealings with the United Mine Workers or else see their business go to southern competitors. They chose the former course and, in so doing, the whole system of collective bargaining was destroyed.

In 1920 the United Mine Workers of America was in a more powerful position than at any previous time in its history. It reported a membership that year of about 400,000 members.[36] It had agreements covering the so-called Central Competitive Field, which included the soft-coal areas of Illinois, Indiana, Ohio, and western Pennsylvania. In 1920 this area produced a little over one-third of the nation's total output of bituminous coal.[37] Almost continuously since 1898, the

[36] This figure was reported by the union as consisting of paid-up membership and "exonerated" membership (workers on strike, unemployed, etc.). The peak in membership for this period was not reached until 1923. Wolman, *op. cit.*, Appendix, table I, p. 173.

[37] *Production of Central Competitive Field and Its Relation to Total Bituminous Production of the Country* (U. S. Geological Survey Weekly Report 259), July 1, 1922, in Isador Lubin, *Miners' Wages and the Cost of Coal* (New York: McGraw-Hill Book Company, 1924), p. 46. According to this source, the Central Competitive Field accounted for thirty-eight per cent of the nation's output in 1920; Dr. Waldo E. Fisher told the writer that his own calculations placed the figure at about thirty-three per cent.

basic provisions of these agreements had been worked out in joint interstate conferences between representatives of the union and of the employers. Wage-rates and other standards decided upon at these conferences guided negotiations in the outlying fields as well. For many years before 1920 the union had agreements which covered the Southwest Interstate Field.[38] In 1920 it was also securely entrenched in the coal-producing areas of central Pennsylvania, certain counties in West Virginia, western Kentucky, Montana, Michigan, Iowa, Wyoming, and a large part of Washington. These areas outside the Central Competitive Field produced about 120 million tons in 1920, or twenty-one per cent of the country's total output.[39] During the war the union had even been able to make a small dent in the traditional non-union fields, so that by 1920 it had a few agreements in Alabama, eastern Kentucky, Tennessee, the Somerset and Connellsville sections of Pennsylvania, and the central and northern fields of West Virginia. In 1920 this area produced nearly forty per cent of the country's entire output; two years later, during the general strike of 1922, it demonstrated that it could supply sixty per cent of the nation's average weekly consumption.[40]

In the 1920 agreement for the Central Competitive Field the union secured the highest wage-rates ever attained. Advances during the war had only partly offset the increases in the cost of living. The union also pointed to sharp advances that had occurred in non-union areas of the industry and in other industries as well. It further argued that the sales and earnings of the coal operators more than justified its claims. A general strike occurred in 1919, and the government established the United States Bituminous Coal Commission. The union and employers agreed that the commission should review the union's demands and that the commission's award would be the basis of a new agreement. This award granted an increase in the basic rate for tonnage men of twenty-four cents a ton, or about thirty per cent more than the 1918 rate. This section of the award was accepted by the union and the employers in 1920. Another section granted an increase of $1.00 a day to day men, which was about twenty per cent above the previous rate. Alleging this was inequitable treatment, the union protested and strikes broke out in Illinois and Indiana, with the result that in August 1920, an increase of $1.50 a day was secured. This brought the basic day rate to $7.50 for an eight-hour day.[41]

According to the calculations of Fisher and Bezanson, average rates for tonnage men in the union fields between 1916 and 1921 in-

---

[38] This field included the states of Oklahoma, Kansas, Missouri, and Arkansas.
[39] Lubin, *op. cit.*, p. 48.
[40] *Ibid.*, p. 47.
[41] *Ibid.*, p. 231.

creased nearly ninety per cent while the average increase for day men was about 183 per cent.[42] Increases during this same period in the non-union fields were relatively greater; thus, average rates for tonnage men in non-union fields increased nearly 124 per cent while rates for day men increased 239 per cent.[43] Later the union pointed to these facts in support of its opposition to wage reductions after 1920. However, despite the greater increases in the non-union fields during this period, wage-rates in these fields were at all times below rates prevailing in the union fields. From 1916 to (but not including) 1921, wage-rates for day men averaged roughly eight cents an hour more in union than in non-union fields.[44] Similar differences existed between union and non-union tonnage rates.[45] After 1920, as shown below, the difference was even greater.

The post-war policy of "No Backward Step" was undertaken in the face of the many difficulties besetting the industry outlined above. For seven years, from 1920 to 1927, the union refused to accept any reduction from the peak level achieved in 1920. The agreement for the Central Competitive Field expired March 31, 1922, and employers in that area exerted great pressure to secure reductions; strikes followed, and finally another agreement was signed reaffirming the existing rates.[46] This agreement, which provided the standards by which agreements in other fields were modeled, ran from March 31, 1922, to April 1, 1924. At the time of expiration of this second agreement, the employers of the Central Competitive Field redoubled their efforts to secure reductions. Although less widespread than before, strikes broke out again and a three-year agreement was finally signed, running from March 31, 1924, to April 1, 1927. Known as the Jacksonville Agreement,[47] it reaffirmed the 1920 rates for another three years. Despite these successes—and no doubt, in part, because of them—the union was confronted with severe obstacles throughout the period. Mounting unemployment took a heavy toll of its members; internal dissension sapped much of its strength; and more and more coal entered the market which had not been produced under its standards of employment.

The first serious attack on the union during the post-war period came in 1920 when operators in Alabama refused to submit possible terms of settlement to the United States Coal Commission. The second major loss occurred in 1921 when many operators in the New

---

42 Fisher and Bezanson, *op. cit.*, table 17, p. 81.

43 *Ibid.*

44 *Ibid.*, table 19, pp. 88-89.

45 *Ibid.*, table 5, pp. 42-43.

46 As previously noted, all agreements signed by the United Mine Workers are available at the office of the international union, Washington, D. C.

47 It received this name because the agreement was reached in the city of Jacksonville, Florida.

River Field of southern West Virginia terminated all dealings with the union, and many producers in Texas, Colorado, and Washington followed suit when efforts to secure wage reductions were unsuccessful. In the state of Washington, for example, the operators announced a return to the wage-scale of October 1919, and when the union refused to accept the reduction, relations between the firms and the union were ended. The year 1922 witnessed even heavier blows against the union's structure of collective bargaining. Operators in Connellsville and Somerset counties of central Pennsylvania terminated dealings with the union. Efforts to hold an interstate conference in the Central Competitive Field for the purpose of drafting another agreement were also unsuccessful that year. As a result, the union was obliged to sign agreements with district organizations and with certain firms individually, although others refused to sign. By that time, too, the union had lost what few agreements it had previously secured in the traditional non-union areas of eastern Kentucky, Virginia, Tennessee, Alabama, Maryland, New Mexico, and Colorado.

The gathering storm came perilously near the union's chief citadel in the Central Competitive Field during the years 1923 and 1924. That was when the last of the union operators in southern West Virginia, notably in the Kanawha field, and in western Kentucky broke away from the United Mine Workers. Northern West Virginia was the only area outside of the Central Competitive Field that remained union, but in 1925 this territory was also lost when operators in the Fairmount Field refused to accept the terms of the so-called Baltimore Agreement.[48]

The stronghold of the United Mine Workers had traditionally been the Central Competitive Field. During 1925 and 1926, however, many of the employers embraced by it, particularly in western Pennsylvania, Ohio, and parts of Indiana, demanded wage reductions. The union still refused and when the Jacksonville Agreement expired on March 31, 1927, a large number of firms would not sign another. Indeed, the only areas in which a majority of employers signed new agreements were Illinois and certain sections of Indiana.[49] By this

---

48 Agreement based on the Jacksonville Agreement, signed at Baltimore, Maryland, in 1924. An important company operating in northern West Virginia was the Rockefeller-controlled Consolidation Coal Company. At the time this firm terminated dealings with the union (1925) a company union was established. It was patterned after the employee representation plan established in The Colorado Fuel and Iron Corporation (another Rockefeller enterprise) in 1916. However, few coal companies during the 1920s followed the Rockefeller example.

49 Significantly enough, agreements signed with employers in these two areas reduced basic day rates from $7.50 to $6.50. Similar reductions occurred in tonnage rates; the pick-mining rate, for example, was lowered from $1.08 to 91 cents an hour. These agreements lasted from September 16, 1928, to March 31, 1932.

year, then, the system of collective bargaining in bituminous coal was pretty well dismembered.

WAGE DIFFERENTIALS

At the very beginning of this seven-year period the non-union operators reduced wage-rates below the level prevailing at the close of the war. While union operators were obliged to maintain existing rates throughout the sharp deflation of 1921 and 1922, non-union firms reduced tonnage rates nearly seven per cent and day rates nearly eleven per cent.[50] The process of disintegration soon became a cumlative one; the greater the number of employers who broke away from the union's standards and reduced the rates, the heavier grew the pressure on other employers to do the same. Moreover, those who initiated the cuts were encouraged to make still further reductions as other employers broke away from the union and cut wages themselves. By contrast, the wage-rates in union firms remained unchanged between 1920 and 1927. In this way a steadily widening gap appeared between union and non-union rates. The available wage data for these years do not allow for a precise measurement of the widening differential. However, a tentative estimate reveals the discrepancy that emerged in the average hourly earnings that prevailed in the three predominantly non-union states of Kentucky, West Virginia, and Virginia, as against the four predominantly union states of Illinois, Indiana, Ohio, and Pennsylvania. In the first period, 1921-1922, average hourly earnings in the non-union states were about eight per cent below comparable rates in the union states. By 1924 they were twenty-one per cent below, and in 1927 they were approximately twenty-two per cent below the union rates.[51]

These circumstances gave to non-union operators in the South a progressively greater advantage over their union competitors in the North. Throughout this period southern operators were for the most part able to sell coal at lower prices than operators in the North; this meant that they were able to gain a larger portion of the national market. In 1920 the average value per net ton of coal at the mine in the three non-union states just mentioned was twenty per cent above average value in the northern states; in 1924 it was seventeen per cent below and in 1927, it was sixteen per cent below the northern figure. Southern output in relation to northern output, on the other hand,

---

50 Fisher and Bezanson, *op. cit.*, table 17, p. 81. This figure represents the net change that occurred between December 31, 1920, and December 31, 1922. The low point during this period was reached in the first half of 1922. *Ibid.*, p. 80.

51 The wage figures, on which these calculations were based, were taken from Berquist and associates, *op. cit.*, vol. I, p. 75. These figures are to be found in the Appendix, table II, of the present study. They were originally secured by the U. S. Bureau of Labor Statistics from the monthly payrolls of a sample number of mining firms.

rose almost steadily during this period. In 1921 production in the three southern states was forty-seven per cent of production in the four northern states. By 1924 it had risen to sixty-three per cent of northern output, and by 1927 it had topped northern output by six per cent.[52]

These figures on the comparative positions of union and non-union coal operators during the post-war period suffer from the difficulty that both areas chosen include some union and non-union firms. Moreover, it is not clear whether the figures concern companies in the North and South which produced the same type of coal and therefore directly competed with one another. Unfortunately, there are no figures on earnings which would remedy this deficiency. For information on prices and production, however, more specific figures are obtainable. Data collected by the United States Bureau of Mines make it possible to compare prices and production in fields in direct competition with one another. It was found, for example, that f. o. b. prices in two fields which produced low volatile coal gave considerable advantage to the southern, non-union operators during these years. At the same time, production in the union field (known as the Central Pennsylvania Field) dropped from about 61,000,000 in 1920 to about 43,000,000 net tons in 1927; output in the non-union field (known as the Southern Low Volatile Field) rose during this period from approximately 34,000,000 to 51,000,000 net tons. The upshot was that the share in the national output going to the Central Pennsylvania Field dropped from about eleven per cent to eight, while the share going to the Southern Low Volatile Field increased roughly from six per cent to ten per cent. Similar shifts are reflected in data for a union and non-union field, both of which produced high volatile coal.[53]

Data on employment for competing fields in the North and South reflect the same influences. Thus, the number of men employed in the Central Pennsylvania Field fell from nearly 77,000 in 1923 to about 60,000 in 1927; the average number of days worked stood at 188 in the former year, 182 in the latter. In the Southern Low Volatile Field, on the other hand, the number of employees rose from about 41,000 in 1923 to 46,000 in 1927; the average number of days worked increased from 168 days in 1923 to 232 days in 1927. Similar changes

---

52 Data on the average value per net ton and output are given in the Appendix, table I. As regards the factor of competitive advantage it would be more accurate to compare delivered prices in the two sections as opposed to f. o. b. prices, since changes in marketing positions depend in the last analysis on the former. Changes in freight rates, for example, could more than offset changes in f. o. b. prices. Price figures at the mine, therefore, only indicate in a general way the advantage which accrued to southern operators during this period. Satisfactory data on delivered prices were not obtainable by this investigator.

53 These figures, available in the office of the U. S. Bureau of Mines, Washington, D. C., are given in the Appendix, Tables III and IV.

occurred in two fields, one union and one non-union, producing high volatile coal.[54]

It seems clear, therefore, that the widening gap between union and non-union wage rates during these years was an important factor in explaining the shift in production from bituminous mines in the North to mines in the South. In turn, the shift put the northern operators under great pressure to reduce wage-rates in order to maintain their position in the national market. The United Mine Workers, however, clung to its policy of "No Backward Step" and refused to grant any reductions in wage rates during the years 1920 to 1927. Behind this decision lay the union's threat to strike, and during this period many serious strikes did, in fact, occur. Strikes also took place in areas that were predominantly non-union, but naturally they were most effective in the regions where the union was strongest. This furthered the shift in output from union to non-union areas.[55] Under these circumstances, operators who had agreements with the United Mine Workers had but two alternatives—either accept the gauge of battle or concede the union's wage demands. They chose the former course. The union, for its part, made no concessions and as a result most of its agreements were terminated.

THE UNION'S POLICY APPRAISED

It is thus apparent that the wage advantage accruing to non-union producers between 1920 and 1927 was an important factor in the breakdown of collective bargaining in this industry. Why, then, did the United Mine Workers pursue a wage policy which did so much to undermine the strength of its own organization? Various answers may be advanced. First, the union's leadership was under considerable pressure to maintain existing wage-rates. Traditional union policy pointed in this direction. The generally prosperous condition of American industry in the post-war years favored such a course. A "high wage" philosophy espoused by such men as Henry Ford came into vogue at this time, a view supported by the Federal government. The government's part in maintaining wage-rates in the bituminous coal industry was particularly noteworthy. It was a government agency, the United States Bituminous Coal Commission, which raised rates to an all-time peak in 1920. It was President Coolidge who used his good offices to end the strike of 1922 by urging that existing

[54] These comparisons are also based on figures available in the office of the United States Bureau of Mines, Washington, D. C.

[55] The strikes of 1922 and 1927 were mostly confined to the northern union fields. In the former year, for example, there were about 18,400,000 man-days lost due to strikes in Pennsylvania and 5,500,000 in Ohio, while the figures for Kentucky and West Virginia for that year were approximately 605,000 and 5,300,000, respectively. In 1927 man-days lost totalled about 6,600,000 in Pennsylvania and 5,600,000 in Ohio; in Kentucky, the year's total was 24,800 and in West Virginia 47,500 man-days lost.

rates be maintained. It was Herbert Hoover, then Secretary of Commerce, who urged employers in 1924 to reaffirm existing wage rates in the conference with union spokesmen at Jacksonville. So in its determination to maintain rates throughout this period the union did not stand alone.

Another influence to which the union's leadership was subject during this period came from within the organization itself. The post-war period was ushered in by an insurgent strike of 25,000 miners in Illinois in 1919. The men demanded the termination of the war-time (Washington) agreement and an upward adjustment of wage-rates. The union leaders made vigorous efforts to suppress the strike, but later that year they themselves called a general strike with the same purpose in view.[56] In 1920 strife within the union centered in Kansas where Alexander Howat, the district president, was leading a strike in opposition to the compulsory arbitration law of that state.[57] At about the same time, he was leading an insurgent campaign against President John L. Lewis; but at the next international convention he was deprived of his office and the protest movement quelled.[58] Other insurgent strikes broke out in Illinois and Kansas during 1920, ostensibly because the majority report of the United States Bituminous Coal Commission recommended greater increases to tonnage men than to day men.[59] Although these strikes were opposed—at least officially—by the international officers, they were supported by the district officers involved and soon afterward the alleged inequalities were removed.[60]

Other internal struggles followed intermittently, the next impor-

---

[56] Selig Perlman and Philip Taft, *History of Labor in the United States, 1898-1932* (New York: Macmillan and Company, 1935), pp. 470-471. The Washington Agreement was to continue "during the continuation of the war, and not to exceed two years from April 1, 1918." The operators interpreted this to mean that the agreement would not terminate until the country had signed the treaty of peace; the union insisted that it should terminate when the country signed the Armistice (November 11, 1918).

[57] The law creating the Kansas Court of Industrial Relations was passed in 1920. Kansas Laws, Special Session, 1920, c. 29, amended by Laws 1921, c. 261. This statute is reprinted in Sayre, *op. cit.*, pp. 918-923. Howat and four other district officers refused to testify before the Industrial Court; brought before a county court, they again refused to testify. The court found them guilty of contempt and sentenced them to jail. *State v. Howat*, 107 Kansas 423, 191 Pac. 585 (1920); upheld, 109 Kansas 376, 198 Pac. 686 (1921); 109 Kansas 779, 202 Pac. 72 (1921); upheld, *Howat v. Kansas*, 258 U. S. 181, 42 Sup. Ct. 277 (1922). Later the law was declared unconstitutional. *Court of Industrial Relations v. Wolff Packing Company*, 114 Kansas 304, 219 Pac. 259 (1923); *Wolff Packing Company v. Court of Industrial Relations*, 267 U. S. 552, 45 Sup. Ct. 441 (1924).

[58] Sayre, *op. cit.*, pp. 475-476.

[59] *Ibid.*, pp. 476-477.

[60] The basic wage for day men was raised from $6 to $7.50 a day at the Cleveland, Ohio, conference in August, 1920. Actually the day men had secured greater advances during the war years than had the tonnage men. See Fisher and Bezanson, *op. cit.*, p. 77.

tant flare-up occurring in 1926. A protest group led by John Brophy, known as the "Save the Union Committee," was formed in opposition to the leadership of President Lewis. They charged that he had been subservient to the demands of the "bosses" and that he had done nothing to solve the basic difficulties confronting the industry. Though unsuccessful in unseating Lewis at the 1927 convention, they continued their attack. In 1928 the insurgents called a conference of their own and elected officers. Soon afterwards President Lewis expelled their leaders from the union, and the movement fell into the hands of more extreme left-wing groups who formed the National Miners' Union in 1929. As the depression in the coal industry deepened, other splinter groups were organized, notably in West Virginia and Illinois, in opposition to the existing leadership of the union.[61]

These pressures had an important, although not always a direct, influence on union policy. To a considerable extent, their presence explains the union's determination to keep wage-rates at their 1920 peak. Despite losses in membership and despite a decline in the number of employers under agreement, the United Mine Workers refused to be dislodged from this position during the years 1920 to 1927. As an explanation of the reasons why the union pursued this policy, the following statement by a prominent employer representative, made in 1922, is significant:

> To have retreated without a show of strength would have spelled the downfall of the officers. Better from their standpoint to have an organized strike with the leaders leading than to have what must most certainly have come about otherwise—unauthorized outlaw strikes, with leaders helpless and protesting. It is conceivable that under different leadership the United Mine Workers could have weathered this storm without resorting to the strike. Such a large percentage of radical membership as was revealed at the Indianapolis meeting in February [1922] would have made such an attempt hazardous, however.[62]

These pressures help explain why the union persevered in its wage policy; they are not, of course, a justification. If the leaders of the union had granted wage reductions in 1922 or 1924, union firms would have been greatly benefited and the pressure to break off dealings with the union would have been reduced. But even if wage reductions had been granted to union firms, there are still grounds for doubting whether this step would have been enough to preserve the industry's system of collective bargaining. For, while it is doubtless true that the wage differential accelerated the shift in production from the North to the South, it certainly was not the only cause. The relation between the southern coal-fields and the rest of the industry at this

---

[61] Perlman and Taft, *op. cit.*, Chapter 41 and pp. 612-614.

[62] Statement of C. E. Lesher, Editor of *Coal Age* (a trade publication), in *Coal Age*, April 13, 1922, quoted in John L. Lewis, *The Miners' Fight for American Standards* (Indianapolis, Indiana: Bell Publishing Company, 1925), p. 163.

time was not altogether unlike the relative positions of Mississippi Valley and New England farm-land at the peak of the westward movement in the preceding century. The shift in output, while more rapid during the period 1920-1927 than ever before, was a long time in coming. Long before the first World War, southern coal had begun to invade certain markets which had been traditionally "northern." In 1898, for example, about eighty-six per cent of the coal trade on the Great Lakes originated in the union districts of Pittsburgh and Ohio; in 1913 the figure had dropped to about sixty-seven per cent. During this same period shipments from West Virginia to the Great Lakes increased from about 40,000 tons, or one per cent of the total, to over 6,000,000 tons, or twenty-three per cent of the total. After 1909 Kentucky coal also figured more prominently in this market.[63] Calculations by Frederick G. Tryon and Bushrod W. Allin show that coal production in the region of the Southern Appalachians approximately doubled between 1905 and 1915. During the same period this region's share in total national output increased from about fifteen per cent to twenty-five per cent.[64] It should not be overlooked, on the other hand, that the Central Competitive Field maintained its share of the national market until the close of the first World War. The rise in output of southern coal was partly due, even in this earlier period, to lower labor costs and greater freedom from strikes. However, in the judgment of the two authorities cited, "primarily it reflected expansion of the railroad net over the latent resources of the mountains."[65] Before this time the trunk lines had been pushed westward through the older coal-fields, leaving the southern fields untouched. Railroad lines first opened the Pocohontas Field in 1883 (westbound shipments in 1893), the Tug River Field in 1900, Winding Gulf in 1907, and Harlan and Elkhorn in 1912. During this period ton-mile freight rates were low enough to allow coal from this region to enter the northern markets.[66]

Once transportation facilities were available, the natural advantages of southern coal-fields assured the area an important place in the nation's industry. Supply was abundant, deposits were fairly accessible, and quality was, on the whole, good. During the post-war period, mining in this area reflected the same favorable factors. Pumping costs were at a minimum since most of the mines, at least in the

---

[63] Edward E. Hunt, Frederick G. Tryon, and Joseph H. Willits, *What the Coal Commission Found* (Baltimore, Maryland: The Williams and Wilkins Company, 1925), p. 233.

[64] Goodrich and others, *Migration and Economic Opportunity* (Philadelphia: University of Pennsylvania Press, 1936), Fig. 17, p. 94, in chapter by Frederick G. Tryon and Bushrod W. Allin. This region comprises the coal plateaus of West Virginia (except for the northern panhandle), eastern Kentucky and eastern Tennessee.

[65] *Ibid.*, p. 94.

[66] *Ibid.*, p. 95.

Southern Appalachian Region, lay above drainage. A minimum of timbering was also required in this region since roof conditions were, for the most part, good. In most cases it was not even necessary to sink shafts, since the coal could be gotten through horizontal drifts or gentle slopes. According to Tryon and Allin, ninety per cent of the coal is now being secured in this way.[67]

Other generalizations about the advantages of southern coal producers over northern competitors are extremely hazardous. In the 1920s, southern mines apparently had no advantage as to thickness of seam, even though a few of the northern mines having the thicker veins of better quality were by this time exhausted. Nor did southern operators have a significant advantage as to quality. The quality of coal in the southern fields varies widely. True, the quality of low volatile coal in the South is on the whole better than in the North. The high volatile coal found in some parts of West Virginia and eastern Kentucky is likewise better than that found in northern fields. But about all that can be safely said is that southern coal averages low in ash and high in heating value. The fact that it runs high in ash-fusing temperature makes it valuable for many purposes. Much of the coal in this area, moreover, is low sulphur coking coal of both low and high volatile content, suitable for almost any type of coke oven. The only northern state which can match southern coal in this respect is Pennsylvania.[68] The superiority of West Virginia and eastern Kentucky over Ohio and Indiana coal is reflected in the following table.

QUALITY OF BITUMINOUS COAL PRODUCED IN WEST VIRGINIA, EASTERN KENTUCKY, OHIO, AND INDIANA*

	West Virginia	*Eastern Kentucky*	*Ohio*	*Indiana*
Average heating value (B.T.U.)	14,090	13,760	12,570	11,620
Average ash content (per cent)	6.1	5.0	8.7	8.8
Average sulphur content (per cent)	1.2	.9	3.0	2.8
Average fusing content (degrees)	2,520	2,640	2,290	2,180
Per cent of output suitable for by-product coke	74.0	79.0	.1	2.0

*The figures are roughly weighted averages of the analyses published by the U. S. Bureau of Mines (mine samples—"as received" basis). They conceal a great range of quality in all the districts shown, but they serve to bring out the exceptional purity of coal from the two southern states.

Source: Goodrich and others, *Migration and Economic Opportunity* (Philadelphia: University of Pennsylvania Press, 1936), table 9, p. 92.

Southern operators during this period apparently derived no significant advantage from the fact that their mines and equipment were comparatively new. But here again generalizations become hazardous. Probably the southern operators were able to capitalize somewhat on the experience of northern producers. Perhaps they were more free to

---

[67] *Ibid.*, p. 92.
[68] *Ibid.*, pp. 92-93.

introduce new and improved methods of management. On the other hand, southern operators were no more active during these years in introducing machinery and other modern equipment than northern producers. Nor is there any evidence to indicate that the development of southern fields was planned any more efficiently or any more wisely than the northern fields. Some mergers and consolidations of properties occurred in the South during the post-war period;[69] but operations in the South were generally no less large-scale than those in the North. It should also be noted that most of the consolidations which occurred in southern fields at this time reflected the penetration of large northern interests.[70]

Nevertheless, considerations of this nature do not afford sufficient ground to justify the union's wage policy during the period. It may be true that the wage advantage which southern producers enjoyed has been exaggerated in explanations of the shift in production from northern to southern fields. Nevertheless, nothing that has been said thus far refutes the contention that the union's wage policy was an important factor in bringing about this result. A third, and final, argument in justification of the union's wage policy is less easy to dismiss.

This argument does not minimize the importance of the wage differential in the shift to southern non-union coal. Rather, it advances the notion that wage concessions to union firms during this period would have done little to remove the differential since southern firms would simply have reduced wages by a corresponding amount. This argument has the disadvantage—or advantage—of not being susceptible to proof or disproof. Perhaps if the union had reduced wages as early as 1922 it would have been more successful in organizing workers in the southern fields. Certainly it would have had a bigger ''war chest'' to carry out such a campaign since employment in the northern fields would probably have fallen less sharply. Furthermore, if southern operators had attempted to cut wages by a corresponding amount, their workers would have been more willing to join the union. Then, too, there was some point below which southern

---

69 See issues of *Coal Age* and *Coal Review* for 1924 and 1925.

70 Some of the most important northern interests having coal properties in the South were: United States Steel Corporation (southern holdings in West Virginia, Kentucky, Tennessee, and Alabama); Pittsburgh Coal Company (southern holdings in Kentucky and West Virginia); Consolidation Coal Company, Rockefeller-controlled (holdings in West Virginia, Kentucky, and Maryland); Bethlehem Steel Corporation (southern holdings chiefly centered in West Virginia); Bertha Consumers Company (holdings in northern West Virginia as well as in Ohio and western Pennsylvania); Cosgrove-Mahan Company (holdings in northern West Virginia as well as in Ohio). *Conditions in the Coal Fields of Pennsylvania, West Virginia, and Ohio*, Hearings before the Committee on Interstate Commerce, U. S. Senate, 70th Cong., 1st sess., pursuant to S. Res. 105 (1928), testimony of Van Bittner, p. 1171.

producers would or could not have pushed wages. The union might have found that the "bottom floor" was higher than it thought. On the other hand, there is some merit in the contention that southern firms would have simply cut wages further. Certainly wage concessions alone would not have removed the wage differential enjoyed by southern operators. Nor would they have prevented the industry's system of collective bargaining from being undermined. The wage concessions would have had to be coupled with a broad organizing campaign, on the one hand, and with other forms of relief to union firms, on the other. The general difficulties confronting the industry make this conclusion inescapable. Nothing short of a broad program of industrial reform would have sufficed.

The course of events after 1927, when wage reductions were finally made in the northern fields, lends support to the latter view.[71] At first—between 1927 and 1929—the wage differential between northern and southern fields narrowed, although rates in both areas declined. Meanwhile, output in the northern fields increased while southern output declined. The change, however, was short-lived. Wage reductions between 1929 and 1933 were greater in the southern than in the northern fields. In 1929 average hourly earnings in the three southern states of Kentucky, West Virginia, and Virginia were approximately thirteen per cent below comparable rates in the four northern states of Illinois, Indiana, Ohio, and Pennsylvania. By 1933 the percentage difference had risen to about eighteen per cent, nearly as much as in 1924 or 1927. Output between 1929 and 1933, moreover, declined less in the South than in the North. In 1929 output in the three southern states was fourteen per cent below output in the four northern states; in 1933 the percentage difference was only about eight per cent.[72]

In order to save its system of interstate agreements the union would apparently have had to do more than grant wage reductions to union operators in the North. Even if it had been successful in organizing the southern fields it could not have afforded to rest content. The union would have had to go beyond these measures and deal with the basic ills afflicting the industry. To these broader problems during most of the 1920s the union's leaders were generally indifferent. The following statement by a union official in regard to the marketing problems of the industry was fairly typical of the union's viewpoint during these years:

> I do not know whether it is possible to work out some general scheme for the proper development of markets in connection with proper mining districts. That is a question for the coal companies to handle and not for the United Mine

---

[71] The one area in which the union retained strength was Illinois. Even here substantial reductions in wage-rates occurred between 1927 and 1933.

[72] The figures are given in the Appendix, tables I and II.

Workers. The United Mine Workers have tried . . . to hold themselves aloof from dealing with that question.[73]

President John L. Lewis, writing at a time when the difficulties of the industry had reached serious proportions and his own organization was rapidly losing strength, had occasion to declare:

> The struggle in the union fields is slowly weeding out uneconomic mines, obsolete equipment and incompetent management. Exactly as was foreseen by the United Mine Workers, the law of supply and demand, now that it can function because strikes and car shortages have been eliminated and no longer serve as props for the unsound parts of the industry, is working a cure. The overdevelopment of the coal business, which all tribunals have agreed is its basic ill, is on the way to elimination.[74]

It was this narrow view of its function within the industry, and not only its wage policy, which constituted the union's most serious error during the post-war years. Not until 1928, by which time the system of interstate agreements had been virtually destroyed, did the union come to grips with some of the industry's basic difficulties. In that year the union sponsored the Watson Bill which provided that coal companies should operate under a system of Federal licensing. Companies which did not comply with the law would receive no license. A Federal commission was proposed which would have power to set maximum—but not minimum—prices. Operators were to be allowed to form selling associations. Collective bargaining rights of union organizations were to be guaranteed. Coming at a time when business generally was prosperous, the bill failed of passage in Congress. In 1932 the union sponsored the Kelly-Davis Bill. Its provisions were substantially the same as those in the Watson measure except that the commission established under its terms was empowered simply to maintain reasonable prices, although no standards of reasonableness were specified. Doubts were raised as to the constitutionality of the Kelly-Davis Bill, and Congress refused to enact it. In 1933 the National Industrial Recovery Act was passed and a code was subsequently established for the bituminous coal industry. This code prohibited certain unfair trade practices, placed restrictions on output, and guaranteed the collective bargaining rights of labor. The United Mine Workers of America actively supported the National Industrial Recovery Act and played an important part in the formulation of the bituminous coal code. In 1933 the union also seized the opportunity afforded by a friendly Federal administration to launch an aggressive organizing campaign. By 1936 the union had brought

---

[73] *Conditions in the Coal Fields of Pennsylvania, West Virginia, and Ohio*, Hearings before the Committee on Interstate Commerce, U. S. Senate, 70th Cong., 1st sess., pursuant to S. Res. 105 (1928), statement by Percy Tetlow, in 1928 statistician for the United Mine Workers of America, p. 1113.

[74] Lewis, *op. cit.*, p. 38.

the greater part of the industry under its standards, including many formerly non-union strongholds in the South.

When the Supreme Court invalidated the N. R. A. in 1935, the union was chiefly responsible for the enactment of legislation which continued the code program for the bituminous coal industry. The Bituminous Coal Conservation Act of 1935 (known as the Guffey-Snyder Act) retained all the features of the code.[75] The Supreme Court, however, held this law to be unconstitutional.[76] In order to meet the court's objections, the wage and hour provisions of the law were omitted, but all other features of the program were continued in new legislation passed in 1937. This legislation is known as the Bituminous Coal Act of 1937 or Guffey-Vinson Act.[77] In 1940 the law was upheld by the Supreme Court in the Sunshine Anthracite Coal Company case.[78] The law establishes machinery for the setting of minimum and maximum prices and specifies numerous acts as unfair trade practices. Authority to carry out these provisions, according to standards set forth in the law, is vested in the Bituminous Coal Division of the United States Department of Interior.[79] All producers in the country are to accept membership in the code organization; those who do not must pay a tax of 19½ per cent of the price for each ton at the mine. This organization is divided into twenty-three district boards which consist of spokesmen of the member-producers. Each of these boards is directed to recommend a list of minimum prices to the Bituminous Coal Division, the prices to "equal as nearly as may be" the weighted average of the total cost of production. The Division, however, is empowered to approve, disapprove, or modify these recommendations as it chooses. The Division's orders are enforceable by court action.[80]

No less significant have been the changes in the union's system of collective agreements. During the 1930s the union brought the great majority of operators, North and South, under its standards. More than this, in 1939 it secured union shop privileges and established the check-off system of dues payment. The only commercial group which refused to grant the union shop was the Harlan County (Kentucky) Coal Operators' Association; but in 1941 even this traditionally anti-union group capitulated. Substantial increases in wage rates were also won. The 1941 Appalachian Agreement estab-

---

[75] 49 Stat. 991 (1935).

[76] *Carter v. Carter Coal Company, et al.*, 298 U. S. 238, 56 Sup. Ct. 855 (1936).

[77] 50 Stat. 72, 15 U. S. C. A. ¶¶ 828-851.

[78] *Sunshine Anthracite Coal Company v. Adkins*, 310 U. S. 381, 60 Sup. Ct. 907 (1940).

[79] Under the original terms of the law, authority was vested in a commission of seven members. The change was made in accordance with a department order, issued under provisions of the President's Reorganization Plan No. 2. This plan was made effective July 1, 1939, by Public Resolution 20, 76th Congress.

[80] Bituminous Coal Act of 1937, 50 Stat. 72, 15 U. S. C. A. ¶¶ 828-851.

lished a basic inside day labor rate of $7.00 a day for a seven-hour day, the same rate to prevail in both the North and South. The previous Appalachian Agreement, signed in 1939, provided for a basic day labor rate of $6.00 in the North and $5.60 in the South.[81] The present rate of $1.00 per hour is the highest hourly rate ever secured by the union, even exceeding the rate prevailing between 1920 and 1927. The 1941 agreement also provided for an increase of twelve cents a ton for tonnage workers and an increase of fifteen per cent for yardage and deadwork. While the agreement removed the southern differential in day-rates, the discrepancy in piece rates between the North and South were continued.[82]

CONCLUSIONS

It is too early to judge whether this program will be successful in solving the problems confronting the union and the industry. Minimum prices as established by the Bituminous Coal Division went into effect only on October 1, 1940, and the increase in wage-rates and the elimination of wage differentials have been in existence a very short time. In addition, the results of these changes have been obscured by the current re-armament drive. The present improvement in business conditions will, of course, make it much easier for the bituminous coal industry to adapt itself to a program of price-fixing, fair trade standards, and higher wage-rates. After the emergency is past, however, the industry will confront the same issues as before. It is difficult to believe that a program of this sort will solve the basic questions confronting the industry.

At bottom, the industry's problem is one of costs and sales. Unless there is improvement in one or both of these aspects of the industry, a program of price-fixing and higher wage-rates is doomed to failure. Some groups within the industry are beginning to realize this fact. During the past few years a number of firms, acting through the National Coal Association, have conducted a joint research program to discover new and more efficient methods of utilizing soft coal. Particular attention has been paid to the selection and preparation of coal for underfeed stokers, to the dustproofing of coal with oil, to the relative economies of house heating with different fuels, to the segregation of coal in industrial power-plant bunkers, to

---

81 *New York Times*, July 7, 1941, p. 1. The Appalachian Agreement covers mines in Pennsylvania, Michigan, Ohio, Maryland, West Virginia, Virginia, northern Tennessee, and eastern Kentucky.

82 Appalachian Agreement, 1941. Included in the agreement is a protective wage clause which gives the union the right to call strikes during the life of the agreement "when necessary to preserve and maintain the integrity and competitive parity of this agreement."

the utilization of coal in pulverized form in steam plants, and to the conversion of coal into gas for industrial and residential use.[83] Efforts are also being made to secure more efficient methods of production and reduce costs in this way. For example, both union and employer representatives are investigating the problem of technological improvements in the industry. Though it is true that most of these plans are still largely on paper, they are at least addressed to the fundamental difficulties besetting the industry. The union and employers confront the choice of assuming their economic responsibilities or shirking them. The record of the 1920s demonstrates beyond any doubt what the latter course would mean.

---

[83] *United Mine Workers Journal*, February 1, 1941, p. 17.

CHAPTER IX

CONCLUSIONS AND RECOMMENDATIONS

This study has analyzed the problem of responsibility under union agreements in a variety of situations. In all of these situations violations of the agreements were frequent; in some, collective bargaining relations were subsequently terminated. The objective has been to discover why these difficulties occurred.

In order to do so, an examination was made of the circumstances surrounding each situation. Despite their seeming complexity these conditions were found to fall into two main categories: first, circumstances where one or both of the parties followed a deliberate policy of disregarding important provisions of the agreements; second, circumstances where economic factors made it difficult or impossible to maintain standards established by the agreements. The first set pertained to a variety of industries or firms where agreements had been recently established and where the agreements did not accurately reflect the bargaining strength of the contracting parties. The second set pertained to two industries in which collective bargaining had been long established and in which competition was keen.

Those facts point to the main conclusion of the study. Obligations are likely to be disregarded under newly established systems of collective bargaining, if the agreements do not accurately reflect the relative bargaining strength of the two parties or if one of the parties feels this to be the case. Similar difficulties are likely to occur under long-established systems if certain firms in an industry or some segments of it are placed under serious competitive handicaps by reason of the agreements. While it is hard to say that this is actually true of most new and old agreements, the situations that have been examined here suggest that there are strong tendencies working in these two directions. It seems quite clear, moreover, that these two sets of circumstances underlie the problem of responsibility under union agreements. In discussing efforts to deal with the problem, therefore, such circumstances must not be overlooked.

Under some recently signed agreements where considerations of power politics still prevail, employers and unions conduct their relations with each other almost as if no agreements were in effect. In such situations employers may disregard their obligations under agreements with a view to weakening the unions' hold on their employees.

The methods used by employers who adopt this policy were discussed in the chapter based on certain National Labor Relations Board cases. In several of these cases the board found employers guilty of discharging workers active in union affairs. In some cases the board also found that the employers sponsored rival labor organizations. In at least two of these cases, according to the findings of the trial examiners, the employers withheld benefits from the unions which had been promised under the agreements. Part of the responsibility for undermining contractual relations in certain of these cases, however, fell on the union leaders. In some instances the union spokesmen pursued policies which alienated important groups of workers. In one case they insisted on an interpretation of the agreement which its terms did not justify. In a few instances they called strikes before steps in the grievance procedures were completed.

The policy of disturbance sometimes pursued by unions under newly won agreements is clearly seen in the automobile industry. Within the last three years the United Automobile, Aircraft and Agricultural Implement Workers of America, C. I. O., has become the dominant labor organization in the industry. Until recently at least, the union has felt it necessary to continue to use some of the tactics pursued before agreements with certain of the large automobile manufacturers were secured. On occasion this has meant calling strikes before grievance procedures were completed; it has meant pressing claims against management which had little or no foundation or which should have been postponed until the agreements had expired; it has meant bringing strong pressure on workers to join the union despite commitments in the agreements to the contrary. At the present time the consideration which primarily determines union strategy seems to be the demand for closed or union shop conditions. For their part, the automobile manufacturers have tried to check the spread of the union's influence in the plants. Since granting the union recognition, violations of the National Labor Relations Act have apparently been rare and, with a few possible exceptions, employers have not openly disregarded their agreements with the union. Rather, employers have pressed for interpretations of the agreements unfavorable to the union's interests. There is some evidence, although not altogether conclusive, that employers have deliberately used issues like seniority to create resentment among the men against the union. On other issues like the timing of operations employers have made vague promises to the union but nothing more.

The question of appropriate remedial action in such situations raises difficult issues. The lines along which action might be taken can only be indicated here. Measures might be adopted by employers, unions, and the government, acting through some administrative agency or the courts. Each group has certain minimum demands or "limits of endurance." Government, speaking for the public as consumers, requires continuous production at "reasonable" prices; employers and owners are determined not to lose all control over their properties or to see their investments destroyed; unions and workers insist that they be allowed to organize, to bargain collectively, and to work under "decent" conditions of employment. Where serious difficulties under newly established systems of collective bargaining are being met, every effort should be made to safeguard these minimum requirements.

To achieve this end under recently established systems of collective bargaining, certain conditions must exist and certain elementary rules of fair play must be observed by unions and employers. Without presuming to name all these conditions and rules, it is believed that the following are of prime importance:

First, neither side must commit acts causing physical injury to others or physical damage to property.

Second, employers must not hire, fire, and grant promotions in ways which discriminate against union members, nor must they try to promote rival labor organizations among their employees.

Third, before securing agreements unions must be able to show that they have the support of a majority of the workers whom they purport to represent.

Fourth, neither side must systematically disregard orderly processes set up by the contracting parties to handle disputes occurring during the life of agreements.

It is relatively unimportant if, by inadvertence, one or more of these four requirements occasionally go unfulfilled. But if they are disregarded as a matter of deliberate policy, either on the part of employers or unions, orderly collective bargaining becomes impossible.

In large measure existing law covers these issues. Property is protected from damage; persons from physical injury; union members from discrimination. Employers are prohibited from promoting or supporting labor organizations. Most courts are prepared to grant redress if the terms of union agreements, including the promise not to strike, are violated. The one principle of those mentioned which is not a definite part of existing law is the requirement that unions, before securing agreements, must show that they speak for a majority of the workers whom they claim to represent. Even this requirement, however, has in large measure been made a matter of public policy under the National Labor Relations Act; if adopted, this proposal would not occasion much of a change in existing law.

The main task confronting government in dealing with such situations seems to be one of more effective enforcement of existing laws. This, of course, is no easy question. In reference to the National Labor Relations Act, for example, some argue that penalties should be imposed on employers who violate the law; others argue that the law should depend upon voluntary acceptance alone. The situations examined in this study, however, would indicate that every effort should be made to accelerate the handling of cases by the National Labor Relations Board. At the present time, if the cases that have been reviewed here are at all typical, decisions are often made too late to affect the outcome of controversies to any important degree. Moreover, if cases were handled more quickly, employers would probably be less prone to disregard orders issued by the board. This recommendation is, of course, made with reference to cases in which union agreements are in effect. If quickening the board's work resulted in no improvement, amendments to the law itself would have to be considered. For example, public policy might be aimed more directly at discouraging deliberate disregard of grievance procedures by unions or employers. With respect to unions in this connection, the Norris-La Guardia Act might be made inapplicable to strikes called before procedures for handling disputes during the life of agreements are exhausted. If this were ineffective the protection afforded by the National Labor Relations Act might be withdrawn from unions in controversies in which they deliberately disregard no-strike clauses in their agreements. In reference to management, public policy as embodied in the National Labor Relations Act already seeks to discourage employers who refuse to negotiate in good faith over controversies arising under agreements. Such a refusal, however, is not specifically included among the unfair labor practices listed in the law. The possibility of changing the act in this way is worth considering, even though the question of effective enforcement raises enormous difficulties.

In dealing with situations in which one party or both deliberately disregard obligations assumed under new agreements, it is suggested that the government should not attempt to go beyond the limits indicated above. There is the further possibility of establishing some form of compulsory arbitration, but this would mean granting government the power to impose wage-rates, hour-schedules, seniority rules, and other employment standards whenever a dispute under an agreement could not be settled. The grant of such broad powers would involve profound alterations in our form of government. It would require a degree of regulation over employment policies which neither unions nor employers would welcome. Particularly in industries where agreements have only recently been established, opposition would probably soon arise and serious problems of administration and enforcement would ensue. These same considerations apply, although with less force, to the conditions created by the present defense program. One thing made clear by an examination of the situations in this study is the impressive degree of power which both unions and employers are able to summon when their interests are threatened. A government which tried to settle labor controversies by means of compulsory arbitration, even during war-time, would have to reckon with this resistance.

It follows that government should attempt to establish or preserve only a few basic conditions like those listed above, which are essential to orderly collective bargaining. So long as these minimum conditions are met, employers and unions should be free to deal with one another under their agreements as they choose. It should be admitted that this approach to the problem has its drawbacks. Violations of agreements, particularly under newly established bargaining systems, would doubtless occur. Bargaining relations might even be terminated. But this is the price that has to be paid so long as collective bargaining under agreements is largely left to the parties immediately involved. Where collective bargaining is on a voluntary basis, the problem of responsibility under agreements rests primarily with the unions and employers themselves.

It is difficult to recommend specific steps which the contracting parties under new agreements might take to preserve orderly procedures of collective bargaining. Perhaps one can only express the somewhat pious hope that the parties to new agreements will henceforth take their responsibilities more seriously. But there are a few simple rules of collective bargaining procedure which, if adopted by all unions and employers, might bring about some improvement. First, controversies arising during the life of agreements should move quickly from spokesmen of less authority to spokesmen of higher authority. The possibility of placing time-limits on the various levels of negotiation should be considered. Second, disputes over issues not covered by the agreements or over demands for immediate changes in the basic terms of agreements should either be deferred until the agreements expire or else sent directly to the parties responsible for drafting the original terms. Third, the agreements should specify in some detail under what circumstances union spokesmen may confer with workers over grievances and under what conditions they may try to gain new members or collect dues. It also seems important to propose that, under certain regulations, union spokesmen should have the power to investigate employment conditions within plants and to consult company records on matters bearing on the agreements.

These tentative recommendations are advanced with newly established systems of collective bargaining primarily in mind. As bargaining relations become better established, further changes to improve the administration of agreements should, of course, be considered. In this connection, the procedures developed under older bargaining systems are worth examining. Under some long-established systems, employer associations play an important part in the formulation and administration of agreements. Under certain systems, money penalties are levied if violations of the agreements occur. Under almost all long-established systems, the last step in the grievance procedure consists of some form of impartial arbitration. More significant than any procedural changes of this sort, however, is the fact that under long-established systems both sides recognize the status of the other. At least during the life of agreements, considerations of power politics and relative bargaining strengths are of minimum importance. Under these circumstances, controversies during the life of agreements become part of the routine of everyday business, concessions are more readily forthcoming, and cases are handled in an atmosphere more conducive to quick and easy settlement.

In this review of the methods of dealing with the problem of responsibility, scant attention has been given to possible changes in the law of union agreements. At least with regard to newly established systems of collective bargaining, the legal aspects of the problem seem to recede to a secondary position. In reference to bargaining relations that are on a more permanent basis, court decisions on such questions as the enforceability of union agreements assume somewhat greater importance. Even under these circumstances, however, the legal aspects of the problem can be easily over-emphasized. Despite the fact that most courts are now prepared to grant redress if a simple breach of a valid union agreement occurs, relatively few actions of this sort are brought. Apparently neither side feels that court action is generally the most effective way to deal with violations of agreements.

Nevertheless, as pointed out earlier in the study, there are certain phases of the law of union agreements where further clarification would be helpful. The criteria which courts have applied to union agreements have frequently been vague and unrealistic. The cases dealing with closed shop agreements afford many striking illustrations of this tendency. Since recent legislative enactments have approved the use of closed shop agreements, it would seem proper for the courts to give similar approval. The only exception should be the occasional case where fraud has been committed or where closed shop agreements are maliciously designed to injure persons or damage property. If the courts were to go further in holding closed shop agreements illegal, they would be assuming functions which belong to the legislatures. Another controversy stems from the "clean hands" doctrine. In some courts equitable relief for violations of agreements is not granted if the aggrieved party has himself committed a violation. It is hard to see why courts should accept this doctrine if the violation committed by the aggrieved party is a relatively unimportant one.

Another point of difficulty has arisen since the passage of the Norris-La Guardia Act. At present, the restrictions on the use of injunctions embodied in this legislation are applicable to strikes called in violation of union agreements. As previously indicated, the proposal to make the law inapplicable to such strikes is worth consideration. Finally, considerable confusion exists over the position of individual union members under union agreements. The various doctrines on which the courts have rested their decisions on this issue have not made for clarity or realism. It has already been proposed that, before signing agreements, unions should be required to show that they have the support of a majority of the workers whom they claim to represent. If this rule were followed, it would be reasonable to consider individual members bound by their union's agreements. Why, indeed, should not the same rule apply to workers who join the union after an agreement is signed? More perplexing is the case of workers who have a genuine desire not to belong to the union. In determining whether such workers should be bound by the agreement, perhaps chief weight should be given to prevailing practice in the particular industry involved. If, in a given industry, non-union workers are not customarily considered bound by agreements, the courts would hardly be justified in ruling otherwise.

Under long-established systems, however, the problem of responsibility is not primarily a matter of grievance procedures or legal safeguards. Nor is it primarily even a matter of relative bargaining powers. The problem is essentially economic in character. This conclusion is based on a detailed investigation of two long-established systems, one in the New York coat and suit industry and another in the bituminous coal industry. In both cases serious difficulties have been encountered in enforcing standards established by agreements. In both, economic factors underlie the problem.

The economic characteristics of these two industries are not such as to make the task of enforcement easy. Employers are numerous; operations are small-scale; the financial position of employers is frequently precarious; trends in the volume of employment have not been favorable. In both industries employers are frequently under great pressure to reduce expenses. Since labor costs are such an important part of total costs, it follows that employers are sometimes ready to go considerable lengths to escape standards established by union agreements. Moreover, so long as some firms are able to operate below union standards, they secure an important competitive advantage which forces other firms to do likewise. These are the factors which have plagued collective bargaining in both of these industries for many years.

In dealing with problems of this nature, union leaders all too frequently follow a policy of economic irresponsibility. They continue to demand higher wage-rates and shorter hours and disregard the problem of how employers will be able to meet the increases in costs. Where they persevere in such policies, violations of the agreements become frequent, and firms are forced to go out of business.

If this happens generally, it requires no great insight to realize that the unions are destroying the basis on which their agreements and their own organizations rest.

In an industry where collective bargaining has been long established, union leaders must be ready to forsake traditional views and accept the economic responsibilities which their position entails. There is a variety of policies which they should be prepared to follow. First, they should take steps to remove any serious competitive handicaps under which union firms are operating. Perhaps an aggressive organizing campaign might encompass this result. Perhaps some concessions to firms already under agreement are required. One thing is clear—unless employment standards in competing firms are substantially the same, difficulties are sure to occur. Second, union leaders should endeavor to remove any serious competitive handicaps under which the industry as a whole may be operating. They should likewise be ready to help remove barriers to expansion in industries in which sales are poor and employment small. Under these circumstances, new and more efficient methods of production should be investigated. There should be efforts to expand sales. There should be an examination of possible sources of government aid. There should be a careful analysis of the industry's wage structure with a view to granting reductions if rates are higher than in comparable lines elsewhere. Whatever the particular steps taken, they perforce must go beyond the interest of any one group in the industry. All parties involved must be reconciled to some concessions.

In the two industries described, in which long-established bargaining systems are in effect, the unions have gone some way toward dealing with these problems. Indeed, the unions have in large measure provided whatever constructive leadership is to be found in the two industries. The International Ladies' Garment Workers' Union, chiefly with the aid of the "inside" manufacturers, has helped to build an elaborate machinery for the peaceful settlement of controversies and for the enforcement of agreements. It has played an important part in the program of the New York coat and suit industry to continue N. R. A. code standards. It has made vigorous efforts to organize non-union shops and to establish uniform employment standards throughout the industry. At present it is actively cooperating with the Board of Stability and Control, recently formed to try to solve some of the industry's problems. The United Mine Workers of America has taken similar steps. In recent years that union has brought a larger proportion of the industry under the standards of its agreements than ever before. These efforts, temporarily at least, have gone a long way toward removing the competitive handicaps under which union employers once labored. The union has also been instrumental in establishing a government-sponsored program of price-fixing, designed to curb competitive practices in the industry. It has taken some steps, chiefly investigatory in nature, to deal with the problem of mechanization.

These are important beginnings, although perhaps in some respects not altogether wise. But their basic weakness is clear. These measures afford insufficient relief to the many firms confronted by financial difficulties. The union leaders must give still more help to these firms. As already indicated, such a policy might require sacrifices. It might alienate certain groups among the unions' membership. It could even lead to an overthrow of the existing union leadership. But the risk cannot be avoided. The choice under these circumstances is not between a few sacrifices and none. Rather is it a choice between sacrifices according to a well-defined plan in which all groups have a part, or sacrifices according to the ruthless and perhaps uneconomic principle of the survival of the fittest.

APPENDIX

Table I

COMPARISON OF AVERAGE VALUE PER NET TON (F. O. B. MINE) AND PRODUCTION OF BITUMINOUS COAL IN TWO GROUPS OF STATES EAST OF THE MISSISSIPPI RIVER—1920-1933[1]

	AVERAGE VALUE			PRODUCTION		
Year	"A" States (Union)	"B" States (Non-union)	Percentage Difference Between "B" and "A"	"A" States Net Thousand Tons (Union)	"B" States Net Thousand Tons (Non-union)	Percentage Difference Between "B" and "A"
1920	$3.54	$4.25	+20.0	334,562	137,040	—59.0
1921	2.73	2.81	+ 2.9	237,879	111,868	—53.0
1922	3.04	2.93	— 3.6	217,703	133,114	—38.9
1923	2.62	2.63	0	317,873	164,439	—48.3
1924	2.23	1.85	—17.0	250,910	157,504	—37.2
1925	2.10	1.72	—18.1	253,096	190,249	—24.8
1926	2.10	1.82	—13.3	273,467	220,567	—19.3
1927	2.06	1.73	—16.0	213,549	227,162	+ 6.4
1928	1.90	1.59	—16.3	219,170	206,713	— 5.7
1929	1.78	1.55	—13.0	246,207	211,730	—14.0
1930	1.68	1.50	—10.7	217,236	183,589	—15.5
1931	1.57	1.31	—16.6	176,668	151,135	—14.5
1932	1.36	1.05	—22.8	135,484	128,600	— 5.1
1933	1.36	1.14	—16.2	150,059	138,622	— 7.6

[1] The "A" states are Illinois, Indiana, Ohio, and Pennsylvania; the "B" states are Kentucky, West Virginia, and Virginia.

Source: U. S. Geological Survey and U. S. Bureau of Mines, figures taken from Fred E. Berquist and associates, *Economic Survey of the Bituminous Coal Industry under Free Competition and Code Regulation* (National Recovery Administration, Division of Review, Work Materials No. 69, 1936), vol. I, p. 65.

Table II

COMPARISON OF AVERAGE HOURLY EARNINGS BETWEEN TWO GROUPS OF STATES EAST OF THE MISSISSIPPI RIVER, SPECIFIED YEARS, 1921-1933[1]

All Men (Day and Tonnage Men Combined)

Periods Studied	Average "A" States (Union)	Average "B" States (Non-union)	Percentage Difference Between "B" & "A"
1921-1922 (10-1-21 to 2-15-22)	$ .894	$ .819[2]	— 8.4
1924 (10-1-24 to 12-31-24)	.885	.699	—21.0
1926-1927 (11-26-26 to 3-22-27)	.860	.670	—22.1
1929 (1st Quarter)	.707	.616	—12.9
1931 (1st Quarter)	.662	.552	—16.6
1933 (February)	.458	.374	—18.3

[1] The "A" states are Illinois, Indiana, Ohio, and Pennsylvania; the "B" states are Kentucky, West Virginia, and Virginia.

[2] Does not include Virginia.

Source: U. S. Bureau of Labor Statistics, figures taken from Berquist and associates, *Economic Survey of the Bituminous Coal Industry under Free Competition and Code Regulation* (National Recovery Administration, Division of Review, Work Materials No. 69, 1936), vol. I, p. 75.

Table III

AVERAGE VALUE PER NET TON (F. O. B. MINE) OF BITUMINOUS COAL, 1923-1927[1]

(Exclusive of Wagon Mines Producing Less than 1,000 Tons Annually)

TWO LOW VOLATILE FIELDS

Year	A. Central Pennsylvania[2] (Union)	B. Southern Low Volatile[3] (Non-union)	Percentage Difference Between B and A
1923	$ 2.87	$ 3.14	+ 9.4
1924	2.37	1.98	—16.5
1925	2.14	1.94	— 9.3
1926	2.14	2.12	— .9
1927	2.05	1.97	— 3.9

TWO HIGH VOLATILE FIELDS

Year	A. Western Pennsylvania[4] (Union)	B. Southern High Volatile[5] (Non-union)	Percentage Difference Between B and A
1923	$ 2.68	$ 2.60	— 3.0
1924	2.22	1.82	—18.0
1925	2.10	1.70	—19.0
1926	2.13	1.80	—15.5
1927	2.06	1.71	—17.0

[1] Figures prior to 1923 are not available.

[2] Includes U. S. Coal Commission Fields No. 6 (Blossburg), 7 (Broad Top), 9, a b c (Central Pennsylvania).

[3] Includes U. S. Coal Commission Fields No. 17 (Tug River), 18 (Pocohontas), 19 (Winding Gulf), 20 (New River), 27 (Virginia Anthracite), 28 (Richmond Basin), 92 (North Carolina).

[4] Includes U. S. Coal Commission Fields No. 1 (Pittsburgh), 2 (Connellsville), 3 (Westmoreland-Ligonier), 4 a b (Freeport), 5 (Butler-Mercer).

[5] Includes all high volatile districts of southern West Virginia, eastern Kentucky, Virginia, and northern Tennessee.

Source: Data prepared by W. H. Young, U. S. Bureau of Mines, February 21, 1934.

Table IV

PRODUCTION OF BITUMINOUS COAL, NET TONS, 1920-1927

(Exclusive of Wagon Mines Producing Less than 1,000 Tons Annually)

TWO LOW VOLATILE FIELDS

	Central Pennsylvania (Union)		Southern Low Volatile (Non-union)		
Year	A. Production (Net Thousand Tons)	B. Percentage of National Production	C. Production (Net Thousand Tons)	D. Percentage of National Production	Percentage Difference Between C and A
1920	60,584	10.7	33,778	6.0	—44.2
1921	42,073	10.1	29,134	7.0	—30.8
1922	38,479	9.2	35,098	8.4	— 8.8
1923	56,349	10.0	37,380	6.6	—33.7
1924	43,244	8.9	39,622	8.2	— 8.4
1925	45,377	8.7	46,884	9.0	+ 3.3
1926	49,871	8.7	53,579	9.3	+ 7.4
1927	43,345	8.4	51,431	9.9	+18.7

TWO HIGH VOLATILE FIELDS

	Western Pennsylvania (Union)		Southern High Volatile (Non-union)		
Year	A. Production (Net Thousand Tons)	B. Percentage of National Production	C. Production (Net Thousand Tons)	D. Percentage of National Production	Percentage Difference Between C and A
1920	100,041	17.7	66,625	11.8	—33.6
1921	68,142	16.4	55,997	13.5	—17.8
1922	67,106	16.0	64,939	15.5	—33.2
1923	109,580	19.5	51,588	14.5	—52.9
1924	81,743	16.9	83,905	17.4	+ 2.6
1925	84,799	16.3	101,470	19.5	+19.7
1926	96,028	16.8	113,711	19.8	+18.4
1927	82,462	15.9	114,799	22.2	+39.2

Source: Data prepared by W. H. Young, U. S. Bureau of Mines, February 21, 1934.

BIBLIOGRAPHY

GENERAL STUDIES

Bernheim, Alfred L., and others. *Labor and the Government.* New York: McGraw-Hill Book Company, Inc., 1935.

Bloch, Louis. *Labor Agreements in Coal Mines.* New York: Russell Sage Foundation, 1931.

Brooks, Robert R. R. *As Steel Goes . . .* New Haven: Yale University Press, 1940.

————. *When Labor Organizes.* New Haven: Yale University Press, 1937.

Caroll, Mollie R. *What Is Collective Bargaining?* New York: Longmans, Green and Company, 1939.

Carsel, Wilfred. *A History of the Chicago Ladies' Garment Workers' Union.* Chicago: Normandie House, 1940.

Cooke, Morris L., and Murray, Philip. *Organized Labor and Producduction.* New York: Harper and Brothers, 1940.

Fisher, Thomas R. *Industrial Disputes and Federal Legislation.* New York: Columbia University Press, 1940.

Fisher, Waldo E., and Bezanson, Anne. *Wage Rates and Working Time in the Bituminous Coal Industry, 1912-1922.* Philadelphia: University of Pennsylvania Press, 1932.

Fitch, John A. *The Causes of Industrial Unrest.* New York: Harper and Brothers, 1924.

Fritz, Wilbert G., and Veenstra, Theodore A. *Regional Shifts in the Bituminous Coal Industry.* Pittsburgh: Bureau of Business Research, University of Pittsburgh, 1935.

Galenson, Walter. *Rival Unionism in the United States.* Washington, D. C.: American Council on Public Affairs, 1940.

Gardiner, Glenn L. *How to Handle Grievances.* New York: Elliott Service Company, 1937.

Goodrich, Carter L. *The Miner's Freedom.* Boston: Marshall Jones Company, 1925.

Goodrich, Carter L., and others. *Migration and Economic Opportunity.* Philadelphia: University of Pennsylvania Press, 1936.

Green, William. *Labor and Democracy.* Princeton: Princeton University Press, 1939.

Greenman, Russell L. *The Worker, the Foreman and the Wagner Act.* New York: Harper and Brothers, 1939.

Haber, William. *Industrial Relations in the Building Industry.* Cambridge: Harvard University Press, 1930.

Hamilton, Walton H., and Wright, Helen R. *The Case of Bituminous Coal.* Institute of Economics of the Brookings Institution. New York: The Macmillan Company, 1925.

Harbison, Frederick H. *The Seniority Principle in Union-Management Relations.* Princeton: Princeton University, Industrial Relations Section, 1939.

Hicks, John R. *The Theory of Wages.* London: Macmillan and Company, Ltd., 1932.

Hinrichs, Albert F. *The United Mine Workers of America and the Non-union Coal Fields.* New York: Columbia University Press, 1923.

Hoxie, Robert F. *Trade Unionism in the United States.* (2nd ed.) New York: D. A. Appleton and Company, 1923.

Hunt, Edwin E., Tryon, Frederick G., and Willits, Joseph H. *What the Coal Commission Found.* Baltimore: The Williams and Wilkins Company, 1925.

Hutt, William H. *The Theory of Collective Bargaining.* London: P. S. King and Son, Ltd., 1930.

Landis, James M. *Cases on Labor Law.* Chicago: The Foundation Press, Inc., 1934.

Leiserson, William M. *Right and Wrong in Labor Relations.* Berkeley: University of California Press, 1938.

Lescohier, Don D. *The Labor Market.* New York: The Macmillan Company, 1919.

Lewis, John L. *The Miners' Fight for American Standards.* Indianapolis: Bell Publishing Company, 1925.

Lieberman, Elias. *The Collective Labor Agreement; how to negotiate and draft the contract.* New York: Harper and Brothers, 1939.

Lorwin, Lewis L. *The Women's Garment Workers.* New York: B. W. Huebsch, Inc., 1924.

Lubin, Isador. *Miners' Wages and the Cost of Coal.* The Institute of Economics of the Brookings Institution. New York: McGraw-Hill Book Company, Inc., 1924.

Magee, Mabel A. *Trends in Location of the Women's Clothing Industry.* Chicago: University of Chicago, 1930.

McCabe, David A. *The Standard Rate in American Trade Unions.* Baltimore: The Johns Hopkins Press, 1912.

McDonald, David J., and Lynch, Edward A. *Coal and Unionism.* Silver Spring, Maryland: Lynald Company, 1939.

McIsaac, Archibald M. *The Order of Railroad Telegraphers.* Princeton: Princeton University Press, 1933.

McPherson, William H. *Labor Relations in the Automobile Industry.* Washington, D. C.: The Brookings Institution, 1940.

National Bureau of Economic Research. *Report of the Committee on Prices in the Bituminous Coal Industry.* Waldo E. Fisher, Chairman. New York: National Bureau of Economic Research, 1938.

Nyman, Richmond C., and Smith, Elliott D. *Union-Management Cooperation in the "Stretch-out."* New Haven: Yale University Press, 1934.

Oneal, James. *A History of the Amalgamated Ladies' Garment Cutters' Union, Local 10.* New York: Local 10, 1927.

Palmer, Gladys L. *Union Tactics and Economic Change.* Philadelphia: University of Pennsylvania Press, 1932.

Parker, Glen L. *The Coal Industry: a Study in Social Control.* Washington, D. C.: American Council on Public Affairs, 1940.

Perlman, Selig. *A Theory of the Labor Movement.* New York: The Macmillan Company, 1928.

Perlman, Selig, and Taft, Philip. *History of Labor in the United States* (John R. Commons and others) Volume 4. New York: The Macmillan Company, 1935.

Rosenfarb, Joseph. *The National Labor Policy.* New York: Harper and Brothers, 1940.

Schneider, David M. *The Workers' Party and American Trade Unions.* Baltimore: The Johns Hopkins Press, 1928.

Segal, Melvin J. *The Norris-La Guardia Act and the Courts.* Washington, D. C.: American Council on Public Affairs, 1941.

Selekman, Ben M. *Postponing Strikes.* New York: Russell Sage Foundation, 1927.

Smith, Elliott D., and Nyman, Richmond C. *Technology and Labor.* New Haven: Yale University Press, 1939.

Teper, Lazare. *The Women's Garment Industry.* New York: Educational Department, International Ladies' Garment Workers' Union, 1937.

Whitehead, Thomas N. *The Industrial Worker.* Cambridge: Harvard University Press, 1938. 2 vols.

Witt, Nathan. *Supplement to Landis' Cases on Labor Law, 1934-1937.* Chicago: The Foundation Press, Inc., 1937.

Witte, Edwin E. *The Government in Labor Disputes.* New York: McGraw-Hill Book Company, Inc., 1932.

Wolman, Leo. *Ebb and Flow in Trade Unionism.* New York: National Bureau of Economic Research, 1936.

Yoder, Dale. *Personnel and Labor Relations.* New York: Prentice-Hall, Inc., 1938.

GOVERNMENT REPORTS AND DOCUMENTS

Attorney General's Committe on Administrative Procedure. *The National Labor Relations Board.* Monograph No. 18. Walter Gellhorn, Director. Washington, D. C.: United States Department of Justice, 1940.

————. *Railway Labor, the National Railroad Adjustment Board and the National Mediation Board.* Monograph No. 17. Walter Gellhorn, Director. Washington, D. C.: United States Department of Justice, 1940.

Final Report of the Automobile Labor Board. Leo Wolman, Chairman. 1935. Copy available at the Business School Library, Columbia University, New York City.

Governor's Advisory Commission, Cloak, Suit and Skirt Industry. *Final Recommendations.* George G. Battle, Chairman. New York: The Commission, 1926. Copy available at the New York City Public Library.

————. *Report of an Investigation by John Dickinson and Morris Kolchin.* New York: The Commission, 1925. Copy available at the New York City Public Library.

Maritime Labor Board. *Report to the President and to the Congress.* Robert W. Bruère, Chairman. Washington, D. C.: Government Printing Office, 1940.

National Labor Relations Board. *Annual Reports,* 1935-1940. Washington, D. C.: Government Printing Office.

National Labor Relations Board, Division of Economic Research. *Governmental Protection of Labor's Right to Organize.* Bulletin No. 1. Washington, D. C.: Government Printing Office, 1936.

————. *Union-Employer Responsibility.* Research Memorandum No. 4. January 16, 1939. Washington, D. C.: The Board.

————. *Written Trade Agreements in Collective Bargaining.* Bulletin No. 4. Washington, D. C.: Government Printing Office, 1940.

National Research Project on Reemployment Opportunities and Recent Changes in Industrial Techniques, Works Progress Administration. *Mechanization, Employment and Output per Man in Bituminous Coal Mining.* Willard E. Hotchkiss, Frederick G. Tryon, Charlotte K. Warner, and others. Philadelphia: Works Progress Administration, 1939. 2 vols.

————. *Production, Employment and Productivity in Fifty-nine Manufacturing Industries, 1919-1936.* Harry Magdoff, Irving H. Siegel, and Milton B. Davis. Philadelphia: Works Progress Administration, 1939.

————. *Trade Union Policy and Technological Change.* Harry Ober. Philadelphia: Works Progress Administration, 1940.

United States Bituminous Coal Commission. *Award and Recommendations.* Henry M. Robinson, Chairman. Washington, D. C.: Government Printing Office, 1920.

——————. *Report.* John H. Hammond, Chairman. 68th Congress, 2nd Session, pursuant to S. Res. 347. Senate Document 195. Washington, D. C.: Government Printing Office, 1925. 5 parts.

United States Department of Labor, Bureau of Labor Statistics. *Adjustment of Labor Disputes.* Florence Peterson, "Monthly Labor Review," November, 1939, Vol. 49, No. 5, pp. 1023-1044.

——————. *Characteristics of Company Unions.* Bulletin No. 635, David J. Saposs and others. Washington, D. C.: Government Printing Office, 1938.

——————. *Grievance Settlement under Union Agreements.* Helen S. Hoeber, "Monthly Labor Review," February, 1940, vol. 50, no. 2, pp. 286-311.

——————. *Handbook of American Trade Unions.* Bulletin No. 618, Estelle M. Stewart. Washington, D. C.: Government Printing Office, 1936.

——————. *Strikes in the United States, 1880-1936.* Bulletin No. 651, Florence Peterson. Washington, D. C.: Government Printing Office, 1938.

——————. *Union-Management Relations in the Women's Clothing Industry.* New York Industrial Area, 1936. Helen S. Hoeber, "Montly Labor Review," July, 1936, vol. 43, no. 1, pp. 24-33.

——————. *Wages and Hours of Labor in Bituminous Coal Mining.* Bulletins No. 454, 516, and 601. Washington, D. C.: Government Printing Office, 1927. Data for selected years, 1922-1929.

United States House of Representatives, Committee on Labor. *Hearings on Proposed Amendments to the National Labor Relations Act, 1939.* 76th Congress, 1st Session, pursuant to H. Res. 2761, 4376, 4400, 4594, 4749, 4990, 5231. Washington, D. C.: Government Printing Office, 1939. Vols. 1-8.

United States House of Representatives, Special Committee to Investigate the National Labor Relations Board. *Intermediate Report.* 76th Congress, 1st Session, pursuant to H. Res. 258. Washington, D. C.: Government Printing Office, 1940.

——————. *Verbatim Record of Proceedings.* Washington, D. C.: The Bureau of International Affairs, 1940.

United States National Recovery Administration, Division of Review. *Economic Survey of the Bituminous Coal Industry under Free Competition and Code Regulation.* Fred E. Berquist and associates. Work Materials No. 69, 1936. 2 vols.

United States National Recovery Administration, Research and Planning Division. *Preliminary Report on Study of Regularization of Employment and Improvement of Labor Conditions in the Automobile Industry.* Leon Henderson, Director. 1935.

United States Senate, Committee on Education and Labor. *National Labor Relations Act and Proposed Amendments.* Hearings before the committee. 76th Congress, 1st and 3rd Sessions, pursuant to S. Res. 1000, 1264, 1392, 1550, 1580, 2123. parts 1-24. Washington, D. C.: Government Printing Office, 1939-1940.

United States Senate, Committee on Education and Labor. *Oppressive Labor Practices Act.* Hearings before a subcommittee. 76th Congress, 1st Session, pursuant to S. Res. 1970. Washington, D. C.: Government Printing Office, 1939.

————————. Report to accompany S. Res. 1970, submitted by Robert La Follette. 76th Congress, 1st Session, Report No. 901. Washington, D. C.: Government Printing Office, 1939.

————————. *Violations of Free Speech and Rights of Labor.* Hearings before a subcommittee. 74th Congress, 2nd Session; 75th Congress, 1st and 3rd Sessions; 76th Congress, 3rd Session; pursuant to S. Res. 266. parts 1-64. Washington, D. C.: Government Printing Office, 1937-1940.

United States Senate, Committee on Interstate Commerce. *Conditions in the Coal Fields of Pennsylvania, West Virginia and Ohio.* Hearings before the committee. 70th Congress, 1st Session, pursuant to S. Res. 105. parts 1-8. Washington, D. C.: Government Printing Office, 1928.

United States Senate, Committee on Interstate Commerce. *Stabilization of the Bituminous Coal Industry.* Hearings before a subcommittee. 74th Congress, 1st Session, pursuant to S. Res. 1417. Washington, D. C.: Government Printing Office, 1935.

LEGAL PERIODICALS

Anderson, Grant T. *Collective Bargaining Agreements.* 15 Oregon Law Review (1936) 229.

Depres, L. M. *Collective Agreement for the Union Shop.* 7 University of Chicago Law Review (1939) 24.

Duguit, Leon. *Collective Acts as Distinguished from Contracts.* 27 Yale Law Journal (1918) 753.

Fraenkel, Osmond K. *Legal Enforceability of Agreements to Arbitrate Labor Disputes.* 1 Arbitration Journal (1937) 360.

Fuchs, Ralph F. *Collective Labor Agreements under Administrative Regulation of Employment.* 35 Columbia Law Review (1935) 493.

Hamilton, Milo F. *Individual Rights Arising from Collective Labor Contracts.* 3 Missouri Law Review (1938) 253.

Magruder, Calvert. *A Half Century of Legal Influence Upon the Development of Collective Bargaining.* 50 Harvard Law Review (1937) 1071.

Mason, Alpheus T. *Organized Labor as Party Plaintiff in Injunction Cases.* 30 Columbia Law Review (1930) 466.

Rice, William G., Jr. *Collective Labor Agreements in American Law.* 44 Harvard Law Review (1931) 572.

———————. *The Legal Significance of Labor Contracts under the National Labor Relations Act.* 37 Michigan Law Review (1939) 693.

Rice, William G., Jr., McCabe, David A., and others. *Collective Bargaining Under the Wagner Act.* 5 Law and Contemporary Problems (1938) 1.

Warm, J. Louis. *A Study of the Judicial Attitude Toward Trade Unions and Labor Legislation.* 23 Minnesota Law Review (1938) 255.

Witmer, T. Richard. *Collective Labor Agreements.* 48 Yale Law Journal (1938) 195.

TRADE UNION DOCUMENTS, NEWSPAPERS, AND PAMPHLETS

Advance, The. New York City: Amalgamated Clothing Workers of America.

A. F. of L. Auto Worker, The. Detroit: United Automobile Workers of America, A. F. of L.

American Federationist. Washington, D. C.: American Federation of Labor.

Automobile Unionism, 1939-1940. Report of the President, R. J. Thomas, to the 1940 convention, St. Louis. Detroit: International Union, United Automobile Workers of America, C. I. O., 1940.

C. I. O. News, The. Washington, D. C.: Congress of Industrial Organizations.

Constitution and By-Laws of the International Ladies' Garment Workers' Union. New York City: The Union, 1932.

Constitution, General Statutes and Subordinate Division Statutes of the Order of Railroad Telegraphers. Cleveland: The Order, 1936.

Constitution of the International Union, United Automobile Workers of America, and Laws Governing Local Unions. Detroit: The Union, 1940.

Constitution of the International Union, United Mine Workers of America. Washington, D. C.: The Union, 1936.

Handbook of Trade Union Methods, with Special Reference to the Garment Trades. New York City: Educational Department, International Ladies' Garment Workers' Union, 1937.

Handling Grievances: a handbook for committeemen of local lodges of the Steel Workers' Organizing Committee. Pittsburgh: The Committee, 1938.

Industry Planning Through Collective Bargaining. New York City: Joint Board of the Dressmakers' Union, I. L. G. W. U., 1941.

Justice. New York City: International Ladies' Garment Workers' Union.

Labor. Washington, D. C.: Publication of fifteen railroad labor organizations, A. F. of L.

Manual of Common Procedure for Local Unions. Indianapolis: United Mine Workers of America.

Pilot, The. New York City: National Maritime Union of America.

Proceedings. First and Second National Conventions, 1937, 1939. New York City: National Maritime Union.

Proceedings of Annual Conventions, International Union, United Automobile Workers of America, C. I. O. Detroit: The Union.

Proceedings of Constitutional Conventions of the United Mine Workers of America, 1920-1940. Washington, D. C.: The Union.

Proceedings of National Conventions, 1920-1940. Summaries reported in "The Railroad Telegrapher." St. Louis: The Order of Railroad Telegraphers.

Proceedings of the First and Second International Wage and Policy Conventions of the Steel Workers' Organizing Committee. Pittsburgh: The Committee, 1937, 1940.

Production Problems: a Handbook for Committeemen of Local Lodges of the Steel Workers' Organizing Committee. Pittsburgh: The Committee, 1938.

Railroad Trainman, The. Cleveland: Brotherhood of Railroad Trainmen.

Report and Record, Conventions, 1920-1940. New York City: International Ladies' Garment Workers' Union.

Revised Constitution. Printed in "The Pilot," July 24, 1939 (vol. IV, no. 28a). New York City: National Maritime Union.

Steel Labor. Indianapolis: The Steel Workers' Organizing Committee.

Summary, Convention Proceedings of the Thirty-first Consecutive Constitutional Convention, U. M. W. A., dealing with Illinois affairs and attempts to foment rebellion and organize a dual union. Indianapolis: United Mine Workers of America.

The Maritime Commission vs. the Seamen. Washington, D. C.: C. I. O. Maritime Committee, 1939.

The N. M. U. Forges Ahead. Article by Joseph Curran, President. New York City: National Maritime Union, 1940.

United Automobile Worker. Detroit: International Union, United Automobile Workers of America, C. I. O.

United Mine Workers' Journal. Washington, D. C.: The Union.

Wage Agreements, Bituminous Coal Industry, 1935-1937. Indianapolis: United Mine Workers of America, 1938.

Wage Agreements, Bituminous Coal Industry and Code of Fair Competition, 1934. Washington, D. C.: United Mine Workers of America, 1934.

INDEX

Adjustment machinery, *see* Grievance machinery.
Ahlquist v. Alaska-Portland Packers' Assn., 71n.
Aircraft industry, 7, 109-111, 200.
Alaska S. S. Co. v. International Longshoremen's Assn., 66n.
Alfred W. Booth v. Burgess, 52n.
Alger, G., 149n.
Allin, B. W., 191-192.
American Federation of Labor, 7, 56-57, 122-123.
American Fur Mfrs.' Assn., Inc., v. Assd. Fur Coat and Trimming Mfrs., Inc., 51n.
Amos, A., 104n.
Anderson, A., 96.
Anderson, C., 105n.
Anderson, H. T., 91.
Anti-injunction laws, 62-64, 69-70, 75; Oregon Anti-Injunction Act, 63; Pennsylvania Anti-Injunction Act, 62, 69n; *see also* Norris-La Guardia Act.
Anti-union practices, 10, 21, 42-43, 78, 82, 86-94, 97-98, 103, 105-106, 113, 116, 118, 200; anti-union statements, 92, 102; "Citizen Committee," 92; move business, threat to, 90-91; runaway shop, 70, 87, 138-139, 141; strikebreakers, 92-93.
Appalachian Agreement, 26n, 27n, 31n, 35n, 41-42, 196-197.
Arbitration, 10, 23-24, 33, 44-45, 98, 133, 145-146, 158; appraisal of types, 34-35; compulsory, 189, 202-203; frequency of cases, 17-18, 45-46, 151-152; impartial chairman, 17, 27-28, 32, 82, 87n, 145, 148-154, 160-164, 167; legal aspects, 68-69; where found, 14.
Arthur v. Oakes, 69n.
Associated Automobile Workers of America, 122.
Assd. Flour Haulers, etc., v. Sullivan, etc., 61n.
Automobile industry, 2-3, 21-22, 24-25, Chapter VI, 134, 200; closed shop, 112-115, 200; economic conditions, 117-121; elections, 120, 123-124; grievance machinery, 16-25, 126; transfers and promotions, 130-131; wage standards, 111-113, 117-118, 120-121, 134; *see also* United Automobile Workers of America.
Automobile Labor Board, 122, 128n.
Automobile Manufacturers Association, 127n.
Automotive Industrial Workers' Association, 122.

Bailey, J. W., 20n.
Baltimore and Ohio Railroad, 171.
Bankruptcy Act, Section 77 B, 88.
Bargaining power, importance of, 9, 12-13, 21, 30, 39, 75, 78, 82-86, 105-106, 111, 118, 199-200.
Barloon, M. J., 113n.
Beatty v. Chicago, Burlington and Quincy Railroad Co., 71n.
Bell, L., 172n.
Bell v. Western Ry. of Alabama, 71n.
Berkhammer v. The Cleveland and Morgantown Coal Co., 58n.
Berquist, F. E., 41n, 174n, 175n, 180n, 181n, 186n.
Berry v. Donovan, 50, 52n.
Bertha Consumers Company, 193n.
Bethlehem Mines Corporation, 171.
Bethlehem Steel Corporation, 193n.
Bezanson, A., 174n, 183, 184n, 186n, 189n.
Bias in labor issues, 1, 7, 53.
Bittner, V., 193n.
Bituminous Coal Act of 1937, 196.
Bituminous Coal Conservation Act of 1935, 196.
Blankenhorn, H. L., 40n.
Bolivian Panama Hat Co., Inc., v. Finkelstein, 60n.
Boot and Shoe Workers' Union, 50, 68n.
Boston and Albany Railroad Agreement, 26n, 28n, 30n.
Boudin, L., 49n.
Bradley, J. D., 173n.
Brescia Construction Co. v. Stone Masons' Contractors' Assn., 51n.
Breslaw, J., 165n.
Brophy, J., 190.
Brown Shoe Co., Inc., etc., and Boot and Shoe Workers' Union, Local No. 655, The Matter of, 79n.
Buffalo Erie Ry. Co., v. Amalgamated Assn. of Street and Electric Ry. Workers of America, The Matter of, 68n.
Buffalo, Rochester and Pittsburgh Railroad, 171.
Building industry, 76; grievance machinery in, 14.
Bulkin v. Sacks, 62n.
Burickson v. Kleen Laundry Service, Inc., 60n.
Burnetta v. Marceline Coal Co., 58n, 71n.

Cannon, B. H., 32n.
Carlson, W. R., 94n.

Carnegie-Illinois Steel Corporation Agreement, 16n, 19n, 20n, 22n, 24n.
Carter v. Carter Coal Co., et al., 196n.
Census of Manufactures, 133n, 134n, 140n, 141n.
Central Competitive Field, 170, 173, 180, 182-185, 191.
Central Pennsylvania Field, 187.
Chafee, Z., Jr., 74n.
Chrysler Corporation, 115, 128.
Chrysler Corporation Agreement, 16n, 19, 22n, 24n, 111n, 112, 124.
Cinderella Theater Co., Inc., v. Sign Writers' Local Union, 62n, 67n.
Citizens' Co. v. Asheville Typographical Union, 63n.
Clarkson v. Laiblau, 65n.
Cloak, Suit and Skirt Manufacturers' Protective Association Agreement, 144n.
Closed shop, 26, 42, 49-54, 73, 81, 87, 89, 110, 112-115, 132, 134, 200, 204; monopolistic aspects, 48-49, 51-53.
Clothing industry, 86; production in, 133-134; wage standards, 134; *see also* Coat and suit industry, Dress industry, International Ladies' Garment Workers' Union.
Coal Age, 190n, 193n.
Coal industry, 76.
 Anthracite, Board of Conciliation of, 14.
 Bituminous, 2-3, 26, 39-46, 76, 86, Chapter VIII, 205-207; Central Competitive Field, 170, 173, 180, 182-185, 191; Central Pennsylvania Field, 187; Connellsville Field, 183, 185; economic characteristics, 175-182; Fairmount Field, 185; grievance machinery, 14, 26-36; Harlan and Elkhorn Field, 191; Kanawha Field, 185; N. R. A. Code, 41; New River Field, 184; Pocahontas Field, 191; Southern Low Volatile Field, 187; Southwest Interstate Field, 170; strikes during agreements, 41-44, 173-174; system of agreements, 170, 174-175, 182-183, 193-194, 196-197; Tug River Field, 191; wage standards, 170-172, 177, 181-188, 193-194, 196-197; Western Pennsylvania Joint Board, 44-46; Winding Gulf Field, 191; *see also* United Mine Workers' Union.
Coal Review, 193n.
Coat and Suit Code Authority, 137n, 141n.
Coat and suit industry, 2-3, Chapter VII, 205-207; arbitration, 133, 145-146, 148-154, 158, 160-164; Board of Stability and Control, 167, 206; enforcement difficulties, 135-144, 153-155, 164-167; failures, 139-140; Labor Bureau, 159-160, 166-167; N. R. A. Code, 155, 159n; size of firms, 140-141, 143, 169; system of production, 133, 135-138, 152-153, 160, 168-169; wage standards, 134, 155, 158-161, 165-166.
Coat and Suit Industry Recovery Board, 149n, 159.
Colonie Fibre Co., and Cohoes Knit Goods Workers' Union No. 21514, The Matter of, 80n.
Colorado Fuel and Iron Corporation, The, 185n.
Commonwealth v. Hunt, 74n.
Competition, 43-44, 76, 135-137, 140; non-union firms, 3, 80-82, 134-135, 138-139, 144, 147-148, 151, 153, 157, 159, 161, 163-165, 167, 170-172, 205-206.
Compulsory arbitration, *see* Arbitration, compulsory.
Congress of Industrial Organizations, 7, 56-57, 122-123.
Connellsville Field, 183, 185.
Connors v. Connolly, 52n.
Consolidated Edison Co., The Matter of, 54n, 55n.
Consolidated Edison Co., v. N. L. R. B., 54, 55n, 56, 115n.
Consolidation Coal Company, 171-172, 185n, 193n.
Consumer's Power Co. and Local No. 740, United Electrical Radio and Machine Workers of America, The Matter of, 80n.
Coolidge, Calvin, 188.
Cornellier v. Haverhill Shoe Mfrs.' Assn., 59n.
Coronado Coal Co. v. U. M. W. A., 64n.
Cosgrove-Mahan Company, 193n.
Court of Industrial Relations v. Wolff Packing Co., 189n.
Crofoot, V., 91.
Curran, J., 20n.
Curran v. Galen, 50n.

Damages against unions, 63-65.
David Adler & Sons Co., v. Maglio, 59n.
Dean v. Mayo, 62n.
Democrat, 44n.
Detroit News, 114n.
Doll and Toy Workers' Union, 87-88.
Dress industry, 133-134, 137, 139, 160n, 168n.
Dubinsky, D., 138n, 147-148, 153.
Dubinsky v. Blue Dale Dress Co., 58n, 60n.

Elk River Coal and Lumber Company, 173n.

Elmira Precision Tool Company, 90.
Employers' associations, 8, 14, 26, 33, 35-36, 40, 73n, 142-146, 152, 166, 203; Automobile Manufacturers Association, 127n; Central Pennsylvania Coal Producers Association, 43, 172; Harlan County Coal Operators' Association, 196; Industrial Council of Cloak, Suit and Skirt Manufacturers, 140, 142, 153, 156, 165-168; Merchants' Ladies' Garment Association, Inc., 144-146; National Coal Association, 197; New York Building Trades Employers' Association, 14; Western Pennsylvania Coal Operators' Association, 44.
Enforcement procedures, *see* Grievance machinery.
Evans, W., 98n.

Fairbanks v. McDonald, 52n.
Fairmount Field, 185.
Farulla v. Freundlich, 58n.
Farulla v. Ralph A. Freundlich, Inc., 87n.
Federal Labor Union 20,090, 88.
Firth Carpet Company, The, 86, 99-103.
Firth Carpet Co. and Textile Workers' Organizing Committee, The Matter of The, 79n, 100n, 101n, 102n, 103n.
Firth Carpet Co. and Textile Workers' Union of America, The Matter of The, 103n.
Firth Workers' Protective Association, 101, 103.
Fisher, W. E., 174n, 175n, 182n, 183-184, 186n, 189n.
Ford, H., 188.
Ford Motor Car Company, 110, 115.
Four Plating Co. v. Mako, 51n.
Fraenkel, O. K., 61n, 68n.
Frankensteen, R. T., 114n.

Garfield Award, 174n.
Garfield, H., 174.
Gellhorn, W., 36.
General Motors Corporation, 19n, 115, 118, 124, 128.
General Motors Corporation Agreement, 19-20, 113n, 117, 128-129.
Goodrich, C. L., 32n, 40n, 169n, 177n, 191n, 192n.
Governor's Advisory Commission (coat and suit industry), 140-142, 143n, 146, 153, 154n.
Grassi Contracting Co., Inc., v. Bennett, 69.
Great International Brotherhood, etc., v. Green, 67n.
Greater City Master Plumbers Assn., Inc., v. Kahme, 62n.
Greenfield v. Central Labor Council, 59n.
Gregg v. Starks, 71n.
Grievance machinery, 1, 8, 10-11, Chapters II, III, 86, 126, 200, 203-204; appraisal of, 46-47; difficulties encountered, 18-21, 30; grievance committee, 2-3, 22, 27-28, 39-40, 127, 129-131, 177; position of representatives, 13, 21-23, 31-33, 117-118, 146; steps in, 13-16, 30, 39-40; time limits, 15, 19, 30-31; union inspection powers, 15, 32; zone of union-employer authority, 10, 19-23, 28-29, 31-32, 111-112; *see also* Union agreements, Long established, Recently established.
Grievance procedures, *see* Grievance machinery.
Guffey-Snyder Act, 196.
Guffey-Vinson Act, 196.

Harbor Boatmen's Union, 95-97.
Harlan and Elkhorn Field, 191.
Harper v. Local Union No. 520, 51n, 58n.
Heit, L., 160n.
Henderson, L., 118n, 120n.
Herket and Meisel Trunk Co. v. United Leatherworkers International Union, 66n.
Hillenbrand v. Bldg. Trades Council, 67n.
Hoban v. Dempsey, 51n.
Hoeber, H. S., 14n.
Hoover, Herbert, 189.
Hotel and Restaurant Employees' International Alliance and Bartenders' International League of America, 16n.
Howat, A., 189.
Howat v. Kansas, 189n.
Hudson Motor Car Company, 110.
Hudson v. C. N. O. and T. P. Ry. Co., 58n.

Ill. Central Ry. Co. v. International Assn. of Machinists, 65n.
Impartial chairman, *see* Arbitration.
Industrial Council of Cloak, Suit and Skirt Manufacturers Agreement, 138n, 152n, 160n, 167n.
Industrial Council v. Sigman, 66n.
Ingersoll, R. V., 143n, 148, 149n, 150-151, 152n, 163-164.
Injunctions, 57-58, 64, 69, 87, 92, 174.
International Association of Machinists, 84.

International Brotherhood of Electrical Workers, 54.
International Ladies' Garment Workers' Union, 27, 32-33, 35-36, 57, 82, Chapter VII, 206; Educational Department, 134n; Local 10, 147-148, 153, 161; membership, 134, 154-155; New York Cloak and Dress Joint Board, 153, 161-162.

Jacksonville Agreement, 76, 172, 184, 189.
Jacob A. Hunkele, The Matter of, 54n.
Jacobs v. Cohen, 50-51.
Jennings v. Lee, 74n.
Joint Board of Western Pennsylvania Coal Operators' Association and District 5, United Mine Workers of America, 44-46.
Jones v. Maher, 66n.
Jordan's Wearing Apparel, Inc., v. Retail Sales Clerk Union, 51n.
Justice, 138n, 141n, 144n, 147n, 148n, 153n, 159n, 161n, 162n, 164n, 165n.

Kanawha Field, 185.
Kansas Court of Industrial Relations, 189n.
Karges Furniture Co. v. Amalgamated Woodworkers L. Union, 63n.
Kelly-Davis Bill, 195.
Kemp v. Division No. 241, 52n.
Kissam v. U. S. Printing Co., 51n.
Klein, S. F., 140n, 143n, 156n, 160n, 165n, 166n, 167n.
Knit Goods Workers' Union, 82.
Knudsen, W. S., 109n.
Kolchin, M., 154n.
Kuznets, S. S., 137n.

La Favorite Rubber Manufacturing Co., and United Rubber Workers of America, The Matter of, 79n, 85n, 101n, 104n, 105n.
La Favorite Rubber Company, 82-83, 85-86, 99-101, 103-105.
Labor disputes, 1, 9, 14; classified, 8, 20-21; meaning under Norris-La Guardia Act, 62; responsibility for, 7-8; slow-down, 124-125; *see also* Lock-outs, Seniority, Speed - up, Strikes, Union agreements, Wage standards.
Labor unions, 8, 9; change in attitude toward, 7-8; federal, 88, 122; importance of, 7; incorporation of, 63-65; leadership, 7-8, 11, 25, 39, 42, 66, 76-77, 102, 104-106, 169, 177; membership, 7, 25, 86, 94, 100-101, 103-104, 106, 110, 113, 115, 123, 134; radical elements, 25, 102, 106, 121, 190; responsibility for members' acts, 65-68; rival organizations, 54-57, 82, 84-86, 92-96, 101, 112-113, 122-124, 157-158; strategy of disturbance, 10, 21, 30, 36-37, 82, 111, 115, 126; working rules, 29, 36-37, 39, 76, 145-146; *see also* specific unions.
Larkin, T. E., 14n.
Lay-offs, 111, 116, 118-119, 125, 128-129.
Leading Cleaners v. Senate, 70n.
Lenox Shoe Co., The Matter of, 54n.
Lesher, C. E., 190n.
Lever Act, 173-174.
Lewis, A. D., 46n.
Lewis, J. L., 42, 46n, 75-76, 171, 189-190, 195.
Lock-outs, 1-2, 10, 16, 33, 35, 41, 82, 156.
Lone Star Gas Co. and Gas Fitters' Auxiliary, etc., The Matter of, 80n.
Lorwin, L. L., 136n, 144n, 145n, 149n.
Louis Hornick and Company, 81-82.
Louis Hornick and Co., Inc., and Textile Trimming Workers' Union, etc., The Matter of, 79n, 81n, 82n.
Lubin, I., 40n, 43n, 182n, 183n.
Lundoff-Bicknell Co. v. Smith, 74n.

M. and J. Tracy, Inc., The Matter of, 56n.
M. and M. Wood Working Co., et al. and Plywood and Veneer Workers' Union, etc., The Matter of, 56n, 80n.
M. and M. Wood Working Co. v. N. L. R. B., 57n.
Magee, M. A., 133n.
Maisel v. Sigman, 58n.
Malin, P. M., 137n, 139n.
Management prerogatives, 10, 19-21, 28-29, 31-32, 111-112.
Marine Employees Committee, 95-97.
Maritime industry, 2; grievance machinery in, 16-25, 79; *see also* National Maritime Union.
Maritime Labor Board, 18n.
Martin, H., 123-124.
Mastell v. Salo, 71n.
Matsin, C., 104n.
Matsin, E., 104n.
McCord v. Thompson-Starrett Co., 51n.
McCoy v. St. Joseph Belt Ry. Co., 58n.
McDonald, W., 101n.
McPherson, W. H., 113n, 123n.
Mechanics Educational Society of America, 19n, 83-84, 122.
Mediation and Conciliation Service, U. S. Department of Labor, 24.

Meltzer v. Kaminer, 65n.
Merchant Marine Institute Agreement, American, 16n, 17, 19, 20n, 22n, 24n.
Merchants' Garment Agreement, 26n, 27n, 31n, 32n, 33n, 36n, 145n, 146n, 155n, 156n, 158n, 159n.
Millis, H. A., 24n, 137n.
Mine B Coal Co., The Matter of, 57n.
Minnesota Labor Relations Act, 63, 69n.
Mississippi Theatres Corp. v. Hattiesburg Local Union No. 615, 58n.
Mohawk Valley Formula, 92.
Moran v. Lasette, 66n.
Morris, J., 98n.
Morrow, J. D. A., 172n.
Murphy v. Ralph, 61n.

N. L. R. B., Petitioner, v. The Sands Manufacturing Co., 84n.
N. L. R. B. v. Pennsylvania Greyhound Lines, Inc., 55n.
Nagler, I., 162n, 164.
National Brotherhood of Painters, Decorators and Paperhangers of America, 15n.
National Bureau of Economic Research, 175n, 178n, 179n, 181n.
National Credit Office, 139.
National Electric Products Corp., The Matter of, 54.
National Industrial Recovery Act, 87, 122, 141, 155, 195, 206.
National Labor Relations Act, 53n, 54-57, 106-107, 112, 118-119, 200; elections, 96-97, 115, 120, 123-124; employer dominated labor organizations, 54-55, 92, 96; proposed changes, 57, 89, 106-108, 201-202.
National Labor Relations Board, 2, 59n, Chapter V, 113n, 114, 200, 202.
National Marine Engineers' Beneficial Association, 95-97.
National Maritime Union, 17, 19, 21-24, 46.
National Mediation Board, 28.
National Miners' Union, 190.
National Organization of Masters, Mates and Pilots, 95-97.
National Railroad Adjustment Board, 28-30, 33, 34n, 36-37; suggested changes, 38-39.
Nederlandsch Amerikaansche Stoomvaart v. Stevedores' and Longshoremen's Benevolent Society, 65n.
Nelson, L., 82n.
New River Field, 184.
New York Central Railroad, 171.
New York Times, 7n, 14n, 19n, 94n, 110n, 111n, 124n, 169n, 197n.
Norris-La Guardia Act, 60-63, 66-67, 202, 204-206; definition of labor dispute, 62.

Office equipment industry, 79, 90; *see also* Remington Rand, Inc.
Order of Railroad Telegraphers, 27-28.
Oregon Anti-Injunction Act, 63.
O'Neill, C., 172.
Overtime, 13, 104.

Packard Motor Car Company Agreement, 126n.
Pennsylvania Anti-Injunction Act, 62, 69n.
Pennsylvania Railroad, 171.
Perlman, S., 189n, 190n.
Perry, H., 101n, 102.
Peterson, F., 7n.
Phillips, P. G., 68n.
Phillips S. and T. P. Co. v. Amalgamated Assn., etc., 66n.
Pickett v. Walsh, 50n, 63n.
Pilot, The, 20n.
Pittsburgh Coal Company, 171, 172n, 193n.
Plant v. Woods, 50.
Playthings and Novelty Workers' Union, 89.
Pocahontas Field, 191.
Preble v. Architectural Iron Workers' Union of Chicago, 69n.
Progressive Miners of America, 57n.

Railroad brotherhoods, 7.
Railroad industry, 2, 26-39, 171-172.
Railway Employees Cooperative Assn. v. Atlanta B. and C. Ry. Co., 61n.
Railway Labor Act of 1926, 28, 29n, 33n.
Ralph A. Freundlich, Inc., 87-89, 99-100.
Ralph A. Freundlich, Inc. and Doll and Toy Workers' Union, The Matter of, 88n.
Ralph A. Freundlich, Inc. and Max Marcus, Tony Armao, et al., The Matter of, 58n, 79n, 87n, 88n, 89n.
Rand, J. H., Jr., 83, 90-92.
Ravitch, A., 89n.
Red Jacket Consolidated Coal and Coke Company, Inc., 172n.
Remington Rand, Inc., 81, 83-85, 89-94.
Remington Rand, Inc., v. Crofoot, 92n.
Remington Rand, Inc., v. Lind, 92n.
Remington Rand, Inc., and Remington Rand Joint Protective Board, etc., The Matter of (1937), 79n, 83n, 85n, 90n, 91n, 92n, 93n.

Remington Rand, Inc., and Remington Rand Joint Protective Board, etc., The Matter of (1940), 79n, 94n.
Remington Rand Joint Protective Board of the Office Equipment Workers, 90, 94.
Reo Motors, Inc., 110.
Responsibility, union-employer, 76, 78, Chapter IX; bargaining strength aspects, 9, 12-13, 21, 39, 75, 78, 82-86, 105-106, 111, 126, 199-200; economic aspects, 8-9, 39, 77, 80-82, 134-135, 137-138, 154-155, 167-170, 205-207; legal aspects, 2, 9, 11, Chapter IV, 204-205; meaning of, Chapter I; and national defense, 11, 110.
Rhoades v. Malta Vita Pure Food Co., 50n.
Rice, W. G., Jr., 55n, 106n.
Rockefeller, J. D., Jr., 171, 172n.
Rogers, H. O., 180n.
Roosevelt, Franklin D., 122.
Rosenblatt, S. A., 149n, 163-164.
Rosenfarb, J., 55n, 108n.
Rubber industry, 79, 109.

S. and K. Knee Pants Co., Inc., and Amalgamated Clothing Workers of America, The Matter of, 80n.
Sadowsky, R., Inc., 149.
Samuel Hertzig Corp., v. Gibbs, 59n.
Sands Manufacturing Co., The, 83-84.
Sands Manufacturing Co. and Mechanics Educational Society of America, The Matter of, 79n, 83n, 84n, 86n.
Saposs, D. J., 120n.
Saxton, J., 42n.
Sayre, F., 174n, 189n.
Schlesinger v. Quinto, 57, 74n.
Schwartz v. Cigar Makers International Union, 58n.
Segenfeld and Kalin v. Friedman, 60n.
Senate hearings, Conditions in the Coal Fields, 76n, 171n, 172n, 173n, 193n, 195n; Violations of Free Speech and Rights of Labor, 120n.
Seniority, 8-9, 15, 22, 78, 83-85, 98, 102, 111, 114, 119, 127-130.
Serrick Corp., The Matter of The, 54n.
Sherman Act, 48-49, 51, 64.
Shinsky v. O'Neil, 50, 51n.
Smith, Alfred E., 135, 146.
Smith, E. S., 103n.
Smith, M., 19n.
Southern Appalachian Region, 191-192.
Southern Low Volatile Field, 187.
Southwest Interstate Field, 170.
Speed-up, 11, 32, 111-112, 125-126.
Spencer, W. H., 28n.
St. Germain v. Bakery & Confectionery Workers' Union, 64n.
State v. Howat, 189n.
Steel industry, 2, 25, 109, 134; grievance machinery in, 16-25.
Steel Workers' Organizing Committee, 7, 17, 19, 22-25.
Stone, N. I., 87n.
Strikes, 1-2, 20; during agreements, 8, 10, 16, 25, 33, 35, 41-44, 57, 60, 62-63, 69, 78, 81-82, 84, 91-92, 124-126, 130, 142-143, 147, 151-152, 155-156, 158, 173-174, 200; frequency during agreements, 10, 41-42, 124, 156, 164; law of, during agreements, 68-70; sit-down, 121.
Sunshine Anthracite Coal Co. v. Adkins, 196.
Superior Electrical Products Co., The Matter of, 56n.

Taft, P., 189n, 190n.
Tailors' and Pressers' Union, 51.
Taylor, F. J., 20n.
Taylor, G. W., 24n.
Teper, L., 137n, 140n, 141n.
Tetlow, P., 195n.
Textile industry, 79, 109.
Textile Trimming Workers' Union, 79, 81.
Textile Workers' Organizing Committee, *see* Textile Workers' Union of America.
Textile Workers' Union of America, 100, 102.
Thomas, R. J., 110, 123.
Thomas v. Cincinnati, N. O. and T. P. Ry. Co., 74n.
Times-Dispatch, 42n.
Tobin v. Shapiro, 62n.
Toy industry, 87.
Trade unions, *see* Labor unions.
Tryon, F. G., 180n, 181n, 191-192.
Tucker, R. S., 141n.
Tug River Field, 191.

U. M. W. A. v. Coronado Coal Co., 63, 64, 67.
Umpire, *see* Arbitration.
Union agreements, 1, 8.
  Breakdown of, 11-12, 36, 78-83, 86, 95, 105-106, 153-155, Chapter VIII.
  Law of, 2, 11, Chapter IV, 204-205; "clean hands" doctrine, 59-60, 204; conspiracy doctrine, 48-49; criticisms, 76-77; enforcement difficulties, 135-144; frequency of cases, 48, 75-76; individual workers, 50-51; position of individual members, 65-75; position of nonmembers, 49-52, 72-73; remedies

against employers, 57-60; remedies against unions, 63-70; restraint of trade doctrine, 48-49; validity, 48-49.
Long established, 11-13, Chapter III, 75, Chapter VII, Chapter VIII.
Number of, 7, 110.
Recently established, 11-12, 16-25, 66, 75, Chapter V, Chapter VI.
Violations, 86, 90-91, 95, 99, 101-104, 106-107, 144; automobile industry, 111-112, 114-117, 124-127; causes of, 42-46; classification of, 8-9; coat and suit industry, 153-154, 156-158, 161-166; coal industry, 170-171, 173-175; penalties for, 15-16, 24-25, 35-36, 44-45, 142, 145-150, 160-161, 174; remedies for, 11, 76-77, Chapter IX; significance of, 9-11, 60.
See also specific agreements.
Union Pacific Stages, Inc., and The Amalgamated Assn. of Street, Electric Ry. and Motor Coach Employees, etc., The Matter of, 2, 80n.
Union shop, *see* Closed shop.
United Automobile, Aircraft and Agricultural Implement Workers of America, *see* United Automobile Workers of America, C. I. O.
United Automobile Workers of America, A. F. of L., 122-123.
United Automobile Workers of America, C. I. O., 2, 15n, 17-19, 22-24, Chapter VI, 200; dues, 113, 126-127; initiation fees, 113; membership, 110, 113-115, 123, 126-127; special assessments, 113; strikes during agreements, 124-126; types of agreements, 110; *see also* Automobile industry.
United Brotherhood of Carpenters and Joiners of America, 16n.
United Electric Coal Cos. v. Rice, 61n.
United Electrical, Radio and Machine Workers of America, 15n.
United Mine Workers' Journal, 198n.
United Mine Workers of America, 7, 25, 27, 31, 41-42, 44, 57, 64, 67, Chapter VIII, 206-207; membership, 182, 190; ''Save the Union Committee,'' 190.
United Rubber Workers of America, 100-101, 105n.
United Shoe Workers of America, 50.
U. S. Bituminous Coal Commission, 174n, 183-184, 188-189.
U. S. Bituminous Coal Division, 196-197.
U. S. Bureau of Internal Revenue, 181.
U. S. Bureau of Labor Statistics, 1-2, 7n, 14n, 42n, 43n, 44n, 156.
U. S. Bureau of Mines, 175n, 176n, 178n, 179n, 180n, 181n, 187n, 188n.
U. S. Department of Justice, Attorney General's Committee on Administrative Procedure, 34n, 37n, 38n, 107n.
U. S. Steel Corporation, 193n.
U. S. Steel Corporation Agreement, 25; *see also* Carnegie-Illinois Steel Corporation Agreement.
United States v. Hayes, 174n.
United Textile Workers of America, 81.
United Traction Co. v. Droogan, 66n.
Unlicensed Marine Employees Committee, 96-97.
Uviller, H., 169n.

Varnado v. Whitney, 64n.

Wage rates, *see* Wage standards.
Wage standards, 8-9, 11, 19, 32, 45, 57, 78, 88, 91, 101, 103, 111-113, 117-118, 120-121, 134, 157-161, 165-166, 170-172, 177, 181-188, 193-194, 196-197.
Walker, J. J., 163.
Walker v. Cronin, 50n.
Wander, H., 144n, 145n.
Washington Agreement, 174, 189.
Watson Bill, 195.
Watson, C. W., 172.
Weber v. Masser, 58n.
Whiting Milk Co. v. Grondin, 70n.
Williams v. Quill, 53n.
Williams Coal Co. and United Mine Workers of America, District No. 23, et al., The Matter of, 80n.
Willits, J. H., 177n, 191n.
Wilson Line, Inc., 81, 83, 85-86, 94-99.
Wilson Line, Inc., and National Marine Engineers' Beneficial Assn., etc., The Matter of, 79n, 83n, 85n, 95n, 96n, 97n, 98n, 99n.
Wilson v. Airline Coal Co., 58n.
Wilson, Woodrow, 171.
Winding Gulf Field, 191.
Wisconsin Employment Peace Act, 54n, 63, 69n.
Witmer, T. R., 48n, 52n, 57, 58n, 68n, 70n.
Witte, E. E., 64n, 65n.
Wolf, F. N., 159n.
Wolff Packing Co. v. Court of Industrial Relations, 189n.
Wolman, L., 122n, 154n.
Women's garment industry, 2, 57, 133, 137; grievance machinery, 14, 26-36; Protocol of Peace, 145n; *see also* Clothing industry, Coat and suit industry, Dress industry.

Yazoo & Miss. Valley Railroad v. Webb, 71n, 72n.
Young v. Canadian Northern Ry., 72n.

Zenite Metal Corp., The Matter of, 54n.

VITA

FRANK COOK PIERSON

Place of birth: Denver, Colorado

Date of birth: November 4, 1911

Educational institutions attended:
East Denver High School, Denver, Colorado
Swarthmore College, Swarthmore, Pennsylvania
Columbia University, New York City

Degrees received:
A.B., Swarthmore College, 1934
M.A., Columbia University, 1938

Positions held:
Assistant bank examiner and research assistant, Federal Reserve Bank of New York
Assistant professor of economics, Swarthmore College